Sunset

Bathrooms
PLANNING & REMODELING

By the Editors of Sunset Books and Sunset Magazine

DESIGNER: LYNN ANDERSON

Built-in vanity houses side-by-side sinks and ample storage; a
wall cabinet adds mirrors and display nooks.

Sunset Publishing Corporation ■ Menlo Park, California

To achieve this dramatic effect, colored joint compound was knife-applied to walls over a lighter tint; a top glaze accents both.

Book Editor
Scott Atkinson

Coordinating Editor
Suzanne Normand Eyre

Design
Joe di Chiarro

Illustrations
Bill Oetinger

Photo Stylist
JoAnn Masaoka Van Atta

Cover: Matching sinks and cabinetry comfortably accommodate two in this colorful master bath. Bathroom design by Osburn Design. Cover design by Naganuma Design & Direction. Photography by Philip Harvey. Photo styling by JoAnn Masaoka Van Atta.

Photography

Jared Chandler: 20 top; **Peter Christiansen:** 28 top, 32 top; **Crandall & Crandall:** 17 top; **Stephen Cridland:** 16 bottom, 27 top; **Jay Graham:** 5, 10, 31 bottom; **Philip Harvey:** 1, 2, 6, 7, 8 top left and bottom left, 9 top, 11, 12, 13, 14, 16 top, 18, 19 top left and top right, 21, 22, 23 top left and top right, 24 top right and bottom, 25, 27 bottom, 28 bottom, 29, 30, 31 top, 32 bottom, 33, 34, 35 bottom left, 37, 46, 48, 51, 64; **David Duncan Livingston:** 15 bottom, 20 bottom, 35 bottom right, 49; **Renee Lynn:** 15 top, 35 top; **Norman A. Plate:** 24 top left, 26 bottom left and bottom right; **Kenneth Rice:** 8 top right; **Brian Vanden Brink:** 19 bottom, 23 bottom, 26 top left; **Tom Wyatt:** 9 bottom, 17 bottom.

Editor, Sunset Books: Elizabeth L. Hogan

First printing April 1994

Time to update your bathroom?

At first glance, a bathroom may seem relatively uncomplicated —a sink, a toilet, and a tub or shower within four walls. But as a look through the pages of this book will prove, there's a lot more to a bathroom than just the basics. Double sinks, whirlpool tubs, stunning tiled surfaces, rich cabinetry—all contribute to turning today's bathrooms into design statements all their own. Now you can achieve the same results.

This new edition offers a wealth of information to guide you, from design ideas for successful floor plans to actual construction techniques. A special section compares the various products on the market today so you can shop wisely for cabinetry, surfacing materials, and fixtures. Whether you're doing the work yourself or hiring professionals for some or all of it, this complete course on bathroom design and construction will provide the help you need.

Special thanks go to Fran Feldman for carefully editing the manuscript. We also wish to thank The Bath & Beyond; Roger Chetrit of Tile Visions; Dillon Tile Supply, Inc.; Menlo Park Hardware Co.; and Plumbing n' Things.

Contents

Special Features

DESIGN IDEAS

Layouts ▪ Materials ▪ Lighting ▪ Storage

Everyone knows a picture is worth a thousand words. That's why this chapter is packed with full-color photos showing bathroom design ideas that you can apply to your own situation, whether you're remodeling an existing bathroom or starting from scratch.

The first section, "Basic layouts" (pages 6–11), presents a variety of floor plans. Even though you may not have a choice of floor plan, study the photos in this section carefully—you're likely to find details that apply to your bathroom. A related section, "Water works" (pages 12–17), deals with the major plumbing fixtures—sinks, tubs, and showers—around which modern bath design revolves.

"On the surface" (pages 18–23) shows good ways to use surfacing materials ranging from faux painting to stone. "Bright ideas" (pages 24–29) explores natural and artificial lighting, almost always subject to improvement when you're remodeling and an important concern if you're designing a new bath. "Storage solutions" (pages 30–35) concludes the chapter.

View across whirlpool tub includes a master suite's sink area and built-in makeup center. Pink marble lines tub pedestal, floor, and countertops. Elegant wall sconces flank ample mirrors, which stretch space and amplify daylight from an overhead skylight.

Basic layouts

ARCHITECT: LAURENCE ALLEN

Stepped glass-block partition defines large walk-in shower in master bath; glass blocks in exterior walls let in soft, diffused light. Twin sinks sitting atop trim gray European-style cabinets are set off by a green marble countertop and backsplash. Nearby dressing area (out of view) links bedroom to bath and features built-in dressers, marble counters, and warm wool carpeting.

DESIGNER: DEBRA GUTIERREZ

Barrier-free shower design is both beautiful and practical. Incorporated into a stylish marble design is an adjustable hand-held shower head, a grab bar, and a comfortable bench.

Kids' bath begins with a riot of colorful tile. Cork floor is slip-proof. Twin sinks, which overhang a space-saving base cabinet, minimize territorial squabbles. A portable step allows for growing to counter height.

DESIGNER: OSBURN DESIGN

■ Basic layouts

ARCHITECT: DAVID WILLIAMS
DESIGNER: RICK SAMBOL / DESIGN CONSULTANTS

DECORATIVE PAINTING: THE BEARDSLEY COMPANY

Powder rooms occasion bold designs that may not be "practical" for day-to-day bathrooms. In an antique vein, room shown above features a formal parquet floor and a wall-hung sink on shiny chrome legs; painted flowers dominate. Limited understair space shown in photo at left gains weight from textured wall-paper and jet black accents.

DESIGNER: LOU ANN BAUER / BAUER INTERIOR DESIGN

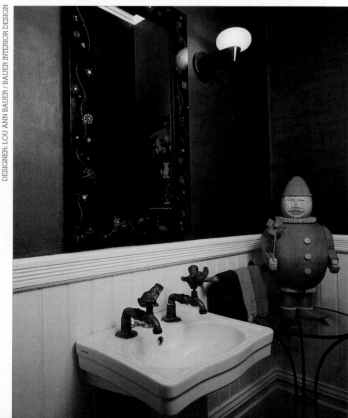

Small washroom combines white wood wainscoting with colorful walls and a hand-painted mirror. Sink fittings atop pedestal sink are actually outdoor faucets.

DESIGNER: ALBERT CAREY, ASID / ACORN KTICHENS & BATHS

With little space to spare, small adult bath has been stretched with mirrors. Hardworking floor plan organizes use areas and incorporates storage by means of vertical dividers.

DESIGNER: RUTH SOFORENKO ASSOCIATES

Tiny white bath has requisite amenities, thanks to careful planning and reliable built-ins. Vanity, sink, tub, and toilet come together in a tight intersection; curves avoid protruding corners that would have blocked foot traffic.

■ Basic layouts

Successful master suite links multiple elements in a single efficient, private retreat. Suite shown above features a stepped glass-block divider that maintains link between bed and bath. Black acrylic soaking tub is on bedroom side of divider; walk-in shower is tucked into a corner. In photo at left, a second suite's exercise area is just a short jog away from soothing tub or seamless shower.

Cedar-lined sauna is a satellite room off a multiroom bath. Twin slat benches, sauna heater, thermostat, and weathertight door are basic equipment. It's a short walk to shower, visible in background.

Water works

ARCHITECT: J. ALLEN SAYLES

Modern pedestal sink lends its smooth lines to a clean white, symmetrical wall. Mirror anchors design; glass shelf provides trim storage for sink-side accessories. Stylish twin wall sconces shed task light from both directions.

ARCHITECT: J. ALLEN SAYLES

Step-down sinks allow two people to use bathroom at once; each countertop is at a comfortable height for user. Recessed sinks are rimmed with dark blue field tiles; vanities below offer plenty of storage space.

Crystal sink bowl sits atop a transparent shelf in a small powder room.
Drain fittings run through transparent glass countertop, providing a design
statement of their own.

■ **Water works**

DESIGNER: GERALD N. JACOBS / JACOBS DESIGN

A holdover from the past, stout free-standing tub highlights a brand-new bathroom. Reconditioned with a chrome spout and handles, tub is ready for many more relaxing soaks.

DESIGNER: MONA BRANAGH / PACIFIC BAY INTERIORS

Molded pedestal tub features a water-fall spout and deck-mounted handles. Tub rises above a built-in platform lined with green marble tiles; color is repeated in striped wallpaper.

ARCHITECT: CHARLES DEBBAS

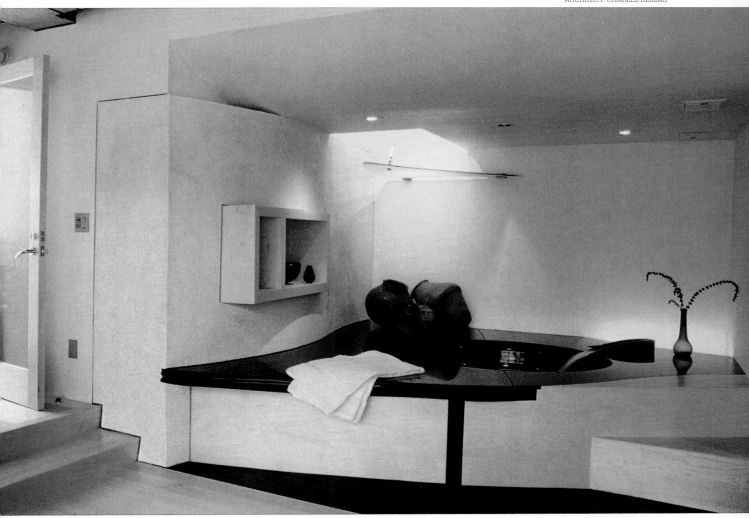

DESIGNER: CHADINE FLOOD GONG / CHADINE INTERIOR DESIGN

Skylighted soaking area occupies a widened section of a private hallway linking master bedroom and guest room/office. Carefully chosen and shaped materials—slate tiles, maple flooring and cabinetry, and a granite-surfaced tub—create an interior evocative of a Japanese landscape.

Japanese soaking tub is tranquil centerpiece of a dramatic bath linking indoors with a small Japanese garden outside. Tub platform, floor, and wall surfaces are covered in multicolored African slate, bringing outdoor feeling inside.

■ Water works

ARCHITECT: DAVID WILLIAMS
DESIGNER: RICK SAMBOL / DESIGN CONSULTANTS

Seamless glass steam shower holds down end of a tub platform housing an oval-shaped whirlpool tub. Second-story picture window offers tub-side views; diamond-shaped shower window combines view with privacy.

Walk-in shower has a striking curved shape that's echoed in floor tiles. Glass blocks bring in light while maintaining privacy; downlights provide auxiliary light.

Step-down shower and platform tub are part of an open suite adjacent to a sunny garden. Step-down reduces shower splash; with no surround, open feeling is maintained. Easy-to-clean tile covers all surfaces.

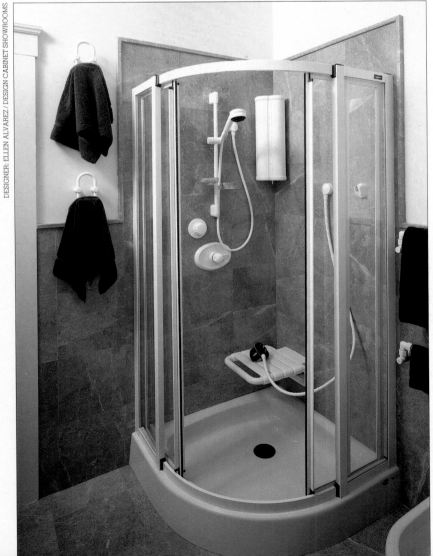

Tucked into a corner of a small bath, sleek European shower unit displays an adjustable shower head and massage unit along with a fold-down seat. Curved sliding doors can be removed for cleaning.

On the surface

Pink wallpaper lends country cheer to walls surrounding a whirlpool tub. White porcelain tiles facing platform front, tub deck, and backsplash contrast with dark-stained oak floor.

DESIGNER: CHARLOTTE BOYLE INTERIORS
ARCHITECT: J. ALLEN SAYLES

DESIGNER: MONA BRANAGH / PACIFIC BAY INTERIORS

Two variations on the pedestal theme: angular adult bath (shown above, at left) gains its fresh effect from a white tile floor and wainscoting punctuated by green trim tiles and chrome accents. Child's bath (shown above, at right) combines a traditional fluted sink with wallpaper and matching cabinet accents; pedestal and floor sport crisp white glazed tile.

Nothing says country comfort like wood—in this case, pine tongue-and-groove paneling, timbers, and window trim. White tile surrounds tub area, heading off moisture damage and allowing for easy cleaning.

■ On the surface

DESIGNER: JOSH CHANDLER

DESIGNER: DAVID LIVINGSTON INTERIORS

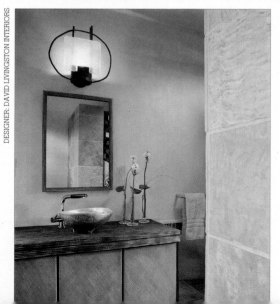

Bathrooms offer a blank canvas for varied creative expression. In photo above, wall sculpture is joined by an eclectic mix that includes a stainless steel countertop and integral sink, a red tub, textured walls, wood rafters and ceiling, and a dark-stained tile floor.

In a softer style, room at left combines a vanity with amazingly varied slate floor and walls. Sink holes cut in bowl and cabinet accommodate plumbing.

Like a torn masterpiece, a marble countertop gives way to granite, and mirrors yield to wall paint. Polished brass fittings, wall sconces, and angular shapes are repeated endlessly in space-stretching mirrors.

■ On the surface

Textured porcelain tiles marked by subtle variations wrap an oval tub in soft color.
Deck-mounted tub fittings are in a matching muted finish; seamless shower recedes
from view and doesn't interrupt sense of space and quiet.

ARCHITECT: MORIMOTO ARCHITECTS

Bold or subtle, flooring makes a supporting statement in bathrooms. Black and white tile mosaic flooring (above left) lends energy to a quiet bath design; tiles are toasty to the touch, thanks to radiant heating pipes below. In photo above, soft white field tiles and matching grout are punctuated by colorful glazed diagonal inserts.

Hardwood wainscoting and chair rail, softened with a white pickling wash, lead the way to a simple European-style pedestal sink. White tile floor and built-in bureau amplify the mood.

Bright ideas

Adding light and design punch while maintaining privacy, glass block is tailor-made for bathroom installation. Curved shower wall shown above left has block below, clear glazing at eye level. Glass-block grouping in photo above delivers soft light to a ground-floor walk-in shower. Single strip of blocks in photo at left brings a flash of light to a child's tub/ shower.

Block walls and an opening skylight team up to provide diffuse light and ventilation in a master bath. Block wraps behind both tub and nearby steam shower; mirrors blur boundaries and amplify brightness. Steam shower offers a glimpse of outside through clear blocks up high and in corner.

■ Bright ideas

ARCHITECT: JOHN MORRIS

Enjoy the view without sacrificing privacy. Shown at left, twin roof windows furnish a sunny, private view from an upstairs bath and provide great ventilation, too. Pop-out greenhouse unit shown below and in inset expands a small bathroom and opens it to garden.

DESIGNER: MOLLY RUTH HALE

Second-story privacy offered an opportunity to open master bath to garden: French doors, matching overhead transoms, tub-side double-hung windows, and a skylight do the trick. Indirect soffit fixtures provide quiet light for a nighttime soak.

Whirlpool tub in a bathroom bay appears to float into surrounding woodland. Decorative windowpanes focus attention on trees and screen bathers from outside view.

■ **Bright ideas**

ARCHITECT: JANICE PREGLIASCO

Window, glass blocks, and mirrors brighten this high-ceilinged bathroom. Lollipoplike mirrors above sinks float on exterior view; they're mounted on hardboard backing and strapped to chrome posts set in backsplash.

Light permeates this bright bath. Sources are all visible in mirror: large ridgeline skylights, glass blocks to help spread light, frosted glass doors, and twin wall sconces to provide plenty of task light around stylish pedestal sink.

ARCHITECT: REMICK ASSOCIATES

ARCHITECT: CHARLES DEBBAS

In temperate climates, why not open up a wall to summer weather? Bathroom suite utilizes a standard garage door and hardware to open up a sitting area near soaking tub to surrounding hills.

Incandescent/fluorescent strip lights form an integral part of sink-side task area; sealed downlights are visible in mirrors. Frosted windows flank sink, aiding privacy; clear skylights bring in extra daylight.

DESIGNER: OSBURN DESIGN

Storage solutions

Seamless white vanity cabinet is built with frame-and-panel faceframe construction; it forms a perfect base for solid-surface countertop and tile detailing. Wall unit features matching flush doors and glass panels; arched valance, topped with crown molding, houses discreet downlights for sink-side tasks.

Stylish European cabinetry built into angle between shower and toilet compartments offers floor-to-ceiling storage and display space on recessed glass shelves. Pinpoint accent lighting comes from low-voltage MR-16 downlights with slot apertures.

Red mahogany cabinets organize every inch of this formal bath done in "club room" style. Base cabinets, lipped shelves, mirror and tub arches, and tub pedestal all match; elegant millwork ties loose ends together.

■ Storage solutions

DESIGNER: CAROLYN VAN LANG

Black-rimmed maple storage unit separates bathroom, with its primary accents, from adjacent bedroom. It's like a kitchen island transported to a bathroom. Jagged marble partition screening bath is reflected in mirror behind sink.

Freestanding deco vanity bridges twin curved pedestals in spacious master suite. Base is veneered with maple; countertop is speckled granite. Twin sinks have waterfall spouts; plumbing is hidden behind pedestal columns.

DESIGNER: GERALD N. JACOBS / JACOBS DESIGN

Dressing area forms a transition zone between bedroom and bath; owners wanted a master suite feel but didn't have space for a separate dressing room. Maple cabinets house plenty of drawers, pegs, cubbyholes, and adjustable shelves; lowered counter section becomes a makeup table.

Antique dresser takes on new life as a bathroom vanity in this traditional setting. Holes were cut in top for a self-rimming sink and deck-mounted fittings; plumbing runs through false drawer.

■ Storage solutions

DESIGN: EUGENE NAHEMOW / LAMPERTI ASSOCIATES

Glass display shelves bring a touch of elegance and openness to a tiny powder room layout. Triple-thick, laminated shelves are supported discreetly at three points; recess saves space.

DESIGN: LINDSTROM CO. AND JC PENNEY

For watching soaps in the suds, television is built into a bathroom wall. Above, cubbyholes hold electronic gear. Ventilation is provided from behind.

Bamboo rods perform as towel bars, bringing nature's forms into bathroom. Double-height unit does double duty.

DESIGN: CURTIS AND EMMONS

DESIGNER: OSBURN DESIGN

Sink-side appliance garage built from bird's-eye maple slides out on heavy-duty drawer guides. Power outlet behind lowered drawer back allows bath appliances to remain plugged in.

Up is down, down is up—electric storage unit floats between symmetrical twin sink areas; besides making a dramatic statement, it provides handy storage right where it's needed. Purple dye stain provides color blast, endlessly repeated in mirrors.

DESIGNER: LOU ANN BAUER / BAUER INTERIOR DESIGN

PLANNING GUIDELINES

Decision-making ▪ Design ▪ Floor plans ▪ Products

The hallmark of today's bathrooms is style; it can be found in elegant powder rooms, gracious guest baths, efficient family bathrooms, and spacious master suites. Inspired by innovative designs, fashionable fixtures and fittings, and a refreshing palette of colors, the zest for home decorating has progressed to the bathroom from other parts of the house. The introduction of new products and materials—stylish yet durable—has added momentum.

But changes in lifestyle and the economy are at the heart of the bathroom remodeling trend. More and more people are deciding to make the most of the home they already own, rather than move to another one. And in the process they're changing the face of the bathroom. Not long ago, the standard bath was simply a room with utilitarian fixtures. Today's bathroom serves many needs. At its best, it can be a sanctuary from the busy world and a place to pamper yourself.

Planning your new bathroom can be one of the most enjoyable aspects of remodeling; it's the first step toward creating the kind of room you want. In this chapter, you'll learn about bathroom planning, from evaluating your existing bathroom to drawing floor plans for a new one, and determining the best ways to launch your project. The varied choices in fixtures, fittings, and materials are discussed in the "Bathroom showcase" (pages 54–63).

Dramatic master bath features his-and-her sinks and vanities, a flush-mounted whirlpool tub, and a two-person walk-in shower. Sponged and streaked walls, custom tiles, and bird's-eye maple set the color scheme. From the bath, it's just a few steps to an oversize dressing room, abundantly fitted with storage racks, drawers, and cubbyholes

Getting started

"Where do I begin?" is one of the most-asked questions about remodeling. The answer is to start with an inventory of your existing bathroom. Once you've assessed the room's current condition and developed some remodeling goals, it will be easier to uncover the room's potential for greater comfort, more convenience, and better appearance.

To decide on your primary goals, complete the inventory below. List all the improvements you'd like to make in their order of importance. To make it easier to establish priorities, you can assign a numerical rating to each improvement or designate each as "must do" or "would like to do." The finished list will help you keep your remodeling goals in focus and guide you in setting a budget, working with professionals, and selecting products and materials.

Trends come and go, and the bathroom is not immune to changing fashion. Perhaps it's time to pull the plug on those outdated fixtures, surface treatments, colors, and accessories. Or you may decide to keep your fixtures and tile and redecorate around them with new paint and wallpaper; this approach can be a surprisingly effective and inexpensive way to update a room's appearance.

To help guide your decisions, start collecting ideas. Study the color photographs in this book. Let

A BATHROOM INVENTORY

To analyze your present bathroom, take the bathroom inventory that follows—it's one of the most important tools in designing your new bathroom. Think of this exercise as a fact-finding process in which you identify specific conditions you'd like to improve, evaluate strengths and weaknesses, and set goals for remodeling.

First, look at the surfaces. Would the bathroom's style be improved if you changed the walls, floor, ceiling, countertops, or cabinetry? Do your doors and drawers need new hardware? Would new windows, a new bathtub, or a new shower door improve the room?

But don't stop when you've examined those relatively superficial elements. Move on to the fundamentals of the room and everything in it—and the way it all works (or fails to work) for the people who use it.

Layout. Consider the following questions in relation to your bathroom's layout: Does the door open into the room? If so, can it inconvenience someone inside? When open, do cabinet or vanity doors and drawers block the door? Can two people use the sink or vanity area at the same time? Would your family benefit from the added privacy of a compartmentalized bathroom, with tub, shower, or toilet separate from each other and from the vanity? Is there ample room for toweling dry without hitting elbows? Are stored items within easy reach?

Fixtures and fittings. Before you rush out to buy new fixtures and fittings, consider whether the existing ones can be cleaned, refinished, or repaired. If not, decide what features you like and dislike about your current equipment. Are you pleased with the sizes, shapes, and materials? Are the faucets easy to turn on and off? Can you adjust water temperature for the sink and shower as easily as you'd like? Are you content with a bathtub, or would you like a shower also? Would you like to add a whirlpool bath?

Walls, floor, and ceiling. Moisture is the enemy of most room surfaces and subsurfaces and can be a particular problem in bathrooms. Water warps flooring, deteriorates paint, and wilts wallpaper. Examine the surfaces in your present bathroom for chips, cracks, bubbles, mold, mildew, and other maladies. Is your tile uneven? Are the grout and caulking in good condition? Have any subsurfaces been damaged by excess moisture?

If any of your surfaces are in poor condition or you want to make a decorative change, be sure to consider moisture-resistance, maintenance, and durability when you choose new materials. The choices in color, pattern, texture, and style are enormous.

Countertops. Do you have ample counter space in your bathroom? If not, decide where you need more room for storage or display, or simply for a convenient place to put things down. Are existing countertops in good condition? Are joints and corners easy to keep clean? Would you prefer a different type of countertop material, or has the present material been satisfactory?

Storage. Before you think about increasing your storage capacity, clean out and organize your bathroom's existing storage areas. If you're still short of space, determine your most pressing storage needs. Would you like a recessed medicine cabinet, better storage for cleaning supplies, a place for dirty laundry, or a tilt-out bin to hold your bathroom scale? Consider adding a vanity, wall cabinets, or even a floor-to-ceiling unit complete with shelves and bins. Can you enlarge the room to gain space? Is it possible to store some items in a hall closet or other nearby space?

Lighting. Old bathrooms rarely have enough properly placed light fixtures. If your bathroom has only one overhead light or a single fixture above the medicine cabi-

them spur your imagination—you're almost certain to find many ideas that you'd like to adapt to your own setting.

Turn, too, to the showcase on pages 54–63, where various types of fixtures and fittings are illustrated and described. Peruse magazines and tour model homes in your neighborhood.

To collect more ideas and get a closer look at new products, visit showrooms and stores displaying bathroom fixtures, cabinetry, light fixtures, wall coverings, tile, and flooring products. As you shop around, try to identify what you like about certain styles. You can obtain catalogues, brochures, and color charts from

stores and from manufacturers. Seek out helpful salespersons and ask questions about products that interest you. The answers and advice you receive can be invaluable.

As you accumulate notes, clippings, photographs, and brochures, file your remodeling ideas in a notebook. Choose a binder with several divisions or file your material in separate 9 by 12-inch envelopes. Organize by subjects, such as best overall style, layouts and plans, pleasing color combinations, fixtures and fittings, lighting, and accessory ideas. Then review your remodeling goals and adapt the categories to suit your project.

---

net, you'll certainly want to give some thought to improving the room's artificial lighting. In additional to upgrading general lighting, would you like to add task lighting? Are you pleased with the appearance of existing light fixtures, and is the kind of light (fluorescent or incandescent) what you want? Consider bringing in more natural light. You can do this by adding a skylight, enlarging an existing window, or creating a new window.

Electrical outlets and switches. Note the location and number of electrical outlets and switches. Are there enough outlets? Are switches and outlets conveniently placed? If you need more electrical outlets, you may want to replace a single outlet with a double one. Plan to substitute circuit-breaking GFCI outlets for standard plugs in all wet areas in the bathroom. For greater convenience in a large space, you can install two and three-way switches for lights.

Heating and ventilation. Basic for bathroom comfort are a controlled temperature and good ventilation. No one enjoys the shock of a chilly bathroom on a cold morning. In a poorly ventilated bathroom, you may gasp for air in the middle of a steamy shower or have to stop to wipe off a foggy mirror while shaving. Note any problems caused by poor heating or ventilation, and don't overlook the problem of mold or mildew.

Water and energy conservation. Heating the bathroom and heating water consume a lot of energy. Are the water heater, pipes, and walls well insulated? Is the shower head equipped with a flow restrictor or shut-off valve? If you plan to buy a new toilet, have you considered a water-saving model?

Privacy. Does the door or window of your bathroom open to a public area? If so, you may want to consider

relocating the opening or designing special window or exterior treatments to increase privacy. You should also check your bathroom for uninsulated pipes, finishing materials that reflect sound, and insufficient floor, wall, or ceiling insulation.

Accessories. Make a list of your bathroom accessories and note any additions or deletions you'd like to make, as well as any changes you want in quality, quantity, or style. Perhaps you'd like to replace mismatched towel bars and other accessories with a coordinated collection in glass, ceramic, or brightly colored plastic. Do you want the finish on towel bars, mirror frames, and cabinet hardware to match existing or new fittings? Also, look at your towels; aside from being functional, do they complement the room's color scheme? Do you have sufficient towel bars, and are they conveniently placed?

Maintenance. Some bathrooms are easier to maintain than others. Evaluate your bathroom's trouble spots, such as soap buildup, discolored grout, and streaked walls. In planning your project, consider installing smooth, seamless or jointless materials (except flooring) and ones especially designed to withstand moisture. If your fixtures are difficult to clean, you may want to refinish or replace them.

Family needs. A bathroom should be easy for everyone to use. Take time to consider the special needs of family members and regular visitors, including children and elderly or disabled persons. Can an adult bathe a small child safely and comfortably? Is the tub and/or shower equipped with a nonskid base and grab bars? If wheelchair access is a consideration, is the entry wide enough, and is there ample space for easy turning? Can all the fixtures be used without assistance? For more information on barrier-free baths, see page 43.

Your present plan

You've taken a critical look at your bathroom, analyzing its good points and noting where you want to make improvements. If your goals point to simple redecorating or minor remodeling, skip ahead to the design information beginning on page 48 and the "Bathroom showcase" on pages 54–63 for help.

For more ambitious remodeling plans, you'll need to measure the room and draw it to scale. The process of measuring the bathroom elements and perimeter will increase your awareness of the existing space. Scale drawings also serve as a foundation for future design and may satisfy the permit requirements of your local building department. Such plans will also help you communicate your ideas to any professional you hire.

The information here will tell you how to measure your bathroom, record those measurements, and draw a two-dimensional floor plan to scale. You'll also learn how to make elevation drawings of each wall.

Measuring the room

Before you begin taking measurements, draw a rough sketch of the bathroom, its various elements, and any adjacent areas that may be included in the remodeling. Make the sketch as large as the paper allows so you'll have ample room to write in the dimensions. Note any suspected deviations from the standard wall and partition thickness (usually about 5 inches). The sketch should also show all projections, recesses, windows, doors, and door swings.

Tools. Listed below are some tools and supplies that will help you with your measuring and drawing tasks. You can find these tools at hardware, stationery, and art supply stores.

■ Retractable steel measuring tape or folding wooden rule

■ Ruler or T-square

■ Triangle

■ Compass

■ Graph paper (four squares to an inch)

■ Tracing paper

■ Masking tape

■ Pencils

■ Eraser

■ Clipboard or pad with 8½ by 11-inch paper

How to measure. It's important to record the dimensions on the sketch as you measure, using feet and inches as an architect would (you may also want to translate certain dimensions, such as those for tubs and shower enclosures, to inches). Measure to the nearest ⅛ inch, since even a fraction of an inch counts in fitting and spacing bathroom elements. All mea-surements should be taken to the wall, not to project-ing wood trim or baseboards.

First, measure the room's dimensions—the floor, ceiling, and walls; measure each wall at counter height. To find out if the bathroom is square, measure the diagonals (corner to opposite corner). Don't worry if the room isn't square; just be sure your drawing reflects any irregularities.

With the overall dimensions recorded on your sketch, measure the fixtures and other elements in the room and the distances between them, and add this information to your sketch. You can use a wall-by-wall approach, or you can measure by category: fixtures, doors, windows, cabinetry, shelves, and accessories.

Depending on the extent of your remodeling goals, your sketch could include locations of the fol-lowing: load-bearing walls and partitions, electrical outlets and switches, light fixtures, drains, pipes, and vents. If you want to enlarge your bathroom—or just add more storage space—show relevant adjacent hall space, closets, rooms, and outdoor areas that you may be able to incorporate.

Note any heights that may affect your remodeling plans. These might include the clearance space under a duct or sloping ceiling, the floor-to-ceiling height, and the distance from the floor to the tops and bottoms of the windows.

Drawing to scale

The secrets to drawing a useful floor plan and eleva-tions are a well-prepared sketch with accurate mea-surements and a reasonable amount of skill at con-verting those measurements to the scale you choose. Your drawings don't have to be works of art, but they should be precise, complete, and easy to read.

Though architects sometimes use a ¼-inch scale (¼ inch equals 1 foot), using a ½-inch scale for your bathroom remodeling drawings is easier, especially when you want to include all the elements of the room and write their dimensions.

How to draw floor plans. With masking tape, attach the corners of the graph paper to a smooth working surface. Use a ruler, T-square, or triangle to draw all horizontal and vertical lines; make right angles exact. Use a compass to indicate door swings.

To complete the floor plan, refer to your sketch and the sample finished floor plan on the facing page. Indicating walls and partitions by dark, thick lines will make the floor plan easier to read.

How to draw elevations. Elevations, or straight-on views of each bathroom wall, show the visual pattern created by all the elements against that wall. Sketch the elements on each wall, measure carefully, and record the figures as you did for the floor plan; then redraw your elevation sketches on graph paper.

SAMPLE FLOOR PLAN & ELEVATION

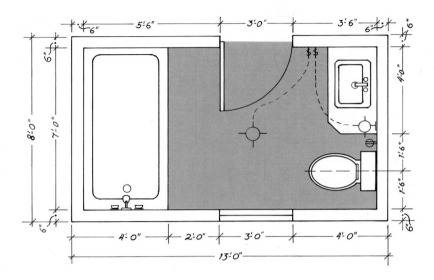

The drawings of your existing bathroom should look like the floor plan above and the elevation sketch at right. Be sure to add the appropriate architectural symbols to your floor plan to indicate outlets, switches, windows, and light fixtures.

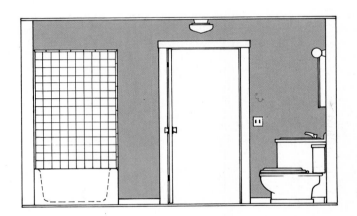

ARCHITECTURAL SYMBOLS

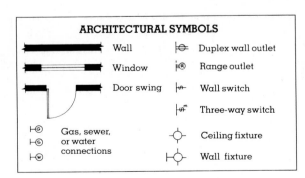

ARCHITECTURAL SYMBOLS

Wall			Duplex wall outlet
Window			Range outlet
Door swing			Wall switch
			Three-way switch
Gas, sewer, or water connections			Ceiling fixture
			Wall fixture

Architects and designers use a set of standard symbols to indicate certain features on floor plans; some of the most common ones are shown at left. It's a good idea to become familiar with these symbols, since you'll want to use them on your own plans. Also, you'll need to know them to communicate with your building department, contractor, or designer.

Basic layouts

Once you've analyzed your present bathroom's assets and liabilities, it's time to start planning your new one. While brainstorming, try to have some basic layout schemes in mind. The floor plans shown below provide a starting point. Keep in mind that these layouts can be combined, adapted, and expanded to meet your needs. For additional ideas, study the photos on pages 6–35.

The "best" bathroom layout doesn't exist—good layouts vary dramatically. Generally, though, a workable floor plan provides for good access to the room, easy movement within the room, and the convenient use of fixtures and storage units.

Here are some layout guidelines categorized by type of bathroom.

Powder room. This two-fixture room, also known as a guest bath or half-bath, contains a toilet and a sink and perhaps some limited storage space. Fixtures can be placed side by side or on opposite or even adjacent walls, depending on the shape of the room. Very small sinks are available for extra-tight spaces.

Because the guest bathroom is used only occasionally and for short intervals of time, it's a good place to enjoy more decorative but perhaps less durable finishes, such as brass, copper, and upholstery. The door should swing open against a wall,

clear of any fixtures. Where space is tight, a pocket door may be the ideal solution.

Consideration should be given to privacy. Preferably, a guest bath should open off a hallway, not directly into the living room, family room, or dining area.

Family bath. The family bath usually contains three fixtures—a toilet, a sink, and a bathtub or shower or combination tub/shower. The fixture arrangement varies, depending on the size and shape of the room. (Several configurations are shown below.) Family baths often have cluster or corridor layouts; they should be at least 5 feet by 7 feet.

To enable several family members to use the bathroom at the same time, consider putting in two sinks. Another possible solution is compartmentalizing, or separating fixture areas. One common arrangement is to isolate the toilet and shower from the sink and grooming area. This configuration can work well to increase privacy when it's not feasible to add a new bathroom.

The family bath is one of the most frequently used rooms in the house. Therefore, be sure to choose durable, moisture-resistant, easy-to-clean fixtures and finishes. Also, be sure to plan adequate storage space for each user's needs.

SAMPLE BATHROOM LAYOUTS

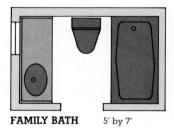

POWDER ROOM
4' by 4'-6"

POWDER ROOM
5' by 5'

POWDER ROOM
3' by 6'

FAMILY BATH   5' by 7'

BACK-TO-BACK   5' by 7' each

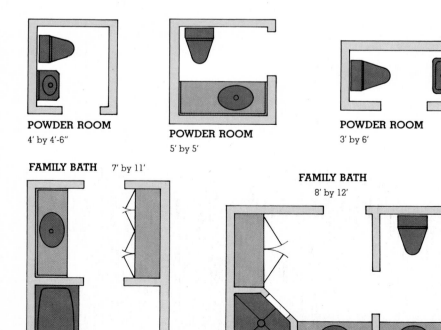

FAMILY BATH   7' by 11'

FAMILY BATH
8' by 12'

Children's bath. Ideally, this bathroom is located between two bedrooms used by children, so there's direct access from each room.

If there's space, you may want to consider shared bathing and toilet facilities and an individual sink and dressing area for each child. When several children are sharing one bath, color coding of drawers, towel hooks, and other storage areas can help minimize territorial battles.

Children's baths require special attention to safety and maintenance. Single-lever faucets reduce the chances of a hot-water burn; slip-resistant surfaces prevent accidents. A timer on the light switch keeps your electrical bill down. Plastic laminate countertops and cabinets are a good choice—they're durable and easy to clean. For more information on safety in the bathroom, turn to page 47.

Master bath suite. The master bath has become more than just a place to grab a quick shower and run a comb through your hair. No longer merely a utilitarian space, today's master bath reflects the personality and interests of its owners. Often, it includes dressing and grooming areas, toilet and bathing facilities, and such other amenities as fireplaces, whirlpool baths, oversize tubs, and bidets. Outside this bath is a natural place for a spa, sunbathing deck, or private garden.

Here are some "extras" that you may want to consider for your master bath. Make sure that you provide adequate ventilation to prevent water damage (from splashes and condensation) to delicate objects and equipment.

- Walk-in dressing room
- Exercise room
- Makeup center
- Reading nook
- Home entertainment center
- Art gallery
- Greenhouse or sun room

Barrier-free bath. If you're remodeling to accommodate a disabled or elderly person, be sure you're aware of that person's special needs. Different heights, clearances, and room dimensions may be required. For example, to accommodate a wheelchair, the room must have specific clearances (see page 45). The door should swing out to allow easy movement in and out of the room. The shower needs to be curbless so a wheelchair can roll in unobstructed. You may also want to install grab bars, use levers in place of round door knobs, and choose fixtures and fittings specifically designed for the disabled.

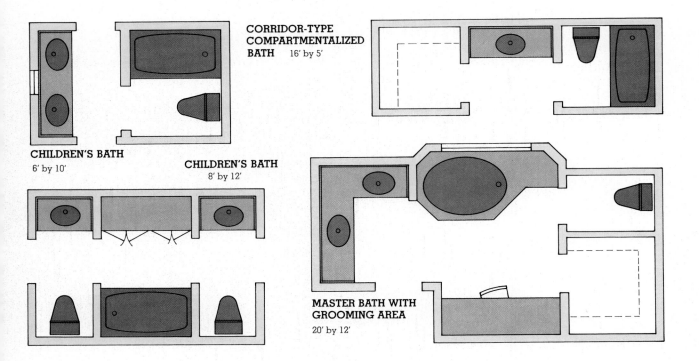

CORRIDOR-TYPE COMPARTMENTALIZED BATH   16' by 5'

CHILDREN'S BATH
6' by 10'

CHILDREN'S BATH
8' by 12'

MASTER BATH WITH GROOMING AREA
20' by 12'

MINIMUM CLEARANCES

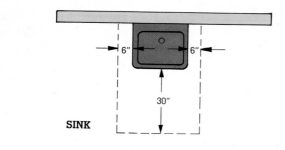

SINK

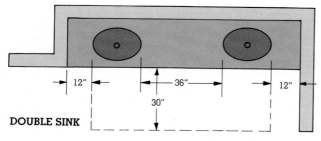

DOUBLE SINK

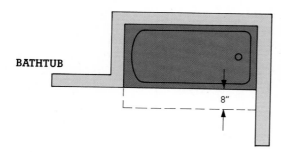

BATHTUB

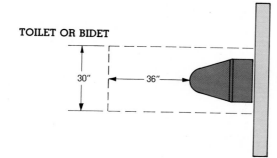

TOILET OR BIDET

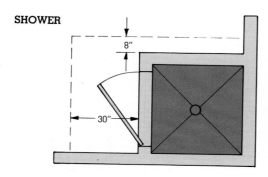

SHOWER

Locating fixtures

Before you can actually plan your bathroom layout and place your fixtures, it's important to understand some basic facts about plumbing lines, minimum heights and clearances, and fixture location. Only then can you plan a layout that makes sense both structurally and economically.

Once you have all the facts at hand, you'll be ready to experiment with layouts. To do this, trace the scale floor plan of your existing bathroom, including any adjoining space you're planning to "borrow." If you're considering removing or relocating walls, eliminate those existing partitions. As you experiment with different arrangements, set aside any plans you like and start fresh with another tracing of the bathroom's perimeter in its future form.

One of the biggest challenges in designing layouts for your new bathroom is keeping track of your ideas. If they're flowing, you won't want to forget your best inspirations just because you didn't get them down on paper.

One answer is to move paper cutouts around your floor plan and then sketch the best plans you devise with them. To use this method, first draw the perimeter of your existing floor plan and any adjacent areas to be included in the project. Then, using graph paper, make cutouts (to scale) of fixtures, cabinets, countertops, and other elements—both existing features you plan to keep and new ones to be added. Move the cutouts around the floor plan; when you hit on a layout you like, sketch it so you'll have a record of it. When you think you've exhausted the possibilities, compare the plans and evaluate them.

The existing structure

You'll keep costs down and simplify construction if you select a layout that uses the existing water supply, drain lines, and vent stack. If that's not possible, you may want to study the how-to section beginning on page 65 to familiarize yourself with the work that plumbing, wiring, and structural changes entail.

If you're adding on to your house, try to locate the new bathroom near an existing bathroom or near the kitchen. It's also more economical to arrange fixtures against one or two walls, eliminating the need for additional plumbing lines.

Generally, you can move a sink a few inches from its present position with only minor plumbing changes. Your existing supply and drain lines can usually support a second sink. You can extend existing supply and drain lines if the distance from the vent is less than the maximum distance allowed by your local code; if not, you'll have to install a secondary vent—a major undertaking.

If your bathroom has a wood floor with a crawl-space, basement, or first floor underneath, it's relatively simple to move both plumbing and wiring. But in rooms with concrete floors, it's an expensive proposition to move plumbing or wiring that's located under the concrete. To gain access to the lines, you would have to go through the laborious process of breaking up and removing the concrete.

Structural changes, especially those entailing work on load-bearing walls, fall into the category of serious remodeling and may require professional help. Relocating a door or window opening may also involve a lot of work, including framing and finishing. Adding a partition wall, on the other hand, is an easier and less expensive job.

Heights & clearances

Building codes specify minimum required clearances between, beside, and in front of bathroom fixtures to allow adequate room for use, cleaning, and repair. To help in your initial planning, check the minimum clearances shown on the facing page.

Generally, you can locate side-by-side fixtures closer together than fixtures positioned opposite each other. If a sink is opposite a bathtub or toilet, keep a minimum of 30 inches between them. Children, elderly, and disabled persons may require assistance or special fixtures; if you anticipate such needs, allow extra space in your layout.

Shown above, at right, are standard heights for countertops, shower heads, and accessories. If you and others using the bathroom are especially tall or short, you may wish to customize the room to your own requirements. However, when planning such a change, keep one eye on your home's resale value: will potential buyers find these alterations as convenient as you do?

Basic height and clearance guidelines for a barrier-free space are illustrated at right. For additional help, look for an architect or designer who specializes in this expanding field.

Fixture arrangement

It's usually best to position the largest unit—the bathtub or shower—first. Be sure you allow space for convenient access, for cleaning, and, if needed, for bathing a child.

Next, place the sink (or sinks). The most frequently used fixture in the bathroom, the sink should be positioned out of the traffic pattern. Be sure to plan for ample room in front for reaching below the sink and give plenty of elbow room at the sides.

Locate the toilet (and bidet, if you have one) away from the door; often, the toilet is placed beside the tub or shower. A toilet and bidet should be positioned next to each other.

Don't forget about the swing-radius for windows and doors. To resolve a conflict, you could either reverse a standard door's hardware from left to right or substitute a pocket door.

STANDARD HEIGHTS

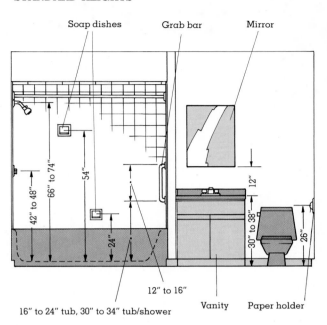

Soap dishes · Grab bar · Mirror

42" to 48" · 66" to 74" · 54" · 24" · 12" · 30" to 38" · 26"

12" to 16"

16" to 24" tub, 30" to 34" tub/shower · Vanity · Paper holder

BARRIER-FREE GUIDELINES

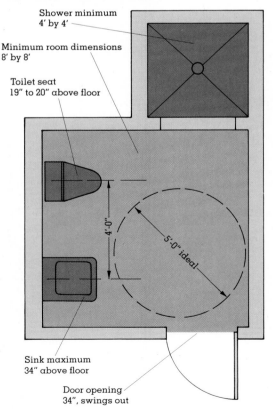

Shower minimum 4' by 4'

Minimum room dimensions 8' by 8'

Toilet seat 19" to 20" above floor

4'-0"

5'-0" ideal

Sink maximum 34" above floor

Door opening 34", swings out

Finishing touches

Once you've decided on a basic layout and marked the design you've worked out onto a clean tracing of your bathroom's floor plan, you can turn your attention to the walls. Begin by drawing an elevation of each wall and marking on those elevations the fixtures you've already located. Then you'll be ready to add all the other elements that go into your bathroom: storage, mirrors, towel bars, amenities, and heating and ventilation details.

To do this, you can use the same cutout technique you used for the fixtures (see page 44). But now you'll be working on an elevation, not a floor plan, and you'll be preparing a different set of cutouts—straight-on views of fixtures, cabinets, mirrors, and other elements. Arrange these cutouts with an eye for line, shape, and scale (see page 48). The plans you sketch as you move the cutouts around will help you visualize the room as a whole and see relationships between horizontal, vertical, diagonal, and curved lines. Be sure to set aside sketches of the arrangements you like so you can compare them later.

Storage needs

After arranging the fixtures, plan your storage space. Consider what you need to store, how much space you need for it, and how best to organize the space. If you're planning to expand your storage capacity, review your notes from the inventory to pinpoint which items require space.

Consider equipping a vanity or cabinet with racks, shelves, pull-outs, or lazy susans for supplies.

Many bathroom items are candidates for open storage—why not display colorful towels or stacks of soap on open shelving? For a look at a variety of successful storage solutions, see pages 30–35.

Filling in the details

Choosing appropriate fixtures, fittings, and cabinetry will block out your bathroom plan quickly, but don't forget the finishing touches that make or break a handsome, comfortable design. Below, you'll find a checklist of bathroom amenities to consider.

Surfaces. Floor, wall, and countertop surfaces should be durable as well as attractive. For details about the characteristics of the various surface materials, including plastic laminate, solid-surface, wood, stone, and tile, see pages 55 and 62–63 in the section "Bathroom showcase."

Saunas and steam showers. These luxurious features, once found mainly in gyms and health clubs, have recently entered the residential bathroom.

A sauna is a small, wood-lined room (often sold prefabricated) that heats itself to around 200°F. In addition to insulated walls, a solid-core door, and double-paned glass (if any), you'll also need an electric or gas sauna heater. Minimum size for a sauna is about 65 cubic feet per person. But don't make the space overly large—you'll just have more space to heat.

New steam units are small enough to be housed in any number of convenient locations—inside a stor-

ARCHITECT: REMICK ASSOCIATES

Heated towel bars keep bath linens toasty and also serve as radiators. Brass rack harnesses old-fashioned hydronic heat; you can also buy electric versions.

PLAYING IT SAFE IN THE BATHROOM

About 25 percent of all home accidents occur in the bathroom. You can reduce the risk of injury by careful planning and by encouraging safe practices. Here are some guidelines.

■ Install sufficient lighting. Include a night-light, especially if you have small children.

■ Choose tempered glass, plastic, and other shatterproof materials for construction and accessories.

■ Install locks that can be opened from the outside in an emergency.

■ Locate clothes hooks above eye level.

■ Select a tub or shower with a nonslip surface. For existing fixtures, use a rubber bath mat.

■ Install L-shaped or horizontal grab bars, capable of supporting a person weighing 250 pounds, in tub and shower areas. Installation must be done properly—bracing between studs may be required. Plaster-mounted accessories don't provide sufficient support.

■ Anchor any carpeting. Choose area rugs or bath mats with nonskid backing.

■ Avoid scalding by lowering the setting of your water heater or by installing a temperature-limiting mixing valve or a pressure-balancing valve to prevent sudden temperature drops.

■ Test the water temperature before stepping into a shower or tub and when assisting a child or elderly person. Place shower controls where they can be accessed quickly and conveniently.

■ Be sure electrical outlets are grounded and protected with GFCI circuit breakers. Outlets should be out of reach from the shower or bathtub. Install safety covers over unused outlets.

■ Avoid using electrical appliances in wet areas. Keep portable heaters out of the bathroom.

■ If children live in or visit your house, buy medicines (and, when possible, household cleansers) in child-proof containers. Store these items in a cabinet equipped with a safety latch. Tape seldom-used non-safety containers closed. Check the contents of your medicine cabinet at least twice a year and discard outdated medicines and those with unreadable or incomplete directions.

■ Keep a first aid kit handy for use in an emergency. Post phone numbers of the nearest emergency rescue unit and poison control center.

---

age cabinet, in an adjacent closet or alcove, or in a tall crawlspace. Besides the steam box, all you need is an airtight shower door, a comfortable bench, and effective ventilation.

Lighting. Don't leave lighting as an afterthought; it should be part of the initial design. A wide range of incandescent, fluorescent, and halogen light sources are on the market today, as well as a huge selection of fixtures to house them.

Design ideas for both natural and artificial light appear on pages 50–51. For a look at how light can be used in bathrooms, see pages 24–29.

Electrical outlets and switches. Tentatively mark the locations of outlets and switches. Every countertop longer than 12 inches should have a two-plug outlet; every wall must have an outlet every 12 feet—or at least one outlet per wall, regardless of size. Be sure that outlets within 6 feet of any wet area are grounded and protected with GFCI circuit breakers.

Switches are usually placed 44 inches above the floor on the open (or latch) side of doorways.

Hardware and accessories. Think now about how you'll coordinate doorknobs, drawer pulls, towel bars, a toilet-paper holder, and other accessories with your fixtures, fittings, and surfaces. Aim for an integrated overall look.

Heating & ventilation

If you want to extend your existing heating system to a new bathroom, check with a professional to be sure your system can handle the added load. You can relocate a hot air register in the floor or in the vanity kickspace by changing the duct work beneath the floor; ducts for wall registers can be rerouted in the stud wall. If you're adding a register, locate it where the duct work can be extended easily from the existing system and where you won't sacrifice wall space.

Hot air duct work is best done by a heating or sheet metal contractor. Extending hot water or steam systems is easier, but it, too, calls for professional help. It may be more practical to equip your bathroom with an electric space heater, which can be recessed in the wall or ceiling, or with an electric heat lamp.

Local building codes may require exhaust fans in certain bathrooms and specify their placement; check the code before you complete your design. Such fans are relatively simple to add or relocate. These units are installed in the ceiling between joists or in the wall between studs, and may require duct work to the outside.

Line, shape & scale

It may never occur to you to consider line, shape, and scale when you draw up your plans. Yet these design elements hold the key to a balanced, visually pleasing design. Take another look at your bathroom elevation sketches to examine these elements. You may want to improve the existing conditions—or perhaps you'll decide to try an entirely new approach.

Line—the dominant theme

Most bathrooms incorporate many different kinds of lines—vertical, horizontal, diagonal, curved, and angular. However, one line usually dominates and characterizes the design. Vertical lines give a sense of height, horizontals add width, diagonals suggest movement, and curved and angular lines impart a sense of grace and dynamism.

Repeating similar lines gives the room a sense of unity. Look at one of your elevation sketches. How do the vertical lines created by the cabinets, vanity, windows, doors, mirrors, and shower or tub unit fit together? Does the horizontal line marking the top of the window align with other horizontal lines in the room, such as the tops of the shower stall, door, and mirror? Clearly, not everything can or should line up perfectly, but the effect is far more pleasing if a number of elements are aligned, particularly when they're the highest features in the room.

Shape—a sense of harmony

Continuity and compatibility in shape also contribute to a unified design. Of course, you needn't repeat the same shape throughout the room—carried too far, that becomes monotonous.

Study the shapes created by doorways, windows, countertops, fixtures, and other elements. Look at patterns in your flooring, wall covering, shower curtain, and towels. Are they different or similar? If they're different, do they clash? If they're similar, are they boring? Consider ways to complement existing shapes or add compatible new ones. For example, if there's an arch over a recessed bathtub, create an arch over a doorway or repeat the arch on the trim of a shelf.

Scale—everything in proportion

When the scale of bathroom elements is in proportion to the overall size of the room, the design feels harmonious. A small bath seems even smaller if equipped with large fixtures and a large vanity. But the same bathroom appears larger, or at least in scale, when equipped with space-saving fixtures, a petite vanity, and open shelves,

Consider the proportions of adjacent features as well. When wall cabinets or linen shelves extend to the ceiling, they often make a room seem top-heavy—and therefore smaller. To counteract this look without losing storage space, place cabinet doors or shelves closer together at the top. Let your floor plan and elevation drawings suggest other ways you can modify the scale of different elements to improve your design.

ARCHITECT: REMICK ASSOCIATES

Squares are everywhere, but size and color contrast set surfaces apart. Easy-to-clean glazed tiles line walls to eye level. Floor mosaics set color accent and lead eye around corner, enlarging sense of space. Tile-high glass-block partition restates square motif and screens shower area while letting light pass through.

Color, texture & pattern

The ways you use color, texture, and pattern play an important part in your design. After you narrow down your selections, make a sample board to see how your choices work together. Color charts for fixtures are readily available, as are paint chips, fabric swatches, and wallpaper and flooring samples.

Choosing your colors

The size and orientation of your bathroom, your personal preferences, and the mood you want to create all affect color selection. Here are some color principles to guide you.

Light colors reflect light, making walls recede; thus, a small bathroom treated with light colors appears more spacious. Dark colors absorb light and can visually lower a ceiling or shorten a narrow room.

When considering colors for a small bathroom, remember that too much contrast has the same effect as a dark color: it reduces the sense of spaciousness. Contrasting colors work well for adding accents or drawing attention to interesting structural elements. But if you need to conceal a problem feature, it's best to use one color throughout the area.

Oranges, yellows, and other colors with a red tone impart a feeling of warmth to a room, but they also contract space. Cool colors—blues, greens, and colors with a blue tone—make an area seem larger. A light, monochromatic color scheme (using different shades of one color) is restful and serene. Contrasting colors add vibrancy and excitement to a design. But a color scheme with contrasting colors can be overpowering unless the tones of the colors are varied. Note, too, that the temperature and intensity of colors will be affected by lighting.

Adding interest with texture & pattern

Texture and pattern work like color in defining a room's style and sense of space. The bathroom's surface materials may include many different textures, from a glossy countertop to smooth wood cabinets to a roughly surfaced quarry-tile floor.

Rough textures absorb light, make colors look duller, and lend a feeling of informality. Smooth textures reflect light and tend to suggest elegance or modernity. Using similar textures helps unify a design and create a mood.

Pattern choices must harmonize with the predominant style of the room. Though pattern is usually associated with wall coverings or a cabinet finish, even natural substances such as wood, brick, and stone create patterns.

While variation in texture and pattern adds interest, too much variety can be overstimulating. It's best to let a strong feature or dominant pattern be the focus of your design and choose other surfaces to complement rather than compete with it.

DESIGNER: FU-TUNG CHENG / CHENG DESIGN

Concrete states an industrial theme, but color and texture add a soft, decorative counterpoint. Clean, cold masonry holds forth on the countertop; masonry is textured and painted on walls and soffits. Variegated slate tiles line floor and tub pedestal.

Lighting guidelines

No matter how beautifully it's decorated, a room with inadequate lighting will be an unpleasant place to be—and difficult to use. In a multiple-use room such as a bathroom, the light levels required range from very soft ambient light to strong directional task lighting. Usually, you can achieve a pleasing level by bringing in natural light through windows and skylights and supplementing it with artificial lighting.

Natural light

To bring natural light into your bathroom, you can use windows and doors (opening to secluded areas) as well as skylights—alone or in combination.

A single window in the middle of a wall often creates a glaring contrast with the surrounding area. To increase the amount of natural light, consider placing windows on adjacent walls or installing a skylight. Either will provide uniform lighting over a larger area. To maximize sunlight, position openings so they face south or west. But to avoid unwanted heat and glare, it's best to locate windows and skylights so they have a northern or eastern exposure.

Windows, available in many styles, may have frames of wood, aluminum, vinyl, or steel. All-vinyl windows and wood windows clad in vinyl or aluminum require the least maintenance.

Though you can have a skylight custom-made, many prefabricated units are available. Some open for ventilation. If there's a space between the ceiling and roof, you'll need a light shaft to direct light to the bathroom below. The shaft may be straight, angled, or splayed.

You can combine glass in different forms (panels and glass blocks, for example) and finishes (clear and translucent) to bring in light and view while still ensuring privacy. Generally, transparent materials are suitable above chin height of the tallest occupant. But be sure to check the heights and locations of neighbors' windows.

Artificial lighting

Artificial lighting can be separated into three categories: task, ambient, and accent. Task lighting illuminates a particular area where a visual activity, such as shaving or applying makeup, takes place. Ambient, or general, lighting fills the undefined areas of a room with a soft level of light—enough, say, for a relaxing soak in a whirlpool tub. Accent lighting, which is primarily decorative, is used to highlight architectural features, set a mood, or provide drama.

Which fixtures are best? Generally speaking, lighting in a bathroom should be small and discreet. Consequently, recessed downlights are very popular. Fitted with the right baffle or shield, those fixtures alone can handle ambient, task, and accent needs.

In a larger bathroom, a separate fixture to light the shower or bath area—or any other distinct part in a compartmentalized design—may be needed. Shower fixtures should be waterproof units fitted with neoprene seals.

Fixtures around a makeup or shaving mirror should spread light over a person's face rather than onto the mirror surface. To avoid heavy shadows, place lights at the sides of the mirror, not just overhead. Wall sconces flanking the mirror not only provide light but also offer an opportunity for a stylish design statement.

And just for fun, why not consider decorative uplights in a soffit or strip lights in a kickspace area? These accents help provide a wash of ambient light and also serve as safe, pleasant night-lights.

Dimmers (also called rheostats) enable you to set a fixture at any level from a soft glow to a radiant brightness. They're also energy savers. It's easy and inexpensive to put incandescent bulbs on dimmers. The initial cost of dimmers for fluorescent lights is greater than for incandescents, and the variety of fixtures with dimmers is limited.

Light bulbs and tubes. Light sources can be grouped in general categories according to the way they produce light.

Incandescent light, the kind used most frequently in homes, is produced by a tungsten thread that burns slowly inside a glass tube. A-bulbs are the old standbys; R and PAR bulbs produce a more controlled beam; silvered-bowl types diffuse light. A number of decorative bulbs are also available.

Low-voltage incandescent lights are especially useful for accent lighting. Operating on 12 or 24 volts, these lights require transformers (which are often built into the fixtures) to step down the voltage from standard 120-volt household circuits.

Fluorescent tubes are unrivaled for energy efficiency; they also last far longer than incandescent bulbs. Older fluorescent tubes have been criticized for noise, flicker, and poor color rendition. Electronic ballasts and better fixture shielding against glare have remedied the first two problems; as for the last one, manufacturers have developed fluorescents in a wide spectrum of colors, from very warm (about 2,700 degrees K) to very cool (about 6,300 degrees K).

Bright, white *quartz halogen* bulbs are excellent for task lighting, pinpoint accenting, and other dramatic accents. Halogen is usually low-voltage but may be standard line current. The popular MR-16 bulb creates the tightest beam; for a longer reach and wider coverage, choose a PAR bulb. There's an abundance of smaller bulb shapes and sizes to fit pendants and undercabinet strip lights.

Halogen has two disadvantages: high initial cost and very high heat. Shop carefully—some fixtures on the market are not UL-approved.

ARCHITECT: MORIMOTO ARCHITECTS

Multiple light sources provide ambient, task, and accent light—day and night. Built-in sink fixture recessed behind "shoji-screen" trim spreads light via diffusing panels. Wall sconces add general light and decorative flair. A skylight brings in welcome sunshine.

Contemporary pendants follow lines of countertop and repeat in backsplash mirrors. Nonglare bulbs provide plenty of ambient and task light.

DESIGNER: OSBURN DESIGN

ARCHITECT: J. ALLEN SAYLES

Well-chosen accent lighting adds pizzazz to a powder room. Diamond-patterned marble border is highlighted by hidden low-voltage strip lights.

Finalizing your plan

The planning process culminates with the drawing of your new floor plan. The floor plan is the basis for the remodeling work, for the preparation of a master list of products and materials, and for the acquisition of any necessary building permits.

Drawing a floor plan

Draw the new floor plan in the same way as you did the existing floor plan (see pages 40–41). On the new plan, include both existing features you want to preserve and all proposed changes, such as new walls, partitions, doors, windows, skylights, light fixtures, electrical switches and outlets, fixtures, cabinets, countertops, and materials. If you prefer, you can hire a designer, drafter, or contractor to draw the final plan for you.

For more complicated projects, your local building department may require additional or more detailed drawings of structural, plumbing, and wiring changes. You may also need to show areas adjacent to the bathroom on the new plan so building officials can determine how the project will affect the rest of your house. Elevation sketches aren't required, but they'll serve as a helpful check in planning the work and ordering materials.

If you're the one ordering the materials for your remodeling project, you'll need to compile a detailed master list. Not only will this launch your work, but it will also help you keep track of purchases and deliveries. For each item that you plan to order, be sure to specify the following information: name and model or serial number, manufacturer, source of material, date of order, delivery date, color, size or dimensions, quantity, price (including tax and delivery charge), and second choice.

Obtaining building permits

To discover which building codes may affect your remodeling project and whether a building permit is required, check with your city or county building department.

You probably won't need a building permit for simple jobs, such as replacing a window with one of the same size, installing a vanity, or changing floor or wall coverings. But for more substantial changes, you may need to apply for one or more of the following permits: structural, plumbing, mechanical heating or cooling, reroofing, or electrical. More complicated projects sometimes require that the design and the working drawings be executed by an architect, designer, or state-licensed contractor.

For your permit, you'll be charged either a flat fee or a percentage of the estimated cost of materials and labor. You may also have to pay a fee to have someone check the plans.

If you're acting as your own contractor, you must ask the building department to inspect the work as it progresses. (A professional contractor handles these inspections without your becoming involved.) The number of inspections depends on the complexity of the job. Failure to obtain a permit or an inspection may result in your having to dismantle completed work.

NEW FLOOR PLAN

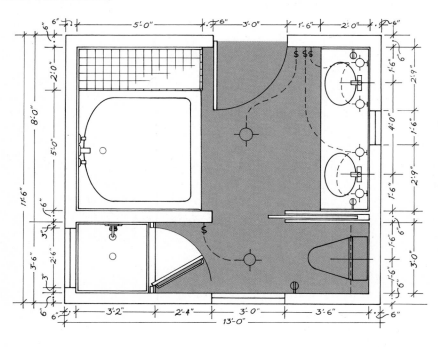

In this redesign of the floor plan shown on page 41, there's one big change: the lower, or outside, wall has been pushed out about 3 feet to house a new shower and toilet alcove. A pocket door seals this space, providing privacy while a second person uses the sink or tub areas.

New fixtures include a 5 by 5-foot platform tub and a second deck-mount sink. New light fixtures and electrical outlets complete the plan.

This project would require a professional to prepare detailed drawings of structural, plumbing, and wiring changes. If your project is less complicated, you could probably draw in all the changes yourself. A key to architectural symbols appears on page 41.

WORKING WITH PROFESSIONALS

Major home remodeling projects are not easy work. If you know how to draw plans but dislike physical labor, you'll need someone else to perform the actual work. If you're able to wield a saw and hammer but can't draw a straight line, you may need professional help to prepare the new floor plan or specifications. Some people do the nonspecialized work, such as clearing the site and cleaning up later, but hire experts for everything else. Others let professionals handle the entire project— from drawing plans through applying the finishing touches.

No matter whom you consult, be as precise as possible about what you want and about your budget. Collect pertinent photographs, manufacturer's brochures, and advertisements. Describe the materials, fixtures, and fittings you want to use. Provide your preliminary plans and a rough figure of how much you plan to spend. If you have questions, write them down as you think of them. The more information you can supply and the more informed you are, the better job a professional will be able to do.

Architect or designer?

Either an architect or a designer can draw plans acceptable to building department officials. Each can send out bids, help you select a contractor, and supervise the contractor's work to ensure that your plans and time schedule are being followed. Some architects and designers even double as their own contractors.

Most states do not require designers to be licensed, as architects must be; designers may charge less for their labor. If stress calculations must be made, designers need state-licensed engineers to design the structure and sign the working drawings; architects can do their own calculations.

Many architects are members of the American Institute of Architects (AIA), and many designers belong to the American Institute of Building Designers (AIBD). If you want to work with a bathroom designer, look for members of the National Kitchen & Bath Association (NKBA) or a Certified Bathroom Designer (CBD). Each association has a code of ethics and sponsors continuing programs to inform members about the latest building materials and techniques.

You may also wish to call on the services of an interior designer for finishing touches. These experts specialize in the decorating and furnishing of rooms. They can offer fresh, innovative ideas and advice. Through their contacts, you have access to materials and products not available at the retail level. Many designers belong to the American Society of Interior Designers (ASID), a professional organization.

Architects and designers may charge for time spent in an exploratory interview. For plans, you'll probably be charged on an hourly basis. If you want an architect or designer to select the contractor and keep an eye on construction, plan to pay either an hourly rate or a percentage of the cost of materials and labor—15 to 25 percent is typical. Descriptions of the services to be performed and the amount of the charges should be stated in advance in writing to prevent expensive misunderstandings later on.

Choosing a contractor

Contractors are responsible for construction and all building operations. Often, they're also skilled drafters, able to draw working plans acceptable to building department officials; they can also obtain the necessary building permits.

If you decide to use a contractor, ask architects, designers, and friends for recommendations. To compare bids for the actual construction, contact at least three state-licensed contractors; give each one either an exact description and sketches of the desired remodeling or plans and specifications prepared by an architect or designer. Include a detailed account of who will be responsible for what work.

Don't be tempted to make price your only criterion for selection; reliability, quality of work, and on-time performance are also important. Ask the contractors for the names and phone numbers of recent clients. Call several and ask them how they feel about the contractor; if you can, inspect the contractor's work. Ask for proof of liability insurance; also check bank and credit references to determine the contractor's financial responsibility.

Though some contractors may want a fee based on a percentage of the cost of materials and labor, it's usually wiser to insist on a fixed-price bid. This protects you against both an unexpected rise in the cost of materials (assuming that the contractor does the buying) and the chance that the work will take more time, adding to your labor costs. Many states limit the amount of "good faith" money that contractors can require before work begins.

Hiring subcontractors

When you act as your own general contractor and put various parts of your project out to bid with subcontractors (plumbers, tile setters, and the like), you must use the same care you'd exercise in hiring a general contractor.

Check the references, financial resources, and insurance coverage of a number of subcontractors. Once you've received bids and chosen your subcontractor, work out a detailed contract for each job and carefully supervise all work.

Bathroom showcase

On the following pages is a wonderland of products and materials for the bathroom. Here you can see and compare at a glance a sampling of styles, installation methods, functions, and materials. Though it's by no means exhaustive, this showcase provides the basic information you'll need as you sketch layouts, gather specifications for contracts or ordering, and develop a budget.

Recognizing the need to conserve resources, many manufacturers today offer a variety of water-saving toilets, faucets, shower heads, and hand-held shower attachments, with price and performance comparable to those of their conventional counterparts. These fixtures and fittings can reduce not only the amount of water used but also the amount of energy needed to heat that water.

CABINETS

Today, as changing lifestyles find new expression and bathrooms become grooming centers, exercise gyms, and spas, storage needs and configurations are also changing. One or more base vanities may still form the backbone of the storage scheme, but bath storage areas have become more stylish, their design integrated with mirrors, sink, lighting, and backsplash treatment. Perhaps you'll wish to add a bank of wall cabinets, let built-ins form knee walls between use areas, or plan a floor-to-ceiling unit.

Traditional American cabinets mask the raw front edges of each box with a 1 by 2 faceframe. On European, or frameless, cabinets, a simple narrow trim strip covers raw edges; doors and drawers usually fit to within ¼ inch of each other, revealing a thin sliver of

trim. Door hinges are invisible. Thanks to absolute standardization of every component, frameless cabinets are unsurpassed in versatility.

You can purchase a vanity cabinet with or without countertop and sink. Some manufacturers produce modular cabinet and shelf units for use with their vanities; other units include laundry bins, medicine cabinets, and closets. Standard width is 30 inches, increasing at 3 or 6-inch intervals, but some are as narrow as 12 inches and as wide as 60 inches. Standard heights range from 28 to 36 inches; depths range up to 24 inches.

If you don't find what you're looking for in the bath department, take a look at kitchen units; the differences between cabinet lines are slowly disappearing.

Styles

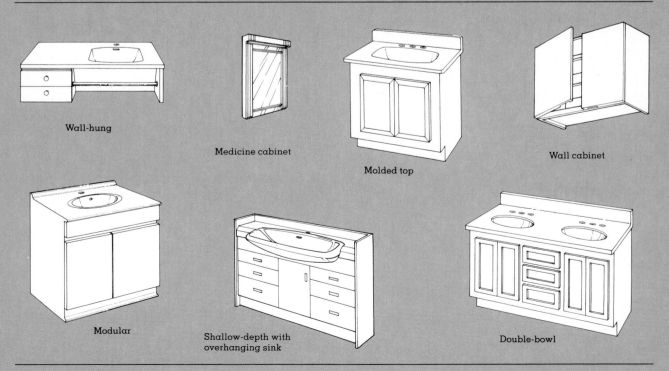

Wall-hung

Medicine cabinet

Molded top

Wall cabinet

Modular

Shallow-depth with overhanging sink

Double-bowl

COUNTERTOPS

Plastic laminate, ceramic tile, solid-surface acrylic, and stone are the four major countertop materials currently in use. Synthetic marble, popular in the past, is losing ground to solid-surface materials. Wood is sometimes used for countertops, too, but the surface must be carefully sealed to prevent water damage.

Style	Characteristics
Plastic laminate	Laminate comes in a wide range of colors, textures, and patterns. It's durable, easy to clean, water-resistant, and relatively inexpensive. However, it can scratch, scorch, chip, and stain. Also, smooth, reflective surfaces tend to show dirt and water marks. Conventional laminate has a dark backing that shows at its seams; new solid-color laminate, designed to avoid this, is somewhat brittle and more expensive. Post-formed tops, premolded and prefabricated, are the least expensive option; a custom top with built-up lip and backsplash looks best but is more costly.
Ceramic tile	Good-looking ceramic tile comes in many colors, textures, and patterns. Installed correctly, it's heatproof, scratch-resistant, and water-resistant. On the other hand, the grout may be hard to keep clean, even when a grout sealer is used. Also, tile's hard, irregular surface can chip delicate glass containers. High-gloss tiles show every smudge. Prices range from modest to extravagant, depending on style, accents, and accessory pieces. Nonporous glazed tiles won't soak up spills and stains.
Solid-surface	Durable, water-resistant, nonporous, and easy to clean, this marblelike material allows for a variety of edge details and sink installations, including integral units. Blemishes and scratches can be sanded out. Solid-surface countertops are expensive and require firm support from below. Until recently, color selection was limited to white, beige, and almond; now, imitation stone and pastels are readily available. Costs go up for wood inlays and other fancy edge details.
Stone	Granite and marble are beautiful natural materials for countertops. In most areas, you'll find a great selection of colors and figures. Stone is water-resistant, heatproof, easy to clean, and very durable. Oil, alcohol, and any acid (even chemicals in some water supplies) can stain marble and damage its high-gloss finish; granite can stand up to all of these. Solid stone slabs are very expensive. Stone tiles, including slate and limestone, are less expensive alternatives.
Synthetic marble	This group of man-made products, collectively known as "cast polymers," includes cultured marble, cultured onyx, and cultured granite. All three are relatively inexpensive and easy to clean. These products are often sold with an integral sink. Synthetic marble is not very durable, and scratches and dings are hard to mend (the surface finish is often only a thin veneer). Quality varies widely; look for Cultured Marble Institute or IAPMO certification.
Wood	Wood is handsome, natural, easily installed, and easy on grooming accessories and glass containers. However, wood is harder to keep clean than nonporous materials. If you use it in areas that will get wet (and that includes many bathroom surfaces), thoroughly protect it on all sides with a good sealer, such as polyurethane. Maple butcherblock, the most popular ready-made top, is sold in 24, 30, and 36-inch widths; installed price is comparable to ceramic or top-of-the-line laminate. Edge-joined oak, redwood, sugar pine, and teak are also used for counters.

SINKS

Sinks come in many shapes, sizes, colors, materials, and styles. The most commonly available styles are deck-mount, integral sink and countertop, pedestal, and wall-hung. Sinks have either no holes for fittings or holes for 4, 6, or 8-inch faucet assemblies; some also have holes for spray attachments and lotion dis-

pensers (see page 59 for more about sink fittings). You'll find a wide selection of sink materials. Vitreous china, fiberglass-reinforced plastic, enameled cast iron, and enameled steel are the most common. Brass and copper sinks make striking accents, but they require zealous maintenance.

Style	Characteristics
Deck-mount, self-rimming	A self-rimming sink has a molded overlap that's supported by the edge of the countertop cutout. The cutout is undersized, allowing the sink rim to sit on the countertop. This style is easy to install and offers the widest range in shapes, including shell, hexagon, and fluted.
Deck-mount, flush	A surrounding metal frame holds a flush-mount sink to the countertop. The frame comes in several finishes to match fittings. Keeping the joints between the frame, sink, and countertop clean requires some vigilance. This style is usually used with plastic laminate countertops.
Deck-mount, unrimmed	An unrimmed sink is recessed beneath the countertop opening and held in place by metal clips. Fittings are mounted through the countertop or directly on the sink. The sink-countertop joint requires a little extra effort to keep clean. This sink is a good choice for use with tile, plastic laminate, or synthetic marble countertops.
Integral sink and countertop	Made of solid-surface material, synthetic marble, vitreous china, or fiberglass, an integral sink and countertop has no joints, so installation and cleaning are easy. This one-piece molded unit sits on top of a vanity. Sink color can either match the countertop or complement it; edge-banding and other border options abound. Double-bowl units are available.
Pedestal	Pedestal sinks are making a big comeback. Typically made of vitreous china in a wide range of traditional and modern designs, these elegant sinks are easy to install. The pedestal usually hides the plumbing. Some models have old-style vanity legs. Pedestal sinks are generally among the highest-priced basins. There's no storage space beneath.
Wall-hung	Like pedestals, wall-hung sinks are enjoying a revival. Materials and styling are similar; in fact, some designs are available in either version. Generally speaking, these are the least expensive and most compact sink options. Wall-hung units are supported by hangers or angle brackets. If you're installing a wall-hung sink for the first time, plan to add a support ledger.

BATHTUBS

Today's bathtub market overflows with styles. The 30 by 60-inch bathtub, which contributed to the predominance of the 5 by 7-foot bathroom, no longer rules. New and more comfortable tub shapes and sizes are available in an array of colors. Tubs can be purchased in whirlpool models and with grab bars and slip-resistant surfaces for safety. A white tub without special features is still the least expensive.

The boxy, familiar tub is enameled steel, relatively inexpensive, and lightweight. But it's also noisy, cold, and prone to chipping. Enameled cast-iron tubs are more durable and warmer to the touch, but they're very heavy. The most innovative tubs are vacuum-formed acrylic or injection-molded thermoplastic like ABS. These lightweight shells retain heat well, but their shiny surfaces can scratch or dull.

Style	Characteristics
Standard 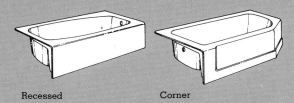 Recessed Corner	Rectangular tubs come in two styles: recessed and corner. Recessed tubs fit between two side walls and against a back wall; they have one finished side. Corner models have one finished side and end and may be right or left-handed. If space allows, choose a longer model rather than the standard 60 inches; a depth of 16 inches or more is more comfortable than the standard 14 inches.
Platform/sunken 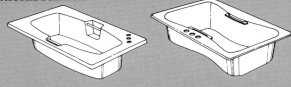	Platform or sunken tubs, most commonly available in enameled cast iron or acrylic, are either set in a raised platform or sunk in the floor. Extra framing is often needed, especially for installation on an upper floor. Interior shapes and features vary. Built-in headrests, seating shelves, and grab bars abound.
Freestanding 	An old-fashioned freestanding tub, such as the enduring clawfoot model, makes a nice focal point for a traditional design. You can buy reproductions or a reconditioned original. Such tubs can double as showers with the addition of Victorian-inspired shower head/diverter/curtain rod hardware. Recently, many new sources for renovators' supplies have sprung up; check specialty shops and antique plumbing catalogues.
Whirlpool 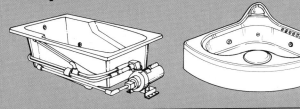	Think of these hydromassage units simply as bathtubs with air jets. Jet designs vary; generally, you can opt for high volume and low pressure (a few strong jets) or low pressure and high volume (lots of softer jets). The best whirlpools are adjustable for water volume, air-water mixture, and direction. Because of their extra weight, whirlpools may need special floor framing. They may also require an extra-capacity water heater or separate in-line heater.
Soaking 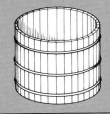	Soaking tubs have deep interiors. Ideal for use in small spaces, they come in recessed, platform, and corner models, with rectangular or round interiors of fiberglass or acrylic. Hot tubs, with their continuous water supply, can present moisture problems in all but the best-ventilated spaces. They're best used outdoors.

SHOWERS

Many shower options are available, including shower and tub/shower kits that come with or without overlapping wall panels, adhesive, and caulking. You can also purchase shower and tub/shower wall kits to use with existing shower bases and tubs. If shower or tub/shower doors don't come with your kit, you can buy them separately. Because of their size, one-piece molded shower or tub/shower surrounds are used primarily in new homes or additions; if you have oversize doors in your house, you may be able to use one of these units.

Size is important; make sure you carefully measure the installation area and the unit before you buy. Units are available in fiberglass-reinforced plastic, acrylic, plastic laminate, and synthetic marble. Shower stalls made of tin or stainless steel are fading from the plumbing scene.

Style	Characteristics
Shower surrounds 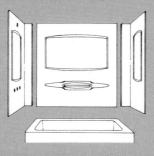	Most shower surrounds require framing for support; you fasten the panel flanges to the framing. The shower base, walls, and door can be purchased individually or in a kit. Some models come with ceilings. For comfort, choose a shower that's at least 3 feet square. Complete assemblies vary in height, but 84 inches is common. Corner and circular shower models are available. Circular showers feature clear or tinted acrylic doors that double as walls.
Tub/shower surrounds 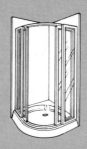	Tub/shower surrounds must also have framing for support. You can purchase the tub, walls, and door in a kit, or buy a separate recessed tub and match it with compatible prefabricated wall panels or a custom wall treatment (such as tile panels). Molded fiberglass wall panels may include molded soap dishes, ledges, and grab bars. You can also add a shower head or install a hand-held shower attachment to convert an existing tub surround to a tub/shower. Shower attachments are mounted to the wall or tub spout.
Shower bases 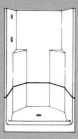 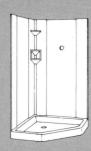 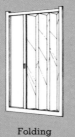 Rectangular Square Corner	A shower base can be purchased separately or in a kit that includes a shower surround. Most bases are made of fiberglass, acrylic, or terrazzo, and come in standard sizes in rectangular, square, or corner shapes; all have a predrilled hole for the drain. It's easy to find a base that matches a tub or another fixture, as many manufacturers make both.
Shower doors    Swinging Sliding Folding	Doors for showers come in a variety of styles: swinging, sliding, and folding, as well as pivot (not shown). Tub/showers typically have sliding or folding doors. Doors and enclosures are commonly made of tempered safety glass with aluminum frames. Frames come in many finishes; you can select one to match your fittings. The glazing can be clear, hammered, pebbled, tinted, or striped. Many sliding doors have towel bars. Swinging, folding, and pivot doors can be installed with right or left openings. Folding doors are constructed of rigid plastic panels or flexible plastic sheeting.

FITTINGS FOR FIXTURES

Fittings are sold separately from fixtures. Select fittings that are durable and easy to use. Cost varies according to material, quality, and design.

Fittings for sinks are available with single, center-set, or spread-fit controls. A single-control fitting has a combined faucet and lever or knob that controls water flow and temperature. A center-set control has separate hot and cold water controls and a faucet, all mounted on a base. A spread-fit control has separate hot and cold water controls and a faucet, each independently mounted. The number of holes in the sink and the distances between them—either 4, 6, or 8 inches—determine which fittings can be used. If fittings are to be attached to the wall or counter, the holes can be placed to suit the fittings.

For tubs and tub/showers, you can use either single or separate controls. Tubs also require a spout and drain. Tub/showers need a spout, shower head, diverter valve, and drain. Water-saver shower heads are readily available. You can purchase single-control fittings with pressure-balancing and temperature-limiting valves.

The best fittings are made of brass and come in several finishes, including chrome, pewter, gold, and bright enamel. Ceramic or nylon-disk designs are generally easier to maintain than older schemes.

Styles

Sink sets

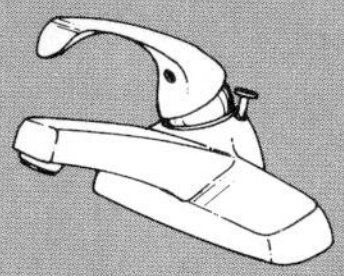

Single-control

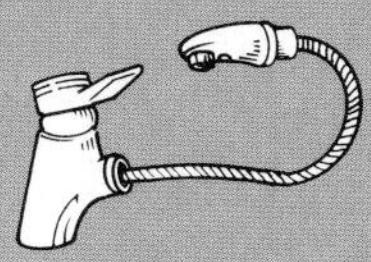

Single-control with pull-out sprayer

Center-set

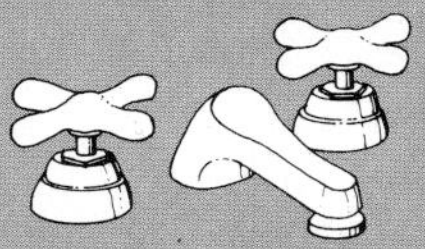

Spread-fit

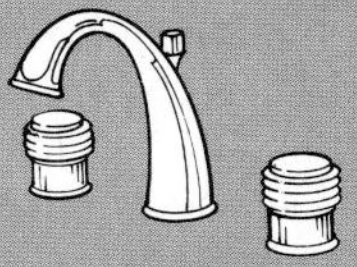

Spread-fit

Shower sets

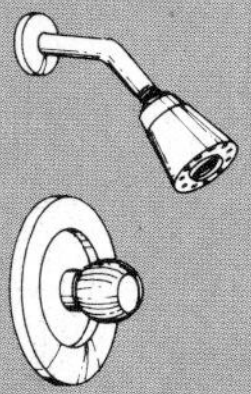

Single-control

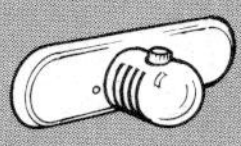

Temperature-limiting

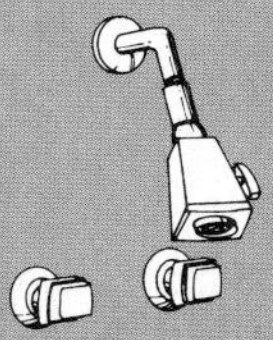

Separate controls

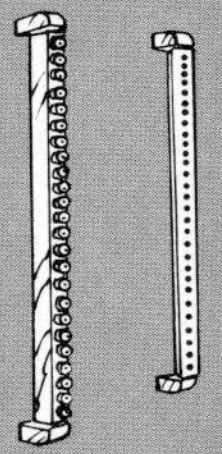

Spray bars

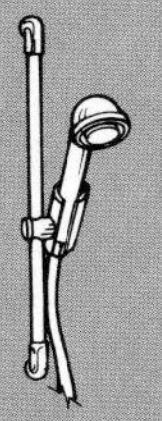

Adjustable-height head

Tub sets

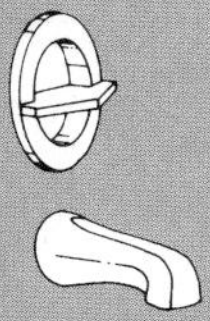

Single-control

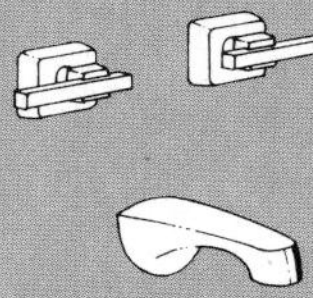

Separate controls

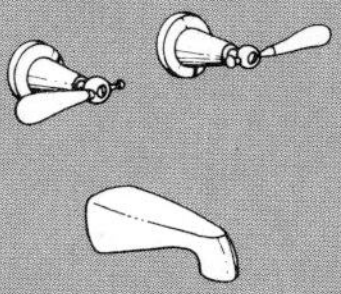

Separate controls

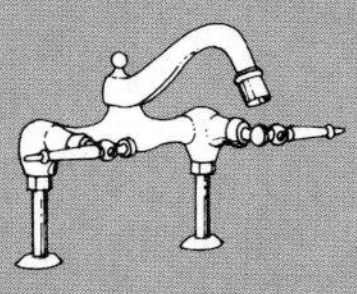

Deck-mount with separate controls

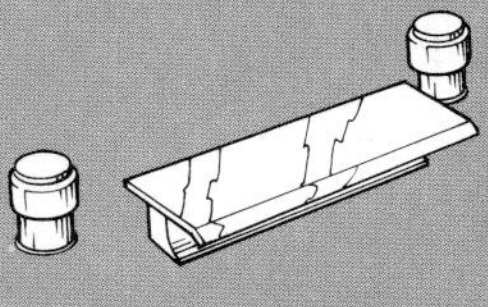

Roman spout with deck-mount controls

Tub/shower sets

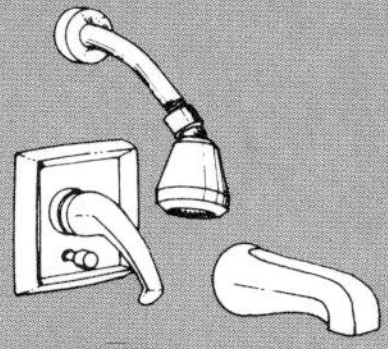

Single-control with diverter

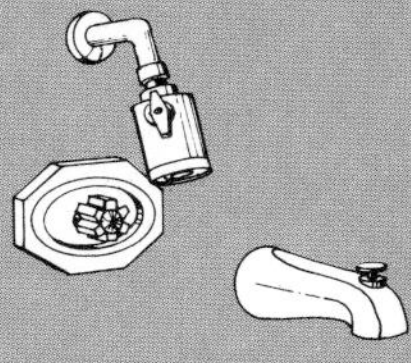

Single-control with spout diverter

Separate controls with handle diverter

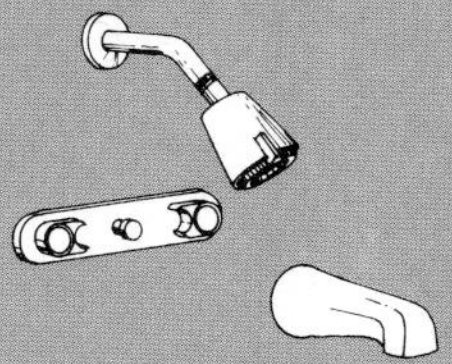

Separate controls with button diverter

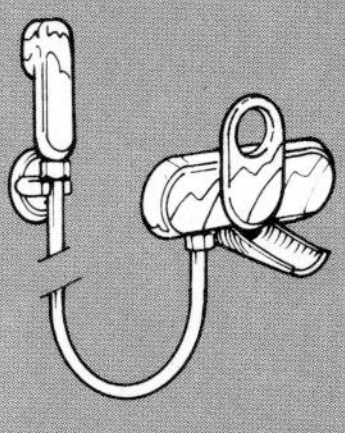

Hand shower

TOILETS & BIDETS

New styling, new colors, and new technologies are updating the tried-and-true water closet. In addition to standard and antique models, toilets now come in sleek European designs, standard or low-profile heights, and rounded or elongated bowl shapes.

A washdown toilet, no longer accepted by many code authorities, is the least expensive, least efficient, and most noisy of the various models. Less noisy is a reverse trap toilet; it has a smaller water area, water seal, and trapway than the washdown.

A siphon jet toilet is quieter and has a larger water surface than the previous two styles, but it's also more costly; because it has a larger trapway, it's less likely to clog.

The new word in toilets is ultra-low-flush. Older toilets use 5 to 7 gallons of water or more per flush. In 1983, codes were changed to require 3½-gallon-per-flush toilets for new construction. But ultra-low-flush (ULF) toilets, which use only 1.6 gallons or less per flush, are already replacing these. Some homeowners complain that ULF toilets require several flushings. One solution to this problem is the pressure-assisted design, which uses a strong air vacuum to power a quick, intensive flush.

A bidet, best installed next to the toilet, is floor mounted and plumbed with hot and cold water. It's used primarily for personal hygiene.

Toilets and bidets are made of vitreous china.

Style	Characteristics
One-piece  Low-profile Wall-hung	One-piece toilets are characterized by their low profile, usually 19 to 26 inches high. These units are designed for floor and wall mounting. Available with round or elongated bowls, one-piece toilets have reverse trap, siphon jet, or ultra-low-flush flushing action. Their design, efficiency, and easy installation make them a popular choice.
Two-piece  Standard  Safety 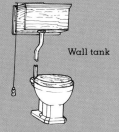 Wall tank  Ultra-low-flush	Two-piece toilets come in many models and can be mounted on the floor or on the wall. A wall-hung toilet, available only in siphon jet and siphon action models, offers easy access to the floor for cleaning. If you don't already have a wall-hung toilet, you'll face fairly major alterations to the wall framing and the floor. If you have special needs, consider special toilet designs. The rim of a higher-seat safety toilet is 18 inches above the floor, compared to the 14-inch height of a conventional bowl. A back-outlet toilet has an above-floor drain. It's most frequently used on concrete floors, where it would be difficult and costly to install other toilets or relocate an existing one.
Bidets Center-fit Spread-fit	Available with wall or deck-mount water controls, a bidet comes with a spray spout or a vertical spray located in the center of the bowl. Some have rim jets for rinsing, to maintain bowl cleanliness. Most models also have a pop-up stopper that allows the unit to double as a foot bath or as a basin for washing clothes.

HEATING & VENTILATION

Nothing spoils the soothing effects of a long, hot soak or shower faster than stepping out into a cool bathroom. A small heater in the wall or ceiling may be just what you need to stay warm while toweling off.

Bathroom heaters warm rooms by two methods: convection (usually boosted by a small fan) and radiation. Convection heaters warm the air in a room; the air, in turn, transfers the heat to surfaces and objects that it contacts. Radiant heaters emit infrared or electromagnetic waves that warm the objects and surfaces they hit without warming the intervening air. If you're installing a new slab or subfloor, you may want to consider radiant heating pipes below.

Most building codes require that bathrooms have either natural or forced ventilation. Forced ventilation, then, is required in windowless bathrooms. In fact, some codes specify that the exhaust fan must be on the same switch as the lights. But even if you have good natural ventilation, an exhaust fan can exchange the air in a bathroom faster than an open window; in bad weather, a fan can keep the elements out and still remove stale air.

Style	Characteristics
Electric heaters  Radiant heater with heat lamps Convection heater with light and fan Radiant or convection wall heater	Wall or ceiling-mounted convection heaters usually have an electrically heated resistance coil and a small fan to move the heated air. Radiant heaters using infrared light bulbs may be surface-mounted on the ceiling or recessed between joists. Radiant heating panels are generally flush-mounted on a wall or ceiling.
Gas heaters   Convection wall heater Freestanding heater	You'll find heaters available for either propane or natural gas. Though most are convection heaters, there is one radiant type: a catalytic heater. Most gas heaters are flush-mounted on a wall, but in a spacious master suite you might consider an attractive, freestanding "stove" unit. Options include electric ignition and wall-mounted thermostats.
Heated towel bars 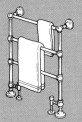 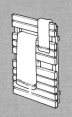 Hydronic towel bar Electric towel bar	Besides gas and electricity, another heat source has reappeared on the bathroom scene: hot water. The original idea was to warm bath towels, but now these hydronic units—wall or floor-mounted—are being billed as radiators as well. You can find electric versions of the towel bar heater, too.
Exhaust fans   Ceiling fan Ceiling fan with light Wall fan	You can buy fans to mount in the wall or ceiling. Some models are combined with a light or a heater, or both. The Home Ventilating Institute recommends that the fan be capable of exchanging the air at least eight times every hour (for details, see page 81). Most fans also have a noise rating measured in sones; the lower the number, the quieter the fan.

FLOORING

Think moisture-resistance when choosing a flooring material for a bathroom. Resilient tiles and sheets, ceramic tile, and properly sealed hardwood and stone are all good candidates. For a touch of comfort, don't rule out carpeting, especially the newer stain-resistant, industrial types.

For safety's sake, a bathroom floor must be slip-resistant, especially in wet areas. Tiles are safest in matte-finish versions. Smaller tiles, with their extra grout spaces, offer more traction than larger tiles. A rubberized mat or throw rug (if it will stay put) can provide firm footing near the tub or shower.

Style	Characteristics
Resilient	Generally made of solid vinyl, rubber, or polyurethane, resilients are flexible, moisture and stain-resistant, easy to install, and simple to maintain. A seemingly endless variety of colors, textures, patterns, and styles is available. Resilient is vulnerable to dents and tears but can be repaired. Tiles can collect moisture between seams if improperly installed.
	Sheets run up to 12 feet wide, eliminating the need for seaming in many bathrooms; tiles are generally 12 inches square. Vinyl and rubber are comfortable to walk on. Polyurethane finish eliminates waxing.
	Vinyl is the least expensive option. Some vinyl comes with a photographically applied pattern, but most is inlaid; the latter style is more expensive but wears better. Tiles are often easier to lay than sheet goods.
Ceramic tile	Made of hard-fired slabs of clay, tiles are usually classified as *quarry* tile, commonly unglazed (unfinished) red-clay tiles that are rough and water-resistant; *pavers*, rugged unglazed tiles in earth-tone shades; and *glazed* tile, available in glossy, matte, or textured finishes and in many colors. Tile sizes run the gamut of widths, lengths, and thicknesses.
	Tile can be cold, noisy, and, if glazed, slippery underfoot. If not properly grouted, tiles can leak moisture. Grout spaces can be tough to keep clean. Cost varies widely; three-dimensional patterns and multicolored glazes can easily double costs. Purer clays fired at higher temperatures generally make costlier but better-wearing tiles.
Wood	Wood contributes warmth to the decor, feels good underfoot, resists wear, and can be refinished. The three basic types are *strip*, narrow tongue-and groove boards in random lengths; *plank*, tongue-and-groove boards in various widths and random lengths; and *wood tile*, often laid in blocks or squares in parquet fashion. "Floating" floor systems have several veneered strips atop each tongue-and-groove backing board. Wood flooring may be factory-prefinished or unfinished.
	Moisture will damage wood flooring; also, an adequate floor substructure is crucial. Bleaching and some staining processes may wear unevenly and are difficult to repair. Wood is moderate to expensive in cost, depending on quality, finish, and installation. Floating systems are generally the most expensive.
Stone	Natural stone, such as slate, flagstone, marble, granite, and limestone, has been used for flooring for centuries. Today, its use is even more practical, thanks to the development of sealers and finishes. Easy to maintain, stone flooring is also virtually indestructible.
	Stone can be used in its natural shape or cut into uniform pieces—rectangular blocks or more formal tiles. Generally, uniform pieces are butted tightly together; irregular flagstone requires grouted joints.
	The cost of most stone flooring is high. Moreover, the weight of the materials requires a very strong, well-supported subfloor. Some stone—marble in particular—is cold and slippery underfoot. Careful sealing is a must; some stones absorb stains and dirt readily.

WALL COVERINGS

In addition to the shower and tub-surround areas, your bathroom will probably include a good bit of wall space. Bathroom wall treatments must be able to withstand moisture, heat, and high usage. These surfaces also go a long way toward defining the overall impact of your bath. (For details on paint, see page 101.)

Style	Characteristics
Ceramic tiles	Wall tiles are glazed and offer great variety in color and design. Generally lighter and thinner than floor tiles, they're used primarily on interior surfaces—walls, countertops, and ceilings. Their relatively light weight is a plus for vertical installation. The glazed surface is water-resistant, though the bodies are porous.
	Standard sizes for wall tiles range from 3-inch squares to 4¼ by 8½-inch rectangles; thicknesses vary from ¼ to ⅜ inch. Other sizes and shapes are available. Many wall tiles come with matching trim pieces for edges, coves, and corners.
	Wall tiles are also available in pregrouted panels, a handy shortcut that reduces installation time and effort. Designed primarily for tub and shower areas, a panel contains up to 64 tiles, each measuring 4¼ inches square. The panels have flexible, water-repellent grout.
	Ceramic mosaic is one of the most colorful and versatile materials in the tile family. Tiles sold under this name are generally small—2 by 2 inches or less. For this reason, they can be installed on curved surfaces. Mosaics come in sheets, with the tiles mounted on thread mesh or paper backing or joined with silicone rubber. Once they're in place, you grout these sheets like any other wall tiles.
Stone	Marble, slate, limestone, and granite, whether as 8 or 12-inch tiles or wider sheets, can perform a role similar to ceramic tile. Stone tiles are expensive but, used as accents, they can go a long way. Most stone, especially marble, should be thoroughly sealed for wall use; untreated, it can be stained or eaten away by acids in cleaning supplies or even household water.
Glass block	If you're looking for some ambient daylight but don't want to sacrifice privacy, consider glass blocks. You can buy 3 or 4-inch-thick square blocks in many sizes; rectangular blocks are available in a more limited selection. Textures can be smooth, wavy, rippled, bubbly, or crosshatched. Mortarless block systems make an often tricky installation job simpler for do-it-yourselfers.
Wallpaper	Wallpaper for the bathroom should be scrubbable, durable, and stain-resistant. Solid-vinyl wallpapers, which come in a wide variety of colors and textures, fit the bill. New patterns, including some that replicate other surfaces (such as linen), are generally subtle; wallpaper borders add visual punch to ceiling lines and openings. Good ventilation is crucial to keep wallpaper from loosening.
Plaster	The textured, uneven, and slightly rounded edges of plaster give a bathroom a custom, informal look. Plaster is especially popular for Southwest-theme designs. If the surface is too irregular, however, plaster is hard to keep clean.
Wood	Tongue-and-groove wood paneling—natural, stained, bleached, or painted—provides a charming accent to country schemes. Wainscoting is the most popular application; the paneling is separated from wallpaper or paint above by the traditional chair rail.
	Moldings are back in vogue. Specialty shops are likely to have a wide selection and will often custom-match an old favorite to order.

REMODELING BASICS

Installation ▪ Removal ▪ Tools ▪ Techniques

After sifting through a wealth of bathroom remodeling ideas, you've probably selected what's right for your family's special needs. Perhaps you've decided on a quick and easy change—a fresh coat of paint in your favorite color. Or maybe this is the time for the major remodel you've been dreaming about—moving a wall, opening the ceiling with a skylight, installing a gleaming new tub and surrounding tile.

This chapter is designed to help you translate your ideas and dreams into changes in your bathroom. From the basics of structural framing, plumbing, and wiring to the fine points of installing the walls, it's all here for you to read and do. Each project begins with general information on planning and procedures, then takes you through the work with illustrated step-by-step instructions.

Though the directions assume that you have some basic knowledge of building terms, tools, materials, and techniques, you needn't be an expert to do most of the projects in this chapter. If you need more detailed information on procedures, take a look at the *Sunset* books *Basic Carpentry Illustrated*, *Basic Plumbing Illustrated*, and *Basic Home Wiring Illustrated*.

Pedestal sinks are making a comeback, and most models are easy to install. Since plumbing hardware will be visible below the sink, you may wish to invest in decorative supply tubing and shutoff valves. For installation details, see pages 84–85.

Before work begins

Are you ready to remodel? Before plunging into a project, you should have a clear idea of the steps required to complete the job, and the sequence in which they should be done. You'll also need to evaluate your own ability to perform the various tasks. One of your first decisions will be whether to do the work yourself or get professional help.

Can you do the work yourself?

What skills do you need to remodel a bathroom? It depends on the improvements you're planning. Projects such as painting, setting wall tile, and installing floors and cabinets are within easy reach of any homeowner with basic do-it-yourself ability. You'll need a few specialized tools to complete some projects, but you can buy them at a building supply or home improvement center, or perhaps even rent them.

If your plans include complex remodeling projects such as moving bearing walls, running new drain and vent pipes, or wiring new electrical circuits and service panels, you may want to hire professionals to do part or all of the job. But many smaller structural, plumbing, and electrical jobs can be done by a homeowner with some basic experience.

Even if there's little you can build, you may discover a talent for demolition—and save some money. But some contractors may not want to relinquish this task. If you do take it on, be sure to finish by the time the remodeling crew is ready to begin.

Planning your project

Putting careful thought into your preparations can save you extra work and inconvenience later. As the scale of your remodeling project increases, the need for careful planning becomes more critical. If your home has only one bathroom, your goal is to keep it in operating order as much of the time as possible. With careful scheduling, the remodeling time will be easier for the entire family.

Be sure to obtain any necessary permits from your local building department. A contractor, if you hire one, will do this job for you. But if you're doing the work yourself, you'll need to secure permits and arrange for inspections. Finally, before you start work, double-check the priorities listed below.

■ Establish the sequence of jobs to be done, and estimate the time needed for completion.

■ If you're hiring professional help, make sure you have legally binding contracts and schedules with contractors and subcontractors.

■ If electricity, gas, or water must be shut off by the utility company, arrange for the cutoff date.

■ Locate an area for temporarily storing fixtures that have been removed.

■ Measure fixtures for adequate clearance through doorways and hallways, or down staircases.

■ Locate a site for dumping refuse and secure necessary permits.

■ Obtain all other required permits.

■ Arrange for timely delivery of materials and be sure you have all the necessary tools on hand.

Note: If you're contracting the work, you can skip the last three steps; they're normally part of the contractor's service.

How to use this chapter

Reading all the sections of this chapter through quickly will help you to get a general feeling for what's involved in bathroom remodeling.

In the first three sections, you'll find an overview of structural, plumbing, and electrical systems. Even if you don't plan to do the work yourself, you may want to review these sections for background information. Understanding basic systems enables you to plan more effectively and to understand the reasons for code restrictions affecting your plans.

Many of your remodeling hours may be spent tearing out old work. To minimize the effort, we've included removal procedures along with installation instructions in the sections on fixtures, wall coverings, flooring, and cabinets.

If you're planning only one or two small projects, turn directly to the applicable sections for step-by-step instructions.

STEPS IN REMODELING

You can use this chart to plan the general order of removal and installation in remodeling your bathroom, though you may need to alter the suggested order, depending on the scale of your job and the materials you select. For more information, read the appropriate sections on the following pages. Manufacturers' instructions will offer additional guidelines as you go along.

Removal sequence

1. Accessories, decorative elements
2. Furniture, if any
3. Contents of cabinets, closets, shelves
4. Fixtures, plumbing fittings
5. Vanity countertops
6. Vanity cabinets, recessed cabinets, shelves
7. Flooring
8. Light fixtures, as required
9. Wall and ceiling coverings

Installation sequence

1. Structural changes: walls, doors, windows, skylights
2. Rough plumbing changes
3. Electrical wiring
4. Bathtub, shower
5. Wall and ceiling coverings
6. Light fixtures
7. Vanity cabinets, countertops
8. Toilets, bidets, sinks
9. Wall cabinets, shelves
10. Flooring
11. Accessories, decorative elements

Structural basics

Understanding your home's structural shell is a good way to begin any home improvement project, including bathroom remodeling.

Your house's framework probably will conform to the pattern of the "typical house" shown in the illustration below. Starting at the base of the drawing, you'll notice the following framing members: a wooden sill resting on a foundation wall; a series of horizontal, evenly spaced floor joists; and a subfloor (usually plywood sheets) laid atop the joists. This platform supports the first-floor walls, both interior and exterior. The walls are formed by vertical, evenly spaced studs that run between a horizontal sole plate and parallel top plate. The primary wall coverings are fastened directly to the studs.

Depending on the design of the house, one of several types of construction may be used above the first-floor walls. If there's a second story, a layer of ceiling joists rests on the walls; these joists support both the floor above and the ceiling below. A one-story house will have either an "open-beamed" ceiling—flat or pitched—or a "finished" ceiling. With a flat roof, the finished ceiling is attached directly to the rafters. The ceiling below a pitched roof is attached to joists.

Removing a partition wall

Sometimes major bathroom remodeling entails removing all or part of an interior wall to enlarge the space.

Walls that define your bathroom may be bearing or nonbearing. A bearing wall helps support the weight of the house; a nonbearing wall does not. An interior nonbearing wall, often called a partition wall, may be removed without special precautions. The procedure outlined in this section applies to partitions only. If you're considering a remodeling project that involves moving a bearing wall, consult an architect or contractor about problems and procedures.

How can you tell the difference in walls? All exterior walls running perpendicular to ceiling and floor joists are bearing. At least one main interior wall may be a bearing wall.

To determine whether the wall you're planning to move is bearing, climb up into the attic or crawlspace and check the ceiling joists. If they are joined over any wall, that wall is bearing. Even if joists span the entire width of the house, their midsections may be supported by a bearing wall at the point of maximum allowable span. If you have any doubts about the wall, consult an architect, contractor, or building inspector.

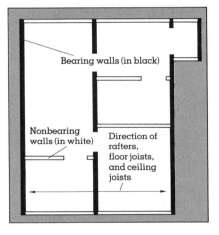

Bearing walls (in black)

Nonbearing walls (in white)

Direction of rafters, floor joists, and ceiling joists

Though removing a partition wall is not complicated, it can be quite messy. Cover the floors and fixtures, and wear a dust mask, safety glasses, and gloves. NOTE: Check the wall for signs of wiring, supply and drain pipes, and heating and ventilation ducts; you'll have to reroute them.

Remove the wall covering. First, if there's a door in the wall, remove it from its hinges. Pry off any door trim, ceiling molding, and base molding.

The most common wall covering is gypsum wallboard nailed to wall studs. To remove it, use a prybar (see "Removing gypsum wallboard," page 98).

If the wall covering is plaster and lath, chisel away the plaster and cut the lath backing—wood strips or metal—so that you can pry off the pieces of lath and plaster.

TYPICAL HOUSE STRUCTURE

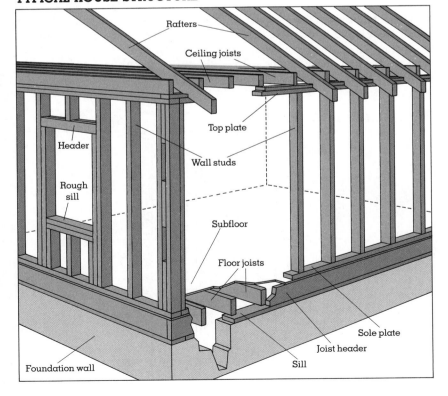

Rafters

Ceiling joists

Top plate

Header

Wall studs

Rough sill

Subfloor

Floor joists

Sole plate

Joist header

Sill

Foundation wall

(Continued on next page)

■ Structural basics

DISMANTLING THE WALL FRAMING

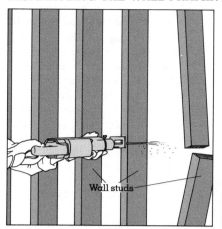

Saw through the middle of the wall studs; bend the studs sideways to free the nails from the top and sole plates.

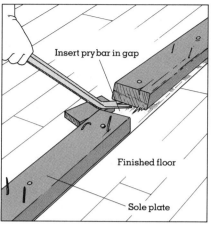

Cut gaps through the sole plate with a saw and chisel; insert a prybar in each gap and lift to free the sole plate.

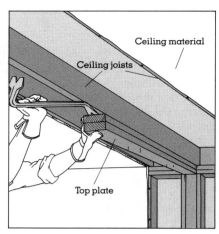

Strip ceiling materials back from the top plate, cut gaps in the plate, and pry out sections of plate.

Dismantle the framing. Remove studs by sawing through the middle of each one; then push and pull them sideways to free the nails (see illustration above).

To remove the sole plate, saw a small section out of the middle down to the finished floor level, chisel through the remaining thickness, and insert a prybar in the gap.

To remove a top plate that lies parallel to the joists, cut ceiling materials back to adjacent joists, and pry off the plate. If the top plate is perpendicular to the joists, you are probably working on a bearing wall and will have to take special precautions (see page 67).

Patch walls, ceiling, and floor. Holes in wallboard and plaster aren't difficult to patch; the real challenge lies in matching a special texture, wallpaper, shade of paint, or well-aged floor. This is not a problem if your remodeling plans call for new wall coverings, ceiling, or flooring. In either case, see the sections "Walls & ceilings" (pages 98–105) and "Flooring" (pages 106–108) for techniques and tips.

Framing a new wall

To subdivide a large bathroom or to enlarge a cramped one, you may need to build a new partition wall or partial wall. Components of wall framing are illustrated below.

Framing a wall is a straightforward task, but you must measure carefully and check the alignment as work progresses. The basic steps are listed below. If you plan to install a doorway, see pages 69–70.

Plot the location. The new wall must be anchored securely to existing ceiling joists, the floor, and, at least on one side, to wall studs. To locate the studs, try knocking with your fist along the wall until the sound changes from hollow to solid.

If you have wallboard, you can use an inexpensive stud finder; often, though, the nails that hold wallboard to the studs are visible on close inspection.

To locate ceiling joists, use the same methods or, from the attic or crawlspace, drill small holes down through the ceiling on both sides of a joist to serve as reference points below. Adjacent joists and studs should be evenly spaced, usually about 16 or 24 inches apart.

WALL FRAMING COMPONENTS

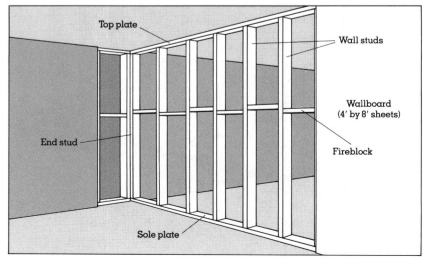

A wall running perpendicular to the joists will demand the least effort to attach. If wall and joists will run parallel, though, try to center the wall under a single joist; otherwise, you'll need to remove ceiling materials between two parallel joists and install nailing blocks every 2 feet (see illustrations at right). If the side of the new wall falls between existing studs, you'll need to install additional nailing blocks.

On the ceiling, mark both ends of the center line of the new wall. Measure 1¾ inches (half the width of the top plate) on both sides of each mark. Snap parallel lines between corresponding marks with a chalk line; the top plate will occupy the space between the lines.

Position the sole plate. Hang a plumb bob from each end of the lines you just marked and mark these new points on the floor. Snap two more chalk lines to connect these points.

Cut both sole plate and top plate to the desired length. Lay the sole plate between the lines on the floor and nail it in place with 10-penny nails spaced every 2 feet. (If you have a masonry floor, use a masonry bit to drill a bolt hole through the sole plate every 2 or 3 feet. Insert expansion anchors for lag bolts and bolt the sole plate to the floor.)

If you're planning a doorway (see "Framing a doorway," below), don't nail through that section of the plate; it will be cut out later.

Mark stud positions. Lay the top plate against the sole plate, as shown in the illustration. Beginning

ANCHORING A TOP PLATE

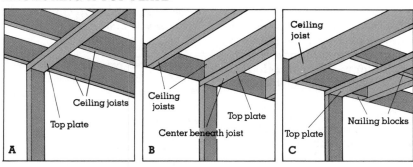

To anchor a top plate, nail to perpendicular joists (A) or to the bottom of the parallel joist (B), or install nailing blocks between parallel joists (C).

at the end that will be attached to an existing stud or to nailing blocks, measure in 1½ inches—the thickness of a 2 by 4 stud—and draw a line across both plates with a combination square. Starting once more from that end, measure and draw lines at 15¼ and 16¾ inches. From these lines, advance 16 inches. Don't worry if the spacing at the far end is less than 16 inches. (If local codes permit, consider a 24-inch spacing— you'll save lumber—and adjust the placement of lines to 23¼ and 24¾ inches.)

Fasten the top plate. While two helpers hold the top plate in position between the lines (marked on the ceiling), nail it to perpendicular joists, to one parallel joist, or to nailing blocks, as shown above.

Attach the studs. Measure and cut the studs to exact length. Attach one end stud (or both) to existing studs or to nailing blocks between studs. Lift

the remaining studs into place one at a time; line them up on the marks, and check plumb with a carpenter's level. Toenail the studs to both top plate and sole plate with 8-penny nails.

Many building codes require horizontal fireblocks between studs. The number of rows depends on the code; if permitted, position blocks to provide an extra nailing surface for wall materials.

Finish. After the studs are installed, it's time to add any electrical outlets and switches (see pages 76–78), as well as any new plumbing (see pages 72–75). It's also time for the building inspector to check your work. Following the inspection, you can finish the walls (see pages 98–105).

Framing a doorway

Your remodeling may call for changing the position of a door and creating a new door opening. Be sure the wall you plan to cut into is a nonbearing wall (see page 67); if it's a bearing wall, consult a professional.

Position the opening. This section assumes that you're installing a standard prehung door and frame. Before starting work, check the manufacturer's "rough opening" dimensions—the exact wall opening required after the new framing is in place.

You'll need to plan an opening large enough to accommodate both

MARKING STUD POSITIONS

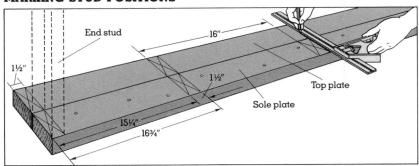

■ Structural basics

the rough opening and the rough door framing—an additional 1½ inches on top and sides. If your door didn't come with rough opening dimensions, add an additional ⅜ inch all around for shimming (adjusting level and plumb) the typical door frame.

Often it's simpler to remove the wallboard from floor to ceiling between two bordering studs (the new king studs) that will remain in place. (This is the method illustrated.) In any case, you'll save work later if you can use at least one existing stud as part of the new framing.

Regardless of the method you choose, use a carpenter's level for a straightedge, and mark the outline of the opening on the wall.

Remove wall covering and studs. First remove any base molding. Cut along the outline of the opening with a reciprocating or keyhole saw, being careful to cut only the wallboard, not the studs beneath. Pry the wallboard away from the framing. To remove plaster and lath, chisel through the plaster to expose the lath; then cut the lath, and pry lath and plaster loose.

Cut the studs inside the opening to the height required for the header (see illustration below). Using a combination square, mark these studs on the face and one side, then

cut carefully with a reciprocating or crosscut saw. Remove the cut studs from the sole plate.

Frame the opening. With wall covering and studs removed, you're ready to frame the opening. Measure and cut the header (for a partition wall you can use a 2 by 4 laid flat), and toenail it to the king studs with 8-penny nails. Nail the header to the bottoms of the cripple studs.

Cut the part of the sole plate within the opening, and pry it away from the subfloor (see "Removing a partition wall," page 67).

Cut trimmer studs and nail them to the king studs with 10-penny nails in a staggered pattern. You'll probably need to adjust the width by blocking out a third trimmer from one side, as shown below right. Leave an extra ⅜ inch on each side for shimming, plus space for the door jambs.

Hang the door. A standard prehung door and frame are predrilled for a lockset. The door comes already fitted and attached to the frame with hinges. Pull out the hinge pins to remove the door before you install the frame. Nail the frame in the rough opening, shimming carefully to make the side jambs plumb and the head jamb level. Rehang the

door and install the lockset; then install stop molding and trim (casing).

Closing a doorway

It's easy to eliminate an existing doorway. Simply add new studs within the opening and attach new wall coverings. The only trick is to match the present wall surface.

First, remove the casing around the opening. Then remove the door from its hinges or guide track, and pry any jambs or tracks away from the rough framing.

Next, measure the gap on the floor between the existing trimmer studs; cut a length of 2 by 4 to serve as a new sole plate. Nail it to the floor with 10-penny nails. (If you have a masonry floor, attach the 2 by 4 with lag bolts and expansion anchors).

Measure and cut new studs to fill the space; position one stud beneath each cripple stud. Toenail the studs to the new sole plate and header with 8-penny nails. Add fireblocks between studs if required by the local code.

Strip the wall coverings back far enough to give yourself a firm nailing surface and an even edge. Then add new coverings to match the existing ones, or resurface the entire wall (see pages 98–105). Match or replace the baseboard molding.

FRAMING A DOORWAY

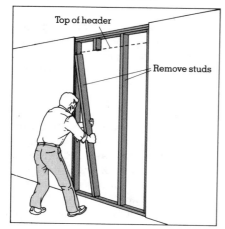

Mark and cut studs within the opening to a height even with the top of the new header, and remove.

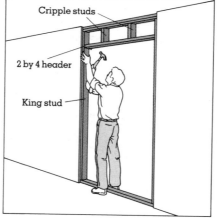

Nail the new header to the king studs, then nail through the header into the ends of the new cripple studs.

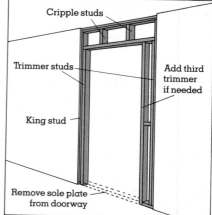

Nail trimmer studs to the king studs; add a third trimmer, if needed, to make the opening the correct width.

SKYLIGHTING THE BATHROOM

A skylight brings light and an open feeling into windowless interior bathrooms or those where uncovered windows would be a privacy problem.

Installing a skylight in a pitched roof with asphalt or wood shingles is a two-part process: you cut and frame openings in both roof and ceiling, and connect the two openings with a vertical light shaft. (You don't even need a light shaft for a flat roof or open-beamed ceiling.) A description of the installation sequence follows; for more detailed information, consult the manufacturer's instructions or your skylight dealer.

Mark the openings. Begin by measuring and marking the location of the ceiling opening. Then drive nails up through the four corners and center so they'll be visible in the attic. You'll save work if you can use one or two ceiling joists as the edges of your opening.

With a plumb bob, transfer the center mark to the underside of the roof. Mark the roof opening suggested by the manufacturer on the underside of the roof and drive nails through the corners.

Frame the roof opening. Exercise extreme caution when working on the roof; if the pitch is steep or if you have a tile or slate roof, you should leave this part to professionals.

If your skylight must be mounted on a curb frame, build the curb first; 2 by 6 lumber is commonly used.

To determine the actual size of the opening you need to cut, add the dimensions of any framing materials to the rough opening size marked by the nails. You may need to remove some extra shingles or roofing materials down to the sheathing to accommodate the flashing of a curb-mount-

BASIC PARTS OF A SKYLIGHT

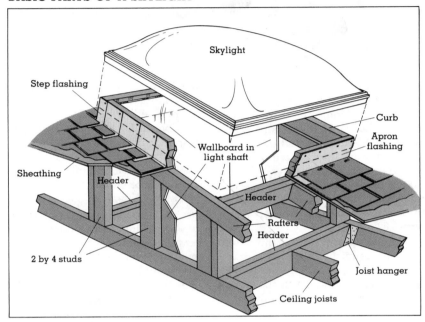

ed skylight or the flange of a self-flashing unit.

Cut the roof opening in successive layers: roofing materials first, sheathing next, and finally the rafters. Before cutting the rafters, support them with 2 by 4s nailed to the ceiling joists below.

To frame the opening, you'll need double headers and possibly trimmers to narrow the width between rafters.

If you're installing a curb-mounted unit, position and flash the curb. Toenail the curb to the rafters or trimmers and to the headers. Flash according to the manufacturer's instructions.

Mount the skylight. For a curb-mounted unit, secure the skylight to the top of the curb with nails and a sealant. Nail a self-flashing unit

through the flange directly to the roof sheathing; then coat the joints and nail holes with roofing cement.

Open the ceiling. Cut through the ceiling materials and then cut the joists. Support joists to be cut by bracing them against adjacent joists. Frame the opening in the manner used for the roof opening.

Build a light shaft. Measure the distance between the ceiling headers and roof headers at each corner and at 16-inch intervals between the corners. Cut studs to fit the measurements and install them as illustrated above. This provides a nailing surface for wall coverings.

To finish, insulate the spaces between studs in the light shaft before fastening wall coverings to the studs. Trim the ceiling opening with molding strips.

Plumbing basics

Whether you're planning to add a single fixture or remodel an entire bathroom, you'll need an introduction to plumbing basics. Replacing an old bathtub, sink, or toilet with a new one at the same location is a straightforward job, but roughing-in (installing) plumbing for fixtures at new locations takes skill and planning.

What follows is an overview of fundamentals—household plumbing systems, plumbing codes, and general procedures for planning, routing, and roughing-in new pipes. This information may help you to decide whether to make your project a do-it-yourself effort or a professional one. If you have doubts, consider a compromise—you might hire a professional to check your plans and install pipes, then make the fixture hookups yourself (see pages 82–97).

If you want to do all the work yourself, read the information that follows before you begin to ensure that you're familiar with the tools and techniques required for the job.

How the system works

Three complementary sets of pipes work together to fill your home's plumbing needs: the water supply system, and the drain-waste and vent (DWV) systems (see the illustration below).

The supply system. Water for your toilet, tub, shower, and sink enters the house from a public water main or from a source on the property. Water from a water company is usually delivered through a water meter and a main shutoff valve. You'll find the meter either in your basement or crawlspace, or outdoors, near your property line. The main shutoff valve—which turns the water for the whole house on and off—is usually situated near the water meter.

At the water service entrance, the main supply line divides in two—one line branching off to be heated by the water heater, the other remaining as cold water. The two pipes usually run parallel below the first-floor level until they reach the vicinity of a group of fixtures, then

head up through the wall or floor. Sometimes the water supply—hot, cold, or both—passes through a water softener or filter before reaching the fixtures.

Supply pipes are installed with a slight pitch in the runs, sloping back toward the lowest point in the system so that all pipes can be drained. Sometimes at the lowest point there's a valve that can be opened to drain the system— essential for vacation homes in cold climates.

Drain-waste and vent systems. The drain-waste pipes take advantage of gravity to channel waste water and solid wastes to the house sewer line. Vent pipes carry away sewer gas and maintain atmospheric pressure in drainpipes and fixture traps. The traps (curved sections in the fixtures' drainpipes) remain filled with water at all times to keep gases from coming up the drains.

Every house has a 3 or 4-inch-diameter main soil stack that serves a dual function. Below the level of the fixtures, it is your home's primary drainpipe; above the stack it becomes a vent with its upper end protruding through the roof. Drainpipes from individual fixtures, as well as branch drains, connect to the main stack. These pipes lead away from all fixtures at a carefully calculated slope—normally ¼ inch per foot. Since any system may clog now and then, cleanouts usually are placed at the upper end of each horizontal section of drainpipe.

A fixture or fixture group located on a branch drain far from the main stack will have a secondary vent stack of its own rising to the roof.

Planning and layout

This section outlines the planning process and explores some of your options in adding new plumbing. When plotting out any plumbing addition you must balance code restrictions, the limitations of your system's layout, design considerations, and, of course, your own plumbing abilities.

A PLUMBING OVERVIEW

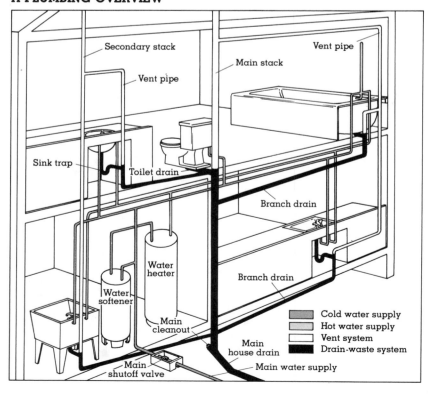

Secondary stack
Vent pipe
Vent pipe
Main stack
Sink trap
Toilet drain
Branch drain
Water heater
Branch drain
Water softener
Main cleanout
Main house drain
Main shutoff valve
Main water supply

Cold water supply
Hot water supply
Vent system
Drain-waste system

Check the codes. Almost any improvement that adds pipe to the system will require approval from local building department officials before you start, and inspection of the work before you close the walls and floor.

Learn what work you may do yourself—some codes require that certain work be done only by licensed plumbers.

Map your system. A detailed map of your present system will give you a clear picture of where it's feasible to tie into supply and drain lines, and whether the present drains and vents are adequate for the use you plan.

Starting in the basement, sketch in the main soil stack, branch drains, house drain, and accessible cleanouts; then trace the networks of hot and cold supply pipes. Also, check the attic or roof for the course of the main stack and any secondary vent stacks. Determine and mark on the sketch the materials and, if possible, the diameters of all pipes (see "Materials," at right).

Layout options. Plan the plumbing for any new fixtures in three parts: supply, drainage, and venting. To minimize cost and keep the work simple, arrange a fixture or group of fixtures so they are as close to the present pipes as possible.

Three economical ways to group your new fixtures (see drawings below) are to:

■ connect an individual fixture to the existing stack (drawing A)

■ add a fixture or group above or below an existing group on the stack

■ tie a fixture (except a toilet) directly into a new or existing branch drain (drawing B)

If your addition is planned for an area across the house from the existing plumbing, you'll probably need to run a new secondary vent stack up through the roof, and a new branch drain to the soil stack (see drawing B below) or to the main house drain via an existing cleanout.

The new vent stack must be installed inside an existing wall (a big job), built into a new oversize or "thickened" wall (see "Build a wet wall," page 74), or concealed in a closet or cabinet. In mild climates, a vent may also run up the exterior of the house, but it must be hidden within a box.

Materials. Decide what kind of pipe you'll need, based on the material of the pipe you'll be tying into.

Your home's supply pipes most likely are either galvanized steel (referred to as "galvanized" or "iron"

pipe) connected by threaded fittings, or rigid copper joined with soldered fittings.

Older DWV pipes probably are made of cast iron, with "hub" or "bell-and-spigot" ends joined by molten lead and oakum. (DWV pipes other than the main stack may be galvanized.)

To extend cast-iron pipes, you may substitute "hubless" fittings (consisting of neoprene gaskets and stainless steel clamps), which are simpler to install than hub fittings.

If you wish to change pipe material in your extension, it's a matter of inserting the appropriate adapter at the fitting end. You might want to change cast-iron or galvanized pipe to copper or plastic pipe. First check your local code, because some areas prohibit use of plastic pipe.

Plumbing codes

Few code restrictions apply to simple extensions of hot and cold water supply pipes, provided your house's water pressure is up to the task. The material and diameter for supply pipes serving each new fixture or appliance are spelled out clearly in the plumbing code. More troublesome are the pipes that make up the DWV system. Codes are quite specific about the following: the size of stacks, drainpipes, and vents serving any new fixture requiring drainage; the critical distance from fixture traps to the stack; and the method of venting fixtures.

Stack, drain, and vent size. The plumbing code will specify minimum diameters for stacks and vents in relation to numbers of *fixture units.* (One fixture unit represents 7.5 gallons or 1 cubic foot of water per minute.) In the code you'll find fixture unit ratings for all plumbing fixtures given in chart form.

To determine drainpipe diameter, look up the fixture or fixtures you're considering on the code's fixture unit chart. Add up the total fixture units; then look up the drain diameter specified for that number of units.

PLUMBING LAYOUT OPTIONS

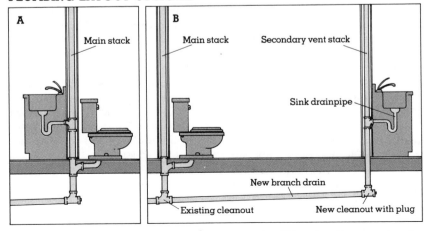

To drain bathroom plumbing additions, you can either (A) tap into the present main stack, if nearby, or (B) install a new branch drain and secondary vent stack.

(Continued on next page)

■Plumbing basics

Vent pipe sizing criteria also include *length* of vent and *type* of vent, in addition to fixture unit load.

Critical distance. The maximum distance allowed between a fixture's trap and the stack or main drain that it empties into is called the critical distance. No drain outlet may be completely below the level of the trap's crown weir (see illustration below)—if it were, it would act as a siphon, draining the trap. Thus, when the ideal drainpipe slope of ¼ inch per foot is figured in, the length of that drainpipe quickly becomes limited. But if the fixture drain is *vented* properly within the critical distance, the drainpipe may run on indefinitely to the actual stack or main drain.

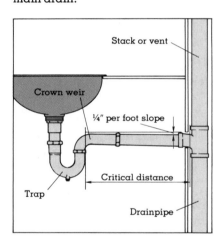

Venting options. The four basic venting options (see illustration above right)—subject to local code—are wet venting, back venting, individual venting, and indirect venting.

■ *Wet venting* is simplest—the fixture is vented directly through the fixture drain to the soil stack.

■ *Back venting (reventing)* involves running a vent loop up past fixtures to reconnect with the main stack or secondary vent above the fixture level.

■ *Individual (secondary) venting* means running a secondary vent stack up through the roof for a new fixture or group of fixtures distant from the main stack.

VENTING OPTIONS

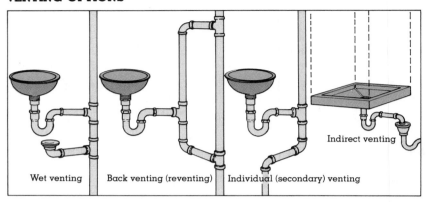

Wet venting   Back venting (reventing)   Individual (secondary) venting   Indirect venting

■ *Indirect venting* allows you to vent some fixtures (such as a basement shower) into an existing floor drain or laundry tub without further venting.

Roughing-in new plumbing

Once you've planned your plumbing additions, you can begin installation.

Locate and tie into existing pipe. In the mapping stage, you determined the rough locations of the pipes. The next step is to pinpoint them and cut away wall, ceiling, or floor coverings along studs or joists to expose the sections you want to tie into. Be sure to cut out holes large enough to allow you to work comfortably. (For information about wall and floor coverings, see pages 98–108.)

Basically, tying into drain-waste, vent, and supply lines entails cutting a section out of each pipe and inserting a new fitting to join old and new pipe. The method you use to tie into the pipes varies with the pipe material.

Route new pipes. With the connections made, the new DWV and supply pipes are run to the new fixture location. Ideally, new drainpipes should be routed below the bathroom floor. They can be suspended from floor joists by pipe hangers, inserted in the space between parallel joists, or run through

notches or holes drilled in joists that are at right angles to the pipe (if allowed by code). If you have a finished basement or your bathroom is on the second floor, you'll need to cut into the floor or ceiling to install pipes between or through joists, hide the pipes with a dropped ceiling, or box them in. (Remember that drainpipes must slope away from fixtures at a minimum slope of ¼ inch per foot.)

Supply pipes normally follow drainpipes but can be routed directly up through the wall or floor from main horizontal lines. Supply pipes should run parallel, at least 6 inches apart. In cold areas, codes may prohibit supply pipes in exterior walls.

Build a wet wall. The main soil stack, and often a secondary stack, commonly hide inside an oversize house wall called a "wet wall."

Unlike an ordinary 2 by 4 stud wall (shown on page 68), a wet wall has a sole plate and a top plate built from 2 by 6 or 2 by 8 lumber. Additionally, the 2 by 4 studs are set in pairs, with flat sides facing out. This creates maximum space inside the wall for large DWV pipes (which often have an outer diameter greater than 3½ inches) and for fittings, which are wider yet.

You can also "fur out" an existing wall to hide added pipes—attach new 2 by 4s to the old ones, then add new wall coverings. Similarly, a new branch drain that can't run below the floor may be hidden by a raised section of floor.

Roughing-in fixtures

Following are general notes on roughing-in new fixtures that require tying into your present DWV and supply systems, or extending them. Note that fixtures may be required to have air chambers—dead-end pipes that minimize noisy water hammer.

Sink. A sink is comparatively easy to install. Common installations are back-to-back (requires little pipe), within a vanity cabinet (hides pipe runs), and side-by-side. A sink can often be wet vented if it's within the critical distance; otherwise it's back vented. Adding a sink has little impact on the drain's present efficiency (a sink rates low in fixture units).

Supply pipes required: Hot and cold stubouts with shutoff valves; transition fittings, if necessary; flexible tubing above shutoff valves (see "Sink faucets," page 92).

Toilet. The single most troublesome fixture to install, a toilet requires its own vent (2-inch minimum) and at least a 3-inch drain. If it's on a branch drain, a toilet can't be upstream from a sink or shower.

The closet bend and toilet floor flange must be roughed-in first; the floor flange must be positioned at the level of the eventual finished floor.

Supply pipes required: Cold water stubout with shutoff valve; flexible tubing above valve (see "Installing a toilet," page 96).

Shower stall and bathtub. Like sinks, bathtubs and showers rate low in fixture units. They're often positioned on branch drains and are usually wet-vented or back-vented; both enter the stack at floor level or below because of the below-floor trap. A shower's faucet body and shower head assembly are installed while the wall is open; tubs and showers may require support framing.

Supply pipes required: Hot and cold supply lines and a pipe to the shower head (see "Bathtub & shower faucets," page 93).

ROUGHING-IN FIXTURES

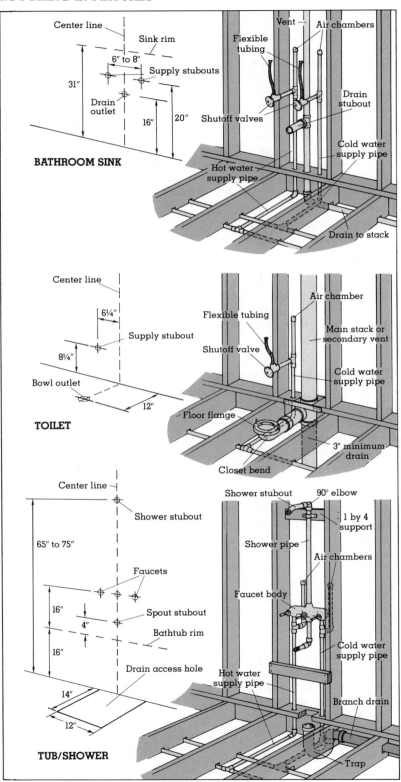

Representative roughing-in measurements. Plumbing components illustrated are a sink, toilet, and tub/shower. Use the measurements to help you plan; check local codes and specific fixture dimensions for exact roughing-in requirements.

Electrical basics

What may appear to be a hopelessly tangled maze of wires running through the walls, under the floors, and above the ceiling of your home is actually a well-organized system composed of several electrical circuits. In your bathroom, those circuits supply power to light fixtures, switches, fans, heaters, and electrical outlets.

This section briefly explains your home's electrical system and offers general information about basic electrical improvements so you can better understand the processes involved in making changes to your electrical system. Techniques for installing light fixtures appear on pages 79–80.

Before you do any work yourself, talk with your building department's electrical inspector about local codes, the National Electrical Code (NEC), and your area's requirements for permits and inspections.

Understanding your system

Today most homes have what's called "three-wire" service. The utility company connects three wires to your service entrance panel. Each of two hot wires supplies electricity at approximately 120 volts. A third wire—a neutral one—is maintained at zero volts. (Don't be misled, though; all three wires are live.)

Three-wire service provides both 120-volt and 240-volt capabilities. One hot wire and the neutral wire combine to provide 120 volts—primarily for lights and plug-in outlets. Two hot wires combine to provide 240 volts, often used for electric heaters.

Service entrance panel. This panel is the control center for your electrical system. Inside the panel, you'll usually find the main disconnect (main fuses or circuit breaker), the fuses or circuit breakers protecting each individual circuit, and the grounding connection for the entire system.

Simple circuitry. The word "circuit" means the course electric cur-

rent travels—in a continuous path from the service entrance panel or a separate subpanel, through one or more devices in your home that use electricity (such as light fixtures or appliances), and back to the panel. The devices are connected to the circuit by parallel wiring. With parallel wiring, a hot, a neutral, and a ground wire (for a 120-volt circuit) run continuously from one fixture box, outlet box, or switch box to another. Wires branch off to individual electrical devices from these continuous wires.

Modern circuit wires are housed together in a cable. Cable contains either one or two hot wires, a neutral wire, and a ground wire—each, except the ground wire, wrapped in its own insulation. (For the best connections, use only cable with all-copper wire.)

Individual wires are color-coded for easy identification. Hot wires are usually black or red, but may be any color other than white, gray, or green. Neutral wires are white or gray. Grounding wires are bare copper or green.

Occasionally, a white wire will be used as a hot wire; it should be taped or painted black near terminals and splices for easy identification.

Grounding. The NEC requires that every circuit have a ground wire. It provides an auxiliary path to ground for any short that might occur in a fixture or appliance. Also, according to the NEC, all bathroom outlets within 6 feet of a water source (sink or tub) must be protected with

ground fault circuit interrupters (GFCI). These cut off power within 1/40 of a second if current begins leaking anywhere along the circuit. They may be special circuit breakers or built into an outlet.

Extending a circuit

To extend an existing electrical circuit, you'll need a knack for making wire connections, and the patience to route new cable.

Before you start work, remember: NEVER WORK ON ANY LIVE CIRCUIT, FIXTURE, PLUG-IN OUTLET, OR SWITCH. Your life may depend on it. Turn off the circuit breaker or remove the fuse and make sure no one but you can turn the electricity back on.

The steps in extending a circuit are outlined below. Generally, you route new cable from box to box; you install new boxes where you want to add outlets, fixtures, or switches; and then you tap into a power source —an existing outlet, switch, or fixture box.

To install a new circuit, the work is much the same, except that you connect into a service panel or subpanel instead of into an existing outlet, switch, or fixture box.

Select a power source. A circuit can be tapped for power at almost any accessible outlet, switch, or fixture box of the appropriate voltage. (The exceptions are a switch box without a neutral wire and a fixture box at the end of a circuit.) The box you tap into must be large enough to hold new wires in addition to exist-

ROUTING CABLE TO OUTLETS

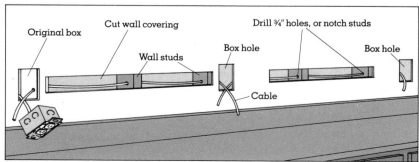

Original box • Cut wall covering • Wall studs • Box hole • Drill ¾" holes, or notch studs • Box hole • Cable

ing wires, and must have knockout holes through which you can run the new cable.

Select and locate new boxes. If wall or ceiling coverings have not yet been installed, choose an outlet or switch box you nail to studs or joists. If wall or ceiling coverings are already in place, choose cut-in boxes that don't have to be secured to studs or joists. Requirements regarding boxes for mounting ceiling fixtures are outlined on pages 79–80.

Unless codes prohibit the use of plastic, you can use either plastic or metal boxes. Metal boxes, though sturdier, must be grounded; plastic boxes cost less and need not be grounded, though the circuit must have a ground wire.

To find a suitable box location, first turn off power to all circuits that may be behind the wall or ceiling. Drill a small test hole and probe through it with a length of stiff insulated wire until you find an empty space.

Unless old boxes are at different levels, place new outlet boxes 12 to 18 inches above the floor, switch boxes or outlet boxes above a counter 44 inches above the floor. Never place boxes near a tub or shower.

If you're adding a new wall, you may be required by code to add an outlet every 12 feet, or one per wall regardless of the wall's length.

When you've determined the correct locations, trace the outline of each box on the wall or ceiling (omit protruding brackets). Then cut along the outlines.

Route and connect new cable. After the box holes are cut, run cable from the power source to each new box location. (Wait until you have the new boxes wired and the outlets, switches, and fixtures connected before you make the actual hookup to the source.)

Where you have access from an unfinished basement, an unfloored attic, or a garage adjacent to the bathroom, it's easy to run cable either attached to the joists or studs

or through holes drilled in them.

Where walls and ceilings are covered on both sides, you'll have to fish cable through them, using electrician's fish tape (illustrated below) or a length of stiff wire with one end bent into a blunt, tight hook.

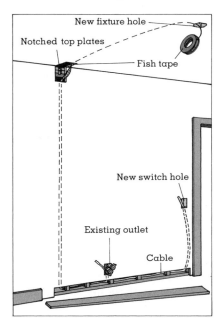

New fixture hole

Notched top plates

Fish tape

New switch hole

Existing outlet

Cable

After routing new cable, secure the cable to each new box. Slip a cable connector onto the end of the cable and insert the cable and connector into a knockout in the box. Fasten the connector to the box, leaving 6 to 8 inches of cable sticking out for wiring connections. Then mount the box to the ceiling or wall and wire as described below.

Wire plug-in outlets. An outlet must have the same amperage and voltage rating as the circuit. If you have aluminum wiring, be sure to use the correct outlet; it will be identified by the letters CO-ALR. An outlet marked CU-AL should be used only with copper wire. If installing a GFCI outlet, follow the manufacturer's directions.

If you're adding a grounded outlet to a circuit that does not contain a grounding wire, you'll have to run a separate grounding wire from the new outlet to a nearby cold water pipe. (One method is shown on page 79; for help, consult an electrician.)

The drawing below shows how to wire a plug-in bathroom outlet with both halves live. The box is assumed to be metal; if you use a plastic box, there's no need to ground the box, but you'll have to attach a grounding wire to each outlet. Simply loop the end of the wire under the grounding screw. Connect the hot wire to the brass screw of the outlet, the neutral wire to the silver screw, and the ground wire to the green screw.

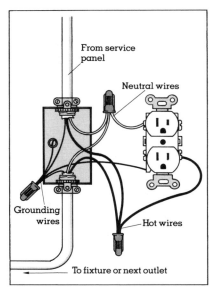

From service panel

Neutral wires

Grounding wires

Hot wires

To fixture or next outlet

Wire single-pole switches. One single-pole switch may control one or more light fixtures, a heater, a ventilating fan, or several outlets.

Like outlets, the switch must have the same amperage and voltage rating as the circuit. If you have aluminum wiring, be sure to use a switch marked with the letters CO-ALR.

When wiring switches, remember that they are installed only on hot wires. The switches illustrated on page 78 have no grounding wires because the toggles on most home switches are made of shockproof plastic. If switches are housed in plastic boxes, the boxes do not need to be grounded. When installing a plastic switch box at the end of a circuit, secure the end of the grounding wire between the switch bracket and the mounting screw. If the switch is in the middle of a circuit,

■ Electrical basics

WIRING SINGLE-POLE SWITCHES

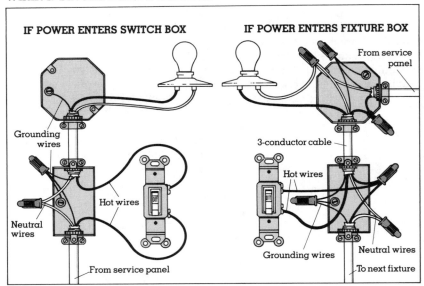

IF POWER ENTERS SWITCH BOX

IF POWER ENTERS FIXTURE BOX

From service panel

Grounding wires

3-conductor cable

Hot wires

Hot wires

Neutral wires

Neutral wires

Grounding wires

From service panel

To next fixture

WIRING A GFCI

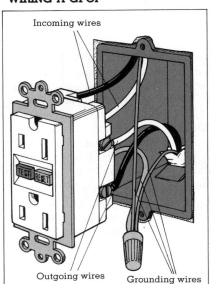

Incoming wires

Outgoing wires

Grounding wires

just twist the ends of the ground wires together and cover them with a wirenut.

Single-pole switches have two screw terminals of the same color (usually brass) for wire connections, and a definite right-side up. You should be able to read the words ON and OFF embossed on the toggle. It makes no difference which hot wire goes to which terminal. The cable can be run first either to the fixture or to the switch—whichever is the more convenient route.

Wire a GFCI. The protection value of an outlet-style GFCI has made it standard in new construction. Depending on the model, the GFCI may also protect all other devices downstream (away from the source) from it, but it will not protect any outlets upstream (toward the source).

A GFCI receptacle is wired like an ordinary outlet, except that you must connect incoming hot and neutral wires to the "line," or input, terminals, and any outgoing wires to the "load" side. If your model includes a built-in grounding jumper, attach it to the other ground wires in the box with a wirenut, as shown above.

Wire into the power source. After you've wired new outlets and switches, you're ready to make the final connections. Connections to three types of boxes used as power sources are illustrated below. Wirenuts join and protect the stripped ends of spliced wires within the boxes.

WIRING INTO A POWER SOURCE

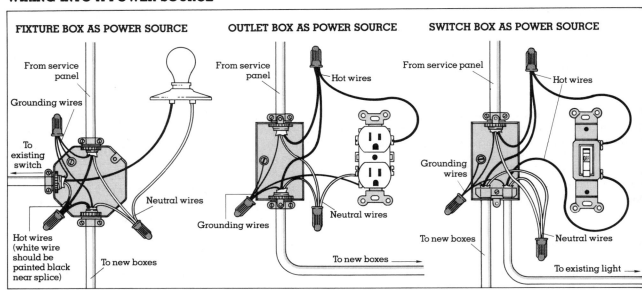

FIXTURE BOX AS POWER SOURCE

From service panel

Grounding wires

To existing switch

Neutral wires

Hot wires (white wire should be painted black near splice)

To new boxes

OUTLET BOX AS POWER SOURCE

From service panel

Hot wires

Grounding wires

Neutral wires

To new boxes

SWITCH BOX AS POWER SOURCE

From service panel

Hot wires

Grounding wires

To new boxes

Neutral wires

To existing light

Installing light fixtures

Most bathrooms need both task lighting for specific areas and general lighting. For a discussion of lighting choices, see page 50.

Basically, to replace an existing light fixture with one of the same type, you disconnect the wires of the old fixture and hook up new wires. Adding a new fixture where there was none before is more complicated. You must first run new cable from a power source and install a fixture box and a switch.

Below are instructions for installing two types of light fixtures—surface-mounted and recessed.

Surface-mounted fixtures.

Attach these fixtures directly to a wall or ceiling fixture box, or suspend ceiling fixtures from a fixture box by chains or cord. New fixtures usually come with their own mounting hardware, adaptable to any fixture box.

Sometimes, though, the weight of the new fixture or the wiring necessary for proper grounding requires that you replace the box before installing the fixture.

Electrical code requirements sometimes allow ceiling fixtures weighing less than 24 ounces to be mounted on cut-in boxes held in position by the ceiling material. For a more secure installation and for heavier fixtures, you must fasten the box to a framing member or a special bracket secured to the joists. Do not attach fixtures heavier than 6 pounds to the box with screws through the fixture's metal canopy; use the hardware supplied by the manufacturer or check with your electrical inspector.

The NEC requires that all incandescent and fluorescent fixtures with exposed metal parts be grounded. If the fixture box is not grounded (as is the case when your present house wiring includes no grounding wire), you'll have to extend a grounding wire from the box to the nearest cold water pipe, as shown above right. The pipe must be metal, unbroken by plastic fittings or runs along its length. Bypass a problem spot or your water meter with a "jumper" wire. It's a good idea to ask a licensed electrician or building inspector to check your work.

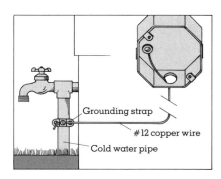

A cord or chain-hung fixture must also have a grounding wire run from the socket to the box. Most new fixtures are prewired with a grounding wire.

Then install your new surface-mounted fixture as described below.

■ **To replace an existing fixture with a new one,** first turn off the circuit. Remove the shade, if any, from the

SURFACE-MOUNTED FIXTURES

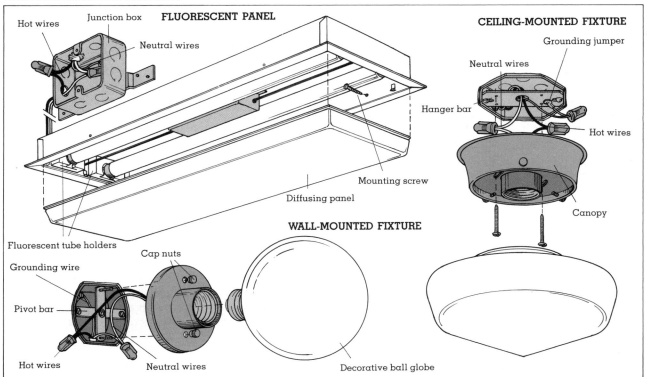

■ Electrical basics

old fixture. Unscrew the canopy from the fixture box, and detach the mounting bar if there is one. Now make a sketch of how the wires are connected. If the wires are spliced with wirenuts, unscrew them and untwist the wires. If the wires are spliced and wrapped with electrician's tape, simply unwind the tape and untwist the wires.

Match the wires of the new fixture to the old wires shown in your sketch, and splice with wirenuts. Secure the new fixtures as recommended by the manufacturer, using any new hardware included.

■ **To install a fixture in a new location,** you must route a new cable from a power source and install new fixture and switch boxes. New cable routed to the fixture box should include a grounding wire to be attached to the box's grounding screw. If more than one cable enters the box (for example, a separate cable from the switch box), you'll need to attach the end of a short length of bare 12-gauge wire (a "jumper") to the grounding screw, and use a wirenut to splice the other end to the ends of the grounding wires in the cables.

RECESSED DOWNLIGHTS

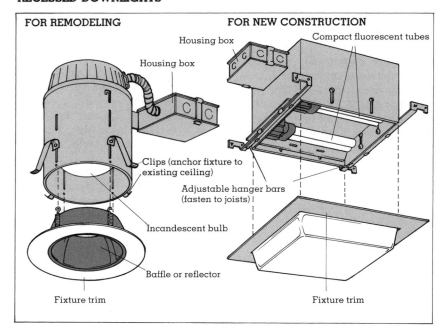

FOR REMODELING

FOR NEW CONSTRUCTION

Compact fluorescent tubes

Housing box

Housing box

Clips (anchor fixture to existing ceiling)

Adjustable hanger bars (fasten to joists)

Incandescent bulb

Baffle or reflector

Fixture trim

Fixture trim

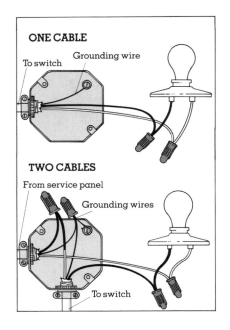

ONE CABLE

Grounding wire

To switch

TWO CABLES

From service panel

Grounding wires

To switch

Once you've routed the new cable and grounded the fixture box, wire in the new fixture—black wire to black, white to white; cap all splices with wirenuts. Then mount the fixture with hardware supplied by the manufacturer.

Recessed ceiling fixtures. Common recessed fixtures include incandescent circular or square downlights and larger fluorescent ceiling, or "troffer," panels. You'll need to cut a hole in the ceiling between the joists, or remove tiles or panels from a suspended ceiling, to install either type. Larger troffer panels may also require 2 by 4 blocking between joists for support.

Recessed fixtures need several inches of clearance above the finished ceiling. They're most easily installed below an unfinished attic or crawlspace. Because of the heat generated by many downlights, you must either buy a special zero-clearance model (type ICT), or plan to remove insulation within 3 inches of the fixture and make sure that no other combustible materials come within ½ inch.

Most low-voltage downlights come with an integral transformer

attached to the frame; if yours doesn't, you'll first need to mount an external transformer nearby and then route wire to the fixture.

If there's no crawlspace above the ceiling, find the joists (see page 68); don't forget to shut off power to any circuits that might be wired behind the ceiling before drilling exploratory holes.

Once you've determined the proper location for the fixture housing, trace its outline on the ceiling with a pencil; use a keyhole saw or saber saw to cut the hole. Brace a plaster ceiling as you cut.

If you don't have access from above, look for a remodeling fixture. The version shown above, at left, slips through the ceiling hole and clips onto the edge of the ceiling. The fixture trim then snaps onto the housing from below. (Hook up the wires to the circuit before securing the fixture and trim.)

So-called new work or rough-in downlights with adjustable hanger bars, such as the model shown above, at right, are easy to install from above. Simply nail the ends of the bars to joists on either side; then clip the trim or baffle into place from below.

CLIMATE CONTROL: HEATING & VENTILATION

Certain elements of your bathroom's climate—steam, excess heat, early morning chill—can be annoying and unpleasant. When you remodel, consider adding an exhaust fan to freshen the air and draw out destructive moisture, and a heater to warm you on cool days. Installing these climate controllers is within the grasp of most do-it-yourselfers. For more details on both fans and heaters, see page 61.

Heating the bathroom

Because electric heaters are easy to install and clean to operate, they're the most popular choice for heating bathrooms. In addition to the standard wall and ceiling-mounted units, you'll find heaters combined with exhaust fans, lights, or both. Many units require a dedicated 120 or 240-volt circuit, so shop carefully.

Gas heaters that can be recessed into a wall between two studs are available in a variety of styles and sizes. Regardless of how they heat, all gas models require a gas supply line and must be vented to the outside.

Choose the location of your heater carefully. Of course, you'll want to place it where someone getting out of the tub or shower will benefit from it (this is particularly true of radiant heaters, which heat objects directly). But don't locate the heater where someone will bump against its hot surfaces, or where it might char or ignite curtains or towels.

Since gas heaters require a vent to the outside, you'll probably want to place the heater on an outside wall. Otherwise, you'll have to run the vent through the attic or crawlspace and out through the roof. It's best to have a professional run gas lines; in any case, you must have the work tested and inspected before the gas is turned on.

Ventilating the bathroom

You can buy fans to mount in the wall or in the ceiling. Some models are combined with a light or a heater; some have both.

It's important that your exhaust fan have adequate capacity. The Home Ventilating Institute (HVI) rec-

ommends that the fan be capable of exchanging the air at least eight times every hour. To determine the required fan capacity in cubic feet per minute (CFM) for a bathroom with an 8-foot ceiling, multiply the room's length and width in feet by 1.1.

For example, if your bathroom is 6 by 9 feet, you would calculate the required fan capacity as follows:

$$6 \times 9 \times 1.1 = 59.4 \text{ CFM}$$

Rounding off, you would need fan capacity of at least 60 CFM. If your fan must exhaust through a long duct or several elbows, you'll need greater capacity to overcome the increased resistance. Follow the dealer's or manufacturer's recommendations.

Ideally, your fan should be mounted as close to the shower or tub as possible. It should also be as far away as possible from the source of replacement air (the door, for instance). In addition, you'll want the exhaust duct to be as short and straight as possible. If you have trouble finding a location that meets all three requirements, you may want to consult a professional.

THREE WAYS TO DUCT EXHAUST FANS

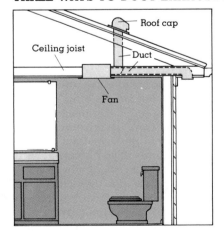

Ceiling fan ventilates through duct either to roof cap on roof or to grill in soffit under the eave.

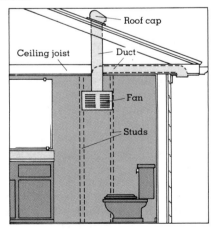

Wall fan on inside wall also ventilates through duct to cap on roof or to grill in soffit under the eave.

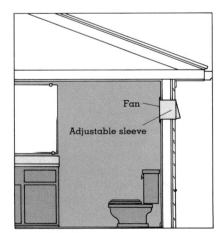

Wall fan on outside wall, installed between wall studs, ventilates through wall directly to outside.

Sinks

Replacing the bathroom sink (also known as a lavatory or basin) is one of the quickest ways to give your bathroom a new look without getting involved in a complex and expensive remodeling project.

This section will show you how to remove and install the four basic types of sinks: integral sink and countertop, pedestal, wall-hung, and deck-mount. For more information on the many sink models and materials, see page 56.

If you're planning to add a sink or to move one, you may want to consult a professional about extending supply, drain, and vent lines (see pages 72–75). But to replace a sink, extensive experience with plumbing isn't a requirement.

REMOVING A SINK

Unless you're installing a new floor covering, be sure to protect the bathroom floor with a piece of cardboard or plywood before you begin work. You'll also want a bucket and a supply of rags or sponges nearby to soak up excess water.

To loosen corroded plumbing connections, douse them with penetrating oil an hour before you start.

Disconnecting the plumbing

If the sink faucet is mounted on the countertop and you don't plan to replace the faucet, it isn't necessary to disconnect the water supply lines. If the faucet is connected to the sink, you do need to disconnect the supply lines.

Be sure to turn off the water at the sink shutoff valves or at the main valve before doing any work. Disconnect the supply lines at the shutoff valves, placing a bucket underneath them to catch any water, and open the faucets so the lines can drain.

If your sink isn't equipped with shutoff valves, disconnect the supply lines at the faucet inlet shanks, as explained on page 92—and plan to add shutoff valves before you connect the plumbing to the new sink (or

have a professional plumber do the work for you).

Next, move the bucket underneath the trap. If the trap has a cleanout plug, remove it to drain the water, then loosen the slip nuts and remove the trap. If there is no cleanout plug, remove the trap and dump the water into the bucket.

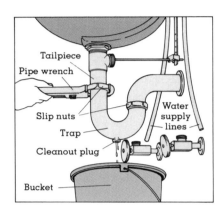

Disconnect the pop-up drain assembly by loosening the clevis screw and then removing the spring clip that connects the stopper and pivot rod to the pop-up rod on the faucet (see "Removing a sink faucet," page 92).

The tailpiece, drain body, and sink flange, as well as the faucet, will now come out with the sink. If you plan to reuse the old faucet, remove it carefully from the sink and set aside.

Removing an integral sink & countertop

An integral sink is molded as part of the countertop, and the unit is secured to the top of a vanity cabinet. Look underneath for any metal clips or wooden braces securing the unit, and remove them. Then lift off the whole unit.

If you can't remove the unit easily, insert the end of a small prybar in the joint between the countertop and vanity cabinet at a back corner. Carefully lift up the prybar to break the sealing material between the countertop and the vanity. If the joint is too narrow to accept the end of a prybar, cut through the sealing ma-

terial with a hot putty knife, then pry or lift up the countertop.

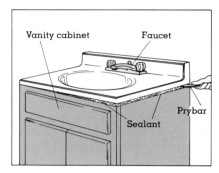

Removing a pedestal sink

Most pedestal sinks are made of two pieces—the sink and the pedestal or base. Look in the opening at the rear of the pedestal to locate a nut or bolt holding the sink down. If you find one, remove it. Lift off the sink and set it aside.

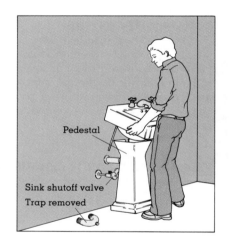

The pedestal is usually bolted to the floor. You may find the bolts on the base, or on the inside of the pedestal (see illustration above right). Undo the bolts and remove the pedestal. If you can't move it after removing the bolts, rock it back and forth, and then lift it out. If the pedestal is recessed into a ceramic tile floor, you may have to remove the surrounding floor tiles with a cold chisel and soft-headed steel hammer. Rock the pedestal back and forth to break any remaining seal with the floor. Lift the pedestal up and set it aside.

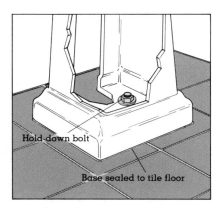

Hold-down bolt

Base sealed to tile floor

Removing a wall-hung sink

To remove a wall-hung sink, first unscrew the legs, if any, that support the front of the sink. Check underneath for any bolts securing the sink to the mounting bracket on the wall (see illustration below), and remove them. Then lift the sink straight up and off the mounting bracket.

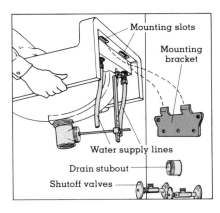

Mounting slots

Mounting bracket

Water supply lines

Drain stubout

Shutoff valves

Removing a deck-mount sink

There are three basic types of deck-mount sinks used in vanity countertops: self-rimming or rimless sinks, flush-mount sinks, and unrimmed or recessed sinks. All may be secured to the countertop with lugs or clamps that must be unscrewed before you remove the sink.

Self-rimming or rimless sinks.

These have a molded flange that sits on the countertop. Once you have removed any lugs or clamps from underneath, just use a hot putty knife or other knife to cut through the

sealing material between sink and countertop; then pry up the sink to break the seal and lift it out.

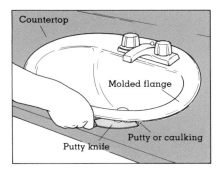

Countertop

Molded flange

Putty or caulking

Putty knife

Flush-mount sinks. Have a helper support the sink while you undo the lugs or clamps that secure the sink's metal rim to the countertop. (If you're working alone, you can support the sink with a 2 by 4 and a wood block tied together through the drain; see illustration below.) After you remove the lugs or clamps, cut through the sealing material between the rim and the countertop with a hot putty knife or other knife. Pry up the rim to free the sink; then lift straight up.

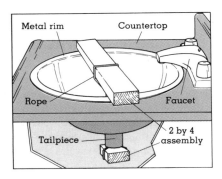

Metal rim   Countertop

Rope   Faucet

Tailpiece

2 by 4 assembly

Unrimmed or recessed sinks. An unrimmed or recessed sink is secured to the underside of the countertop. The easiest way to remove the sink is to first take off the countertop. Check underneath for any brackets and remove them. Then insert a prybar into the joint between the countertop and the vanity cabinet near a rear corner, and pry up. Turn the countertop bottom side up and rest it on a padded surface. Undo the lugs or clamps securing the sink, and lift it off the countertop.

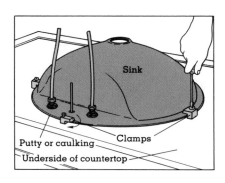

Sink

Putty or caulking   Clamps

Underside of countertop

When the countertop is tiled, the flange usually rests on top of the plywood base for the tile. Look underneath; if you don't see any clips or brackets, you'll have to remove the tile surrounding the edge of the sink. With a soft-headed steel hammer and cold chisel, remove enough tile so that you can lift the sink from the countertop. (Be sure to protect your eyes with goggles.) If you can't find matching replacement tile and need to reuse the old tiles, remove them carefully to avoid breaking them.

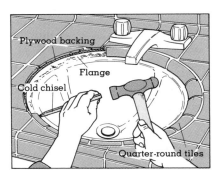

Plywood backing

Flange

Cold chisel

Quarter-round tiles

INSTALLING A SINK

If you're installing a sink at a new location instead of replacing an existing one, you'll need to extend the supply, drain, and vent pipes (see pages 72–75).

If you'd like your sink to be higher than standard, you can raise the vanity of an integral or deck-mount sink by building a base under it. If you're installing a wall-hung sink, simply mount the bracket higher. You can't adjust the height of a pedestal sink, but you may be able to buy a taller model.

(Continued on next page)

■Sinks

MOUNTING A DUAL-HANDLE FAUCET

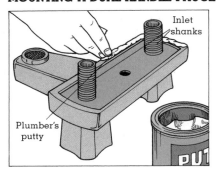

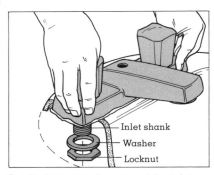

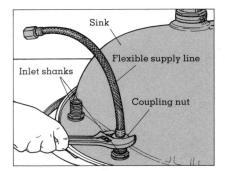

Apply putty to bottom edge of the faucet if there is no rubber gasket to seal it to sink's surface.

Set the faucet in place, insert the inlet shanks through the sink holes, and press down. Add washers and locknuts.

Attach flexible supply lines to the faucet's inlet shanks, using pipe joint compound and coupling nuts.

Before installing the sink, you'll need to install the faucet and the sink flange.

Installing the faucet & sink flange

Whether the faucet is to be mounted on the countertop or on the sink itself, you'll find it easier to install the faucet before you set the sink in place. The main steps are illustrated above. First make sure that the mounting surface is clean. If your faucet came with a rubber gasket, place it on the bottom of the faucet. For a faucet without a gasket, put a bead of plumber's putty around the bottom edge of the faucet.

Set the faucet in position, and press it down onto the sink or countertop surface. Assemble the washers and locknuts on the inlet shanks, and then tighten the nuts. Remove excess putty from around the faucet. Connect the supply lines to the inlet shanks and tighten the coupling nuts. For more information on installing faucets, see pages 92–93.

Now install the sink flange and drain. To attach the flange, run a bead of plumber's putty around the drain hole of the sink. Press the flange into the puttied hole. Put the locknut, metal washer, and flat rubber washer on the drain body in that order. Insert the threaded end of the drain body into the bottom of the sink and screw it onto the flange. Then tighten the locknut until it is snug (do not overtighten).

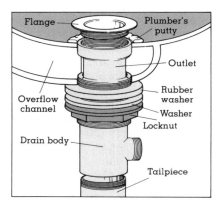

Installing an integral sink & countertop

Cover the top edges of the vanity cabinet with a sealant recommended by the manufacturer. Place the countertop unit on the cabinet flush with the back edge. Make sure the overhang—if any—is equal on the left and right. Press along the countertop edges to complete the seal, and check around the perimeter, removing any excess sealant.

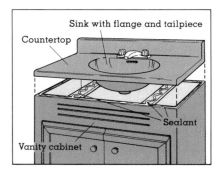

If your unit came with mounting brackets, use them to secure the countertop to the vanity. Seal the joint between the countertop and the wall with caulking compound.

Installing a pedestal sink

Position a *dual-handle faucet* as shown above. Assemble the washers and locknuts on the inlet shanks; then tighten the nuts. Remove excess putty from around the faucet. Connect the supply lines to the inlet shanks.

Most *single-lever faucets* include short supply tubes; simply tighten the locknuts on the threaded stubs from below. For details, see pages 92–93.

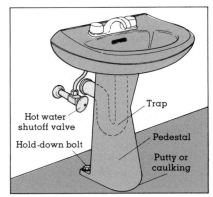

Position the sink on top of the pedestal and, if required by the manufacturer, bolt the two together as directed.

Installing a wall-hung sink

For new installations, you'll need to remove the wall coverings and wallboard. Notch two studs directly behind the sink's proposed location, and nail or screw a 1 by 6 or 1 by 8 mounting board flush to the stud fronts; then re-cover the wall.

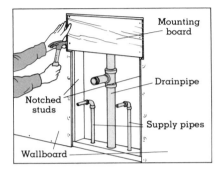

Before you attach the mounting bracket to the wall mounting board, check to see that it fits the sink. Refer to the manufacturer's instructions to properly position the bracket. Generally, you center the bracket over the drainpipe, then level it at the desired height from the floor. Fasten the bracket to the mounting board with woodscrews, making sure that it's level. Then carefully lower the sink onto the mounting bracket.

Because the mounting bracket can bend or break under the weight of a large wall-hung sink, the manufacturer may recommend that adjustable legs be inserted into the holes under the front corners of the sink. Screw the legs down until the sink is level; be sure to keep the legs plumb.

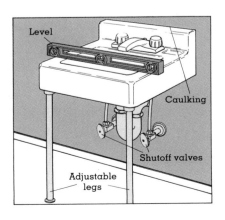

Seal the joint between the back of the sink and the wall with caulking compound.

Installing a deck-mount sink

If your countertop doesn't have a hole for the sink, you'll need to cut one. For a self-rimming or an unrimmed sink, mark the hole, using the templates supplied with the sink. If you didn't receive a template, cut one from paper; it should fit loosely around the outside of the sink bowl where the bowl meets the flange.

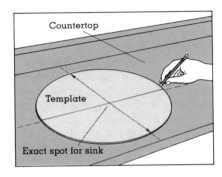

For a flush-mount sink, trace the bottom edge of the sink's metal framing rim directly onto the spot where the sink will sit in the countertop.

After you mark the location of the cutout, drill a starting hole, then use a saber saw to cut the opening.

Install your deck-mount sink as described below.

Self-rimming or rimless sinks.

First, run a bead of caulking compound or plumber's putty around the underside of the flange. Set the sink on the countertop and press it down until the putty oozes out. Install any lugs or clamps according to the manufacturer's instructions. Remove excess putty.

Flush-mount sinks. Apply a bead of caulking compound or plumber's putty around the sink lip. Fasten the metal framing rim around the lip, following the manufacturer's directions. Next, apply a bead of caulking compound or plumber's putty

around the top edge of the countertop sink opening, and set the sink and rim in place. Secure the sink and rim to the underside of the countertop with the lugs or clamps provided. Wipe off excess putty.

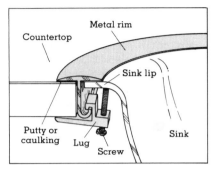

Unrimmed or recessed sinks.

Turn the countertop upside down and apply plumber's putty or caulking compound on the underside, around the edge of the sink opening. Set the sink in place, checking from the other side to be sure it is centered in the opening. Anchor the sink as recommended by the manufacturer. If you're finishing the countertop with ceramic tile, you can mount the sink atop the plywood base and then edge it with tile trim.

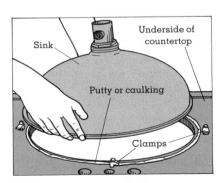

Connecting the plumbing

Once the sink is installed, connect the water supply lines to the shutoff valves and tighten the coupling nuts. Then connect the trap to the drainpipe and tailpiece, and tighten the slip nuts (see drawing, page 82). Connect the pop-up stopper to the faucet pop-up rod (see page 93). Turn on the water at the shutoff valves or main shutoff; check for leaks.

Bathtubs

Installing or replacing a bathtub can be a complicated job—one that takes careful planning. But a gleaming new tub in your bathroom is well worth the effort.

Your tub choices range from porcelain-enameled cast iron or steel to lightweight fiberglass-reinforced plastic. The waterproof wall covering around a tub (called a surround) can be tile or panels of fiberglass-reinforced plastic or coated hardboard.

If you're building a new bathroom, you can create an entire bath area with a tub and surround manufactured as a one-piece unit. These units are not recommended for remodeling projects, though, since they are usually too large to fit through a door and must be moved in before the bathroom walls are framed. For remodeling, your best choice is a tub with separate wall panels or tiles.

Before you install a tub in a new location, check local building codes for support requirements; a bathtub filled with water is extremely heavy and needs plenty of support. You should also check the plumbing code requirements for extending the water supply and drain-waste and vent systems (see page 73). Consider getting professional help to build the framing and to rough-in plumbing for a new installation.

In this section, you'll find general directions for removing and installing bathtubs and wall coverings. For detailed product information, see page 57.

REMOVING A BATHTUB

There are three main steps to this job: disconnecting the appropriate plumbing, removing part or all of the wall covering, and removing the tub itself.

Disconnecting the plumbing

Generally it's not necessary to turn off the water unless you're replacing the faucet body. If you do need to turn off the water, do so at the fixture shutoff valves (if you can reach them through an access door in an adjoining room or hallway) or at the main shutoff valve. Open the faucets to drain the pipes.

Next, remove any fittings—spout, faucet parts, shower head, and diverter handle—that will be in the way. To remove the tub, you'll also have to unscrew and remove the overflow cover and drain lever. By pulling out this fitting, you'll also remove the bathtub drain assembly if it's a trip-lever type.

If you have a pop-up stopper, pull it out with the rocker linkage after removing the overflow cover (see illustration below).

If there's an access door or access from the basement or crawlspace, use a pipe wrench to loosen the coupling nuts from behind the tub; disconnect the trap and waste tee, as shown below, at right. If you can't get access to the drain plumb-

ing, you can work from inside the tub; disconnect the tub from the overflow pipe and drainpipe by unscrewing the overflow retainer flange and drain flange.

Removing the wall covering

Most bathtubs are recessed; that is, they are surrounded by walls on three sides. Depending on whether you want to replace the tub only, or the tub and the wall covering, you'll need to remove all or part of the surrounding tiles or panels. Before doing this, remove any fittings, such as the shower head, that are in the way (if you haven't yet done so).

Tile. If there are wall or floor tiles along the edge of the tub, free the tub by chipping out approximately **4** inches to the nearest grout joint (see illustration above right). On the walls, remove the plaster or gypsum wallboard backing at the same time, so that several inches of the wall studs are exposed. Use a cold chisel and soft-headed steel hammer to remove the tile, and be sure to protect your eyes from fragments by wearing goggles.

If you're removing a recessed tub, you must also remove enough tile (and other obstructions) from the floor and walls to be able to slide the tub out of its recess.

Fiberglass panels. Take out the wall panels by first removing the

DISCONNECTING THE PLUMBING

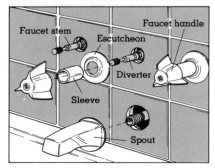

Remove faucet and diverter parts and spout, leaving stubout for spout and faucet and diverter stems.

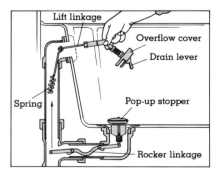

Unscrew overflow cover, then pull out drain assembly—first the overflow cover and lift linkage, then the pop-up stopper.

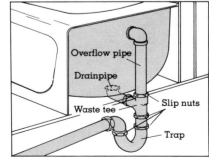

Loosen slip nuts and remove trap from underneath tub; then disconnect and remove overflow pipe.

REMOVING WALL COVERINGS

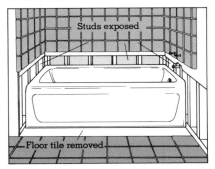

For tile walls, chip away a 4-inch strip of tile and backing from walls; remove an equivalent strip from a tile floor.

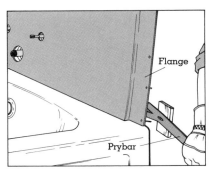

For fiberglass panels, pry panel flange and pull panel and any backing off the wall studs.

gypsum wallboard or molding from the panel flanges. With a prybar, pry the panels, along with any backing, off the studs. Once the end panels are removed, you can take out the back panel, leaving the exposed wall studs (see illustration above).

Removing the tub

The tub's bulk will make this one of your biggest jobs. To get the tub out, you may first have to remove the bathroom door or even cut a hole in the wall opposite the tub plumbing. Plan exactly how you'll route the tub through and out of the house. You'll need helpers to move it, especially if it's a heavy steel or cast-iron fixture.

Steel or cast-iron tubs. Locate and remove from the wall studs any nails or screws at the top of the tub's flange (lip) that may be holding the tub in place. With at least one helper (probably three for a cast-iron tub), lift up the tub with a prybar and slide two or three soaped wooden runners under it (see illustration at right). Then slide the tub out of the recess.

Fiberglass tubs. To remove a fiberglass or plastic tub, pull out all nails or screws driven into the wall studs through the flange. Reach between the studs and grasp the tub under the flange (see illustration far right); with the aid of a helper, if necessary, pull the tub up off its supports and out of the recess.

INSTALLING A BATHTUB

If you're replacing an old tub with a new one, carefully inspect the subfloor where the tub will be installed for level and for moisture damage, and make any necessary repairs or adjustments.

If you're installing a tub in a new location, you'll do the framing and rough-in the plumbing first (see "Structural basics," pages 67–70, and "Plumbing basics," pages 72–75).

Setting, leveling & securing the tub

This is the most crucial part of the installation process. A tub must be correctly supported and carefully secured in a level position so that it will drain properly and all plumbing connections can be made easily.

MOVING THE TUB

To move a steel or cast-iron tub, slide it across floor on soaped wooden runners. You'll need several helpers .

Steel or cast-iron tubs. These heavy tubs require either vertical or horizontal wood supports (see "Four ways to support a tub" on the following page). Horizontal supports are 1 by 4s or 2 by 4s, nailed across the wall studs so that the tub's flange rests on them. Vertical supports are 2 by 4s nailed to each stud. Position the supports so that the tub will be level both from end to end and from back to front.

If your tub is steel, you can attach prefabricated metal hangers to the studs with woodscrews to support the tub.

When you've attached the appropriate supports, slide your new tub along soaped wooden runners into position (see illustration below). With the aid of several helpers, lift it so that the flanges rest on the supports. Check the tub at both ends to see that it's level. If not, insert shims between the tub and wall supports or floor to level it. To prevent the tub from slipping, anchor it by driving nails or screws into the studs tight against the top of the flange.

Fiberglass tubs. If necessary, temporarily remove any protruding stubouts. Then, with a helper, set the tub on wood supports, tight against the rear studs.

Once the tub is in position, check on top for level at both ends, shimming where needed, as for steel and cast-iron models. Drill holes in the tub flange and carefully nail or screw through the holes into the studs.

(Continued on next page)

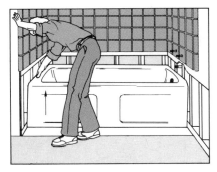

To move a fiberglass tub, grasp it under back of the flange and lift it up and out. A helper will make the job easier.

■Bathtubs

Connecting the plumbing

Once the tub is secured in position, reconnect the overflow pipe, trap, and drain assembly. (Be careful not to overtighten the nuts and crack the tub's surface.) Make sure you connect the overflow pipe with the tub drainpipe on the side of the trap nearest the bathtub, not on the far side.

If you're reusing existing wall coverings, install the faucet and spout, plus a diverter and shower head as required. If you plan on a new wall covering (see below), connect the fittings afterwards.

Installing the wall covering

Before patching or re-covering the walls with either tile or panels, turn on the water and check the drain and supply pipes for leaks.

If you plan to install a tiled wall, see pages 103–105. If you're starting from scratch, it's best to use cement backer board as a base.

To install new fiberglass panels, cover any exposed studs with gypsum wallboard (cut to accommodate the plumbing) or cement backer board. Then follow the procedure below.

Drill pipe holes. To install a panel over pipe stubouts and faucet and

FOUR WAYS TO SUPPORT A TUB

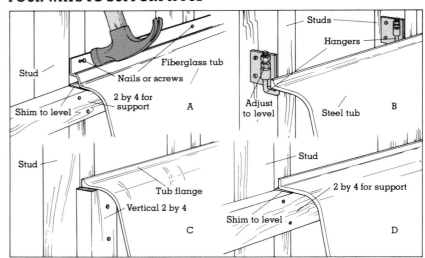

Support a new tub in one of these ways: nail or screw fiberglass tub flange to studs (A); support steel tub with metal hangers (B); nail vertical 2 by 4s to studs to support metal tubs (C); nail horizontal 2 by 4s to support metal tubs (D).

diverter stems, you'll need to mark and drill it accurately (see illustration below). Measure and mark the panel by holding it up against the stubouts and stems. Drill slightly oversized holes in the panel with a spade bit, backing the panel with a wood plank to prevent splintering.

Set panels. Apply mastic in S-patterns to the backs of the panels (see illustration below), and press

the panels in place around the top of the tub, according to manufacturer's directions. If panels are to be nailed or screwed to the studs, predrill all nail holes.

Finish and seal panels. Seal all gaps between the wall covering and the stubouts and stems with silicone caulk. Finally, attach the faucet and diverter parts, spout, and shower head.

INSTALLING PANELS AROUND A TUB

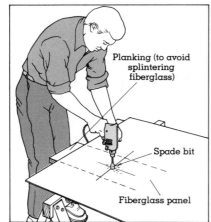

After carefully marking one panel to fit over the stubouts and faucet and diverter stems, drill holes in it with a spade bit.

Apply mastic to panel in S-patterns while panel rests on planks laid across a pair of sawhorses.

Press panel into place on the wall, fitting it over stubouts and faucet and diverter stems.

Showers

From elegant ceramic tile to easy-to-install fiberglass or plastic panels, your choices are many when it comes to replacing or adding a shower in your home. And if you're installing a completely new bathroom, you can also choose a molded one-piece shower enclosure. (These are not recommended for remodeling projects because they won't fit through most bathroom doors.)

In this section you'll find instructions for removing all types of showers (including the older metal units) and for installing tile and fiberglass-reinforced or plastic-paneled showers. For more details on the various models, see page 58.

REMOVING A SHOWER

Most showers consist of three walls with waterproof wall covering, such as tile or panels, and a separate base, mounted in a wood frame. Removing a shower is a three-step procedure: disconnecting the plumbing, removing the wall covering, and removing the base. If the shower is a one-piece unit, you'll also have to cut a hole in a wall to get it out, unless you cut the unit into pieces.

If you're changing the location of a shower or permanently removing it, you'll probably want to dismantle the wood frame and remove the plumbing.

Disconnecting the plumbing

First remove the shower door or the rod and curtain. Then turn off the water supply at the fixture shutoff valves (sometimes accessible through an access door in an adjoining hallway or closet) or at the main shutoff valve. Open the faucets to drain the pipes. Then sponge the shower base dry.

Remove the faucet handles and other trim parts, leaving the faucet stems. Then remove the shower head with a pipe wrench tape-wrapped to avoid scarring the fixture (see illustration above).

DISCONNECTING SHOWER PLUMBING

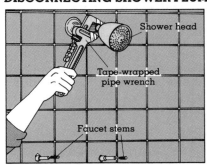

Use pipe wrench wrapped with tape to remove shower head. (Faucet parts have already been removed.)

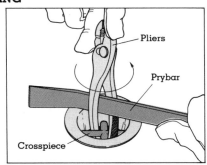

After removing drain cover, use pliers and prybar to unscrew crosspiece from drain.

Unscrew and pry up the drain cover, and with a pair of pliers and a small prybar, unscrew the crosspiece (see illustration). If you're removing a one-piece shower enclosure, you'll also have to disconnect the drainpipe and remove protruding faucet stems and fittings that might get in the way when you tip the unit to pull it out. Finally, plug the drain opening with a rag to prevent debris from falling into it.

Removing the wall covering

The removal procedure you'll follow depends on whether you have a tiled shower, walls covered with fiberglass panels, or an older metal shower.

After you've removed the wall covering, check for moisture damage to the frame and to any soundproofing insulation secured across the inside of the frame. Repair or replace if necessary.

Tile. Ceramic tile is the most difficult wall covering to remove. If the existing tile is clean, smooth, and securely attached, you can avoid removing it by using it as a backing for a new tile surface. If you must remove it, proceed with caution and wear goggles while you work.

(Continued on next page)

REMOVING SHOWER WALLS

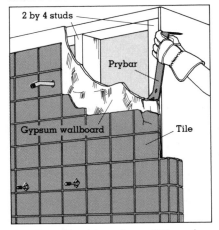

For tile walls, chip and pry off tile and wallboard backing to expose entire frame of shower.

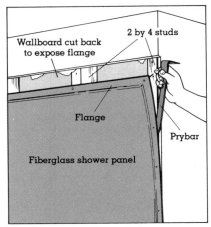

For panel walls, remove any wallboard or molding covering panel flanges; then pry panels off frame.

■Showers

To remove tile set in mortar, you must break up the tile, mortar, and any backing with a sledge hammer. Remove it down to the wood frame, being careful not to hit and damage the wall studs. You may want to hire a tile professional for this part of the project.

If the tile is set on wallboard with adhesive, use a cold chisel and soft-headed steel hammer to chip away small sections of tile and backing. Then insert a prybar and pry off large sections of tile and backing until the entire frame is exposed (see illustration, page 89).

Fiberglass panels. First remove any molding or wallboard covering the panel flanges. Then pry panels, along with any backing and nails, off the wood frame (see illustration, page 89). If you're removing a one-piece enclosure, you may have to cut it apart to get it out (a saber saw with a plastic-cutting blade will do the job quickly).

Metal showers. Remove metal shower walls by unscrewing them at the edges and then at the front and back corners. These screws hold the shower walls to each other and sometimes to a wood frame. If the screws are rusted, cut the screw heads off with a hacksaw or cold chisel; then separate the walls with a hard pull.

Removing the base

The base may be tile on a mortar bed, or it may be a fiberglass unit. Tile is difficult to remove because it's laid in mortar; fiberglass bases are simply pried out.

After you've removed the base, inspect the subfloor and framing for moisture damage, and repair where necessary.

Tile on mortar. As with tile walls, check first to see if you can lay the new tile over the old. If not, use a sledge hammer to break up and remove all tile and mortar down to the subfloor. You may be able to pry up one side of the base and slip a wedge under it to make it easier to break up. Wear goggles to protect your eyes from tile or mortar fragments.

Fiberglass. Remove all nails or screws from the flange around the top of the base. Pry the base off the floor with a prybar; lift it out.

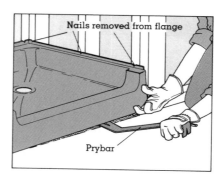

Nails removed from flange

Prybar

INSTALLING A SHOWER

When you replace an old shower, the plumbing—and probably the wood frame—will already be in place.

If you're putting a shower in a new location, you must first frame the shower walls using 2 by 4s (see "Structural basics," pages 67–70). Make accurate measurements (follow the manufacturer's directions to frame a fiberglass shower); keep framing square and plumb.

Once the frame is complete, you'll also need to rough-in supply and drain lines, and install the faucet and pipe for the shower head (see pages 72–75 and 94).

Now you're ready to install the shower—first the base, then the walls.

Installing the base

Installing a watertight tiled base on a mortar bed is a highly complicated project not recommended for beginners. If you want this type of base in either a tile or panel shower, consider having a professional build it.

To install a fiberglass or plastic base, position it over the drain outlet. Connect the base to the drain by screwing in the crosspiece (see illustration, page 89), and cover the opening with rags to keep debris from falling in. Follow the manufacturer's directions to secure the base to the frame (nailing is shown below). Later, remove the rags and attach the drain cover.

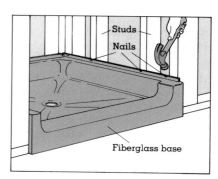

Studs

Nails

Fiberglass base

Installing the wall covering

Once the base is secured, you're ready to cover the shower's side and back walls with tile or panels.

Tile. Like a tile base, tile walls can be tricky to install. If you want tile on a mortar bed, you may want to hire a tile contractor to install it. If you're planning to back the tile with either water-resistant wallboard or cement backer board, you may decide to do the job yourself.

First, prepare the backing. Cut holes for the shower head stubout and faucet stems; then nail the backing to the frame (see illustration above right).

Plan the layout of your tile by marking horizontal and vertical working lines on the shower wall (see illustrations above right). Using thin-set adhesive, tile the back wall. Then move on to the sides, cutting tiles to fit around the shower stubout and faucet stems.

Set ceramic tile accessories. Allow the tile to set (for the required time, consult the adhesive manufacturer's instructions) before grouting all the joints between the tiles. When the grout has set, you can seal it. For more information on establishing working lines, setting tile, and grouting joints, turn to pages 103–105; or ask your tile dealer.

INSTALLING TILE ON SHOWER WALLS

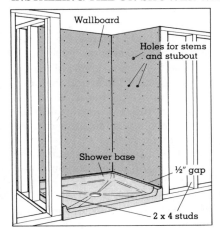

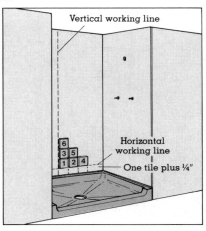

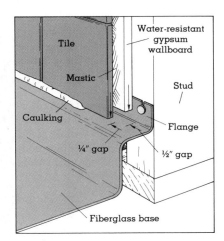

To attach wallboard or backer board to a wood shower frame, nail along the length of the 2 by 4 studs.

Mark working lines, both horizontal and vertical, then set tile on shower walls in a pyramid pattern.

Backing is positioned to leave ½-inch gap above base; leave ¼-inch gap for caulking tile.

Fiberglass panels. Shower panels of fiberglass usually come with manufacturer's directions for installation. Some require no backing (except perhaps soundproofing insulation); others require separate water-resistant wallboard backing.

For both types of panels, measure and mark on one panel the locations of the shower head stubout and faucet stems. Lay the marked panel across two sawhorses, and with a spade bit, drill slightly oversized holes for your fittings. Support the panels with wood planks so you don't splinter them as you drill (see illustration below).

If the base of your shower has channels on the outside edges for sealant, clean out any debris from them. Then fill the groove at the back with the sealant recommended by the manufacturer (see illustration below). Also apply adhesive to the reverse side of the back panel according to manufacturer's directions.

Install the back panel by fitting it into the groove on the base, then pressing it against the frame to make a complete seal. Next, fill the other grooves on the base with seal-

ant and install the side panels; they may snap or clip to the back panel. Screw or nail the flanges of the panels to the framing. Install cover moldings over the nails or screws, if required.

Connecting the plumbing

Once you've installed the wall coverings, caulk around all openings; then re-attach the shower head, escutcheons, and faucet handles.

Finally, hang the shower door, or mount a curtain rod and hang a shower curtain.

INSTALLING FIBERGLASS SHOWER PANELS

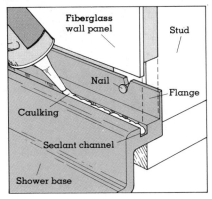

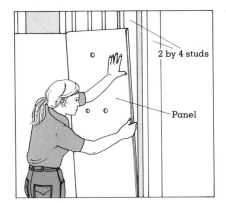

Mark a panel for stubout hole and faucet stem, set panel on supporting planks and sawhorses, and drill holes.

Channel in shower base holds panel tightly in place; sealant prevents moisture from getting behind panels.

Press panel to the frame, guiding head stubout and faucet stems through holes; nail or screw panel flange to frame.

Faucets

Whether you're replacing an old faucet or selecting fittings for a new sink or bathtub, you'll find a wide variety of faucet types and styles from which to choose. The product information on page 59 can help you make your selection.

In this section, you'll find information on removing and installing two different types of widely used bathroom faucets: deck-mount models for sinks, and wall-mount models for bathtubs and showers.

SINK FAUCETS

In choosing a deck-mount faucet, be sure that the faucet's inlet shanks are spaced to fit the holes in your sink. If you're replacing a faucet, it's wise to take the old one with you when you shop. You'll also need new water supply lines, so take them with you, too.

Choose a unit that comes with clear installation instructions, and make sure that repair kits or replacement parts are readily available.

Removing a sink faucet

Before removing the faucet, turn off the water at the sink shutoff valves or main shutoff valve. Place a bucket under the valves and use a wrench to remove the coupling nuts connecting the water supply lines to the valves. Open the faucet and allow the water to drain from the lines.

If your sink has a pop-up drain, you'll need to disconnect it before removing the faucet. Unfasten the clevis screw and spring clip that secure the pivot rod to the pop-up rod, and remove the pop-up rod from the faucet body (see drawing on facing page).

With an adjustable or basin wrench, reach up behind the sink and remove the coupling nuts holding the supply lines to the inlet shanks on the faucet (see illustration above). Use the wrench to remove the locknuts from the shanks. Take off the washers; then lift up the faucet and remove it from the sink or countertop.

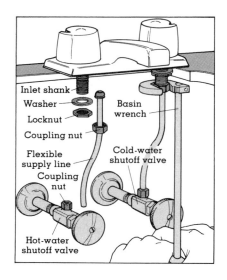

Inlet shank
Washer
Locknut
Coupling nut
Flexible supply line
Coupling nut
Hot-water shutoff valve
Basin wrench
Cold-water shutoff valve

Installing a sink faucet

Before you start, have an adjustable wrench on hand. If your new faucet doesn't come with a rubber gasket, you'll also need a supply of plumber's putty.

If you're installing a new faucet on an old sink, make sure the area around the faucet is free of dirt and mineral buildup.

The basic steps in installing a sink faucet are outlined below, but since procedures vary with the type of faucet, you should also look carefully at the manufacturer's instructions.

Mounting the faucet. If your new faucet doesn't have a rubber gasket on the bottom, apply a bead of plumber's putty around the underside of the outside edge.

The faucet may have either inlet shanks or inlet tubes and threaded mounting studs. Insert the inlet shanks or tubes down through the holes in the mounting surface; press the faucet onto the surface. For a faucet with inlet shanks, screw the washers and locknuts onto the shanks by hand (see illustration at left); tighten with a wrench. If your faucet has tubes, assemble and tighten the washers and nuts on the mounting studs (see drawing below).

Connecting the plumbing. Two types of flexible supply lines are available: chrome-plated corrugated metal tubing and plastic tubing. Because it's a little better looking, metal tubing is usually used when the supply lines are visible. Gaskets and coupling nuts are sold separately, so be sure they fit the faucet and the shutoff valves. Plastic tubing is sold with gaskets and coupling nuts already assembled.

Before connecting the supply lines, apply pipe joint compound to the threads on the inlet shanks and shutoff valves, or to the threads on the fittings at the ends of the tubing.

INSTALLING A SINGLE-LEVER FAUCET

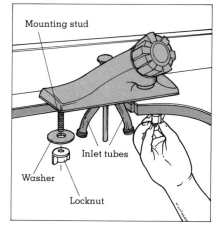

Mounting stud
Inlet tubes
Washer
Locknut

Position the faucet, threading inlet tubes through the sink hole; then tighten the locknuts on mounting studs.

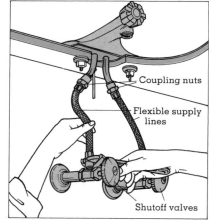

Coupling nuts
Flexible supply lines
Shutoff valves

Extend flexible tubing from inlet tubes as required; attach it to shutoff valves with an adjustable wrench.

Then connect the supply lines to the inlet shanks or tubes (see illustration on facing page). Tighten the coupling nuts with a wrench. Gently bend the supply lines to meet the shutoff valves, and secure them to the valves with coupling nuts. Tighten the nuts with an adjustable wrench, then turn on the water and check for leaks.

If you're installing a new pop-up drain assembly, follow the manufacturer's instructions. Connect the pop-up rod to the new pivot rod, using the fastenings supplied with the new drain assembly.

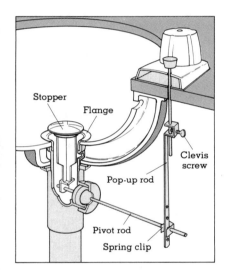

BATHTUB & SHOWER FAUCETS

Faucets for bathtubs and showers are either compression models (usually with separate hot and cold water controls) or washerless models (with a single lever or knob to control the flow and mix of hot and cold water). In both types (see illustration above right), the faucet body is mounted directly on the water supply pipes inside the wall.

You can either renovate a bathtub or shower faucet, or completely replace it. If the faucet body is in good condition, you may simply want to replace some of the faucet parts. If the faucet body is in poor condition, or if you want to change the type of

TWO TYPES OF BATHTUB AND SHOWER FAUCETS

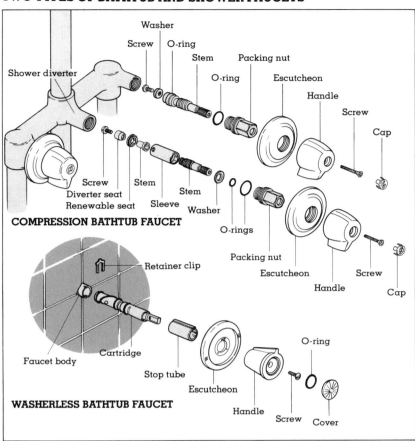

COMPRESSION BATHTUB FAUCET

WASHERLESS BATHTUB FAUCET

faucet you have, you may have to replace the entire assembly. You'll also need to replace the complete faucet if you want to add a shower head above an existing bathtub (see "Adding a shower faucet," page 94). The following sections tell you how to renovate or replace a faucet.

Renovating a bathtub or shower faucet

To renovate a faucet, you can replace faucet parts—stems, handles, and trim (such as escutcheons)—and the tub spout or shower head. In a tub, you might also replace the diverter—the mechanism that redirects water to the shower pipe. To find the correct replacement parts, it's a good idea to disassemble the old faucet first, then take the parts with you to the store when you shop for new ones.

Before you start work, turn off the water at the bathtub or shower shutoff valves or at the main shutoff valve. (Bathtub or shower shutoff valves may be accessible through a panel in an adjoining room, hall, or closet.)

The drawings on this page show you how typical compression and washerless faucets are put together, but the assembly may vary with individual models. As you disassemble your faucet, take notes and make a sketch of the parts and the sequence of assembly so you'll be able to put the faucet back together. First remove faucet handles, trim, and stem parts; then remove the diverter (if necessary). Finally, remove the tub spout or shower head with a tape-wrapped pipe wrench.

When you're ready to assemble the new fittings, simply reverse the procedure.

(Continued on next page)

■Faucets

REMOVING A BATHTUB FAUCET

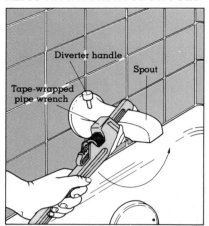

Remove spout from wall stubout by turning counterclockwise with a tape-wrapped pipe wrench.

Remove faucet body from supply pipes by unscrewing or unsoldering the connections.

Replacing a bathtub or shower faucet

Replacing a complete bathtub or shower faucet involves cutting away the wall covering and removing the faucet body from the supply pipes with wrenches or a small propane torch. You'll need to take the old faucet body with you when you buy a new one, to be sure of getting the correct size. If you've never done any pipefitting, you may want to get professional help to install the new faucet body.

Getting to the faucet body. First remove the faucet handles and trim, and the shower head or tub spout and diverter. To work on the faucet body and the pipes behind the wall, open the access door or panel if one is available. If not, cut a hole in the bathroom wall large enough to allow you to work on the faucet body and pipes comfortably (see illustration at right). Then turn off the water at the bathtub shutoff valves or main shutoff valve.

Removing the faucet body. The illustration above shows how a bathtub or shower faucet body is mounted onto the water supply pipes. It may be attached with either threaded or soldered connections. If you find threaded connections, un-

screw them. Use one wrench on the supply pipe to hold it steady, and one wrench on the coupling, turning it counterclockwise. If you find soldered copper connections, unsolder them, using a small propane torch.

Installing the faucet body. If your tub or shower is not equipped with individual shutoff valves, you may want to add them now (or consult a professional plumber for help). To install a faucet body on threaded pipe fittings, apply pipe joint compound to the male threads of the pipes and screw the connecting coupling nuts down tight.

For copper pipe, solder couplings to the pipes and screw them onto the faucet body. If the faucet body must be soldered directly to the pipe, first remove the valve and diverter stems.

After the pipes are connected to the faucet body, turn the water on and check for leaks. To make certain the pipes can't vibrate when the water is turned on and off, anchor them and the faucet body firmly to the wall studs or support with pipe straps before patching and re-covering the wall.

Carefully measure and mark the positions of the new faucet, spout, and shower head stubouts on the replacement wall covering. Then

prepare and replace the wall covering, and attach the new fittings.

Adding a shower faucet

To add a shower head above your old bathtub, you'll have to replace the old faucet assembly with one equipped with a shower outlet and diverter valve. In addition, you'll have to install a shower pipe in the wall, as shown below.

If your tub surround is tiled, the tile will have to be removed so you can add the shower pipe. Cut your access hole large enough to install the shower pipe. From the shower outlet on the faucet body, run a ½-inch pipe up the wall to the desired height (see illustration, page 75) and top it with an elbow. Nail a 2 by 4 wood support behind the elbow and anchor the pipe to it with a pipe strap.

To avoid scratching the shower arm while you're repairing the wall covering, thread a 6-inch galvanized nipple into the elbow in place of the shower arm.

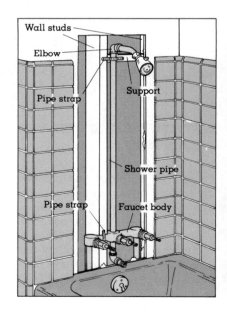

Finally, clean the pipe threads and install the shower arm and shower head, using pipe joint compound on the male threads of the fittings. Repair or replace wall coverings as required (see pages 98–105).

Toilets & bidets

Removing or installing a toilet or bidet is not very complicated, especially when the plumbing is already in place. During major remodeling involving the floor or walls, remember that toilets and bidets are the first fixtures to remove and the last to install.

For product information on various models, see page 60.

TOILETS

Conventional two-piece toilets have a floor-mounted bowl with a tank mounted on the bowl. Older types with floor-mounted bowls may have the tank mounted on the wall. One-piece toilets, with the bowl and tank mounted on the floor as a single unit, are becoming increasingly popular with homeowners. (One-piece wall-hung models that connect directly to the stack in the wall are also available.) This section deals primarily with conventional floor-mounted toilets.

Before you begin work, be sure to check any code requirements for a new or replacement toilet.

Removing a toilet

The procedure for removing a toilet varies with the type of fixture. For a two-piece toilet, you remove the tank first, then the bowl. (For a one-piece toilet, you remove the tank and bowl at the same time.)

Disconnect the water supply. Before you begin work, turn off the water at the fixture shutoff valve or main shutoff valve. Flush the toilet twice to empty the bowl and tank; then sponge out any remaining water. To remove the toilet seat and lid, unfasten the nuts on the two bolts projecting down through the bowl's back edge. Unfasten the coupling nut on the water supply line (see illustration below) underneath the tank. If the line is kinked or corroded, replace it when you install the new toilet.

Remove the tank. If you're removing a bowl-mounted toilet tank, detach the empty tank from the bowl as follows: Locate the mounting bolts inside the tank at the bottom. Hold them stationary with a screwdriver while you use a wrench to unfasten the nuts underneath the tank (see illustration below). You'll find it easier to remove the nuts if a helper holds the screwdriver. Then lift up the tank and remove it.

In a wall-mounted tank, a pipe usually connects the tank and bowl. Loosen the couplings on the pipe and remove it. Then reach inside the tank with a wrench and unscrew the nuts on the hanger bolts—these attach the tank to the hanger bracket on the wall. Now you can remove the tank.

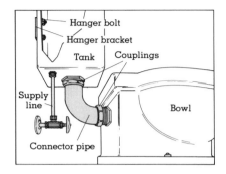

Remove the bowl. The following instructions apply to most floor-mounted toilet bowls. At the base of the bowl near the floor, pry off the caps covering the hold-down floor bolts. Unscrew the nuts from the bolts. If the nuts have rusted on, soak them with penetrating oil or cut the bolts off with a hacksaw.

Gently rock the bowl from side to side, breaking the seal between the bowl and the floor. Lift the bowl straight up, keeping it level so any remaining water doesn't spill from its trap (see illustration below).

Stuff a rag into the open drainpipe to prevent sewer gas from escaping and to keep debris from falling into the opening.

(Continued on next page)

REMOVING A FLOOR-MOUNTED TOILET

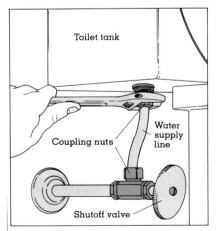

Loosen the coupling nut on the water supply line at the bottom of the tank, using a wrench.

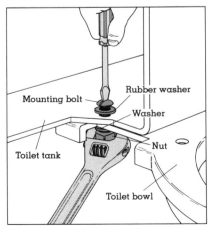

Detach the tank from the bowl by loosening mounting bolts with a screwdriver and a wrench.

Lift the bowl straight up off the floor flange, keeping it level to avoid spilling any remaining water.

■Toilets & bidets

Installing a toilet

The amount of work needed to install a new toilet depends on whether it will be in a new location. Hooking up a toilet in a new location is a challenging project because you must extend supply, drain, and vent pipes (see pages 72–75). You may want to have a professional run the piping to the desired spot and then complete the installation yourself.

Replacing an old fixture with a new one at the same location is a one-afternoon project that you can do yourself. The only crucial dimension you need to check on a new toilet is its roughing-in size—the distance from the wall to the center of the drainpipe (most are 12 inches).

You can usually determine roughing-in size before removing the old bowl—just measure from the wall to one of the two hold-down bolts that secure the bowl to the floor. (If the bowl has four hold-down bolts, measure to one of the rear bolts.) Your new toilet's roughing-in size can be shorter than that of the fixture you're replacing, but if it's longer, the new toilet won't fit.

Once you' e determined that the fixture will fit, you're ready to install it. The following general instructions apply to two-piece floor-mounted toilets. The key steps are illustrated at right. (For a one-piece, floor-mounted toilet, install the bowl as described below, then connect the water supply.)

Prepare the floor flange. This fitting connects the bowl to the floor and drainpipe.

Remove the rags and, with a putty knife, scrape off the wax bowl ring that formed the seal between the bowl and the flange. Thoroughly scrape the flange so that the new ring will form a leakproof seal.

If the old flange is cracked or broken, or if its surface is rough, replace it with a new flange, matched to the existing drainpipe material. (Use a plastic flange with plastic pipe, cast iron with a cast iron pipe.) Remove the old hold-down bolts from the floor flange, then insert the new bolts through the flange. If necessary, hold them upright with plumber's putty. Align the bolts with the center of the drainpipe.

Install the bowl ring. Turn the new bowl upside down on a cushioned surface. Place the new bowl ring over the toilet horn (outlet) on the bottom of the bowl, and apply plumber's putty around the bowl's bottom edge.

Place the bowl. Check that all packing material has been removed from the new bowl, and all rags from the drainpipe. Then gently lower the bowl into place over the flange, using the bolts as guides. To form the seal, press down firmly while twisting slightly.

Check the bowl with a level—from side to side and from front to back; use copper or brass washers to shim underneath the bowl where necessary. Be careful not to break the seal. Hand tighten the washers and nuts onto the hold-down bolts; you'll tighten them permanently after the tank is in place.

Attach the tank. For a bowl-mounted tank, fit the rubber gasket

INSTALLING A FLOOR-MOUNTED TOILET

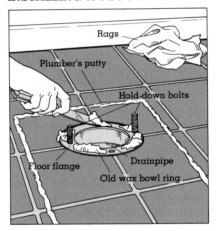

Thoroughly scrape the old bowl ring from the floor flange, using a putty knife or similar tool.

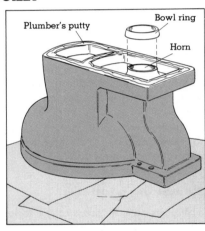

Position the new bowl ring over the toilet horn on the bottom of the bowl as it rests on a cushioned surface.

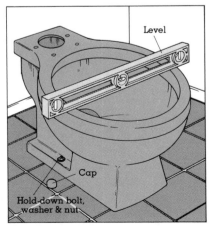

Level the bowl once it's in place, using small copper or brass washers to shim underneath, if necessary.

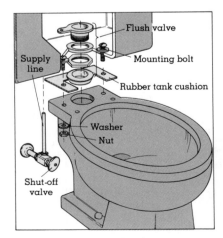

Attach the tank to the bowl using mounting bolts, with rubber gasket and tank cushion in place.

over the end of the flush valve that projects through the bottom of the tank. Place the rubber tank cushion on the rear of the bowl. After positioning the tank on the bowl, insert the mounting bolts through their holes in the bottom of the tank so they pass through the tank cushion and the back of the bowl. Then tighten the nuts and washers onto the bolts. (Secure wall-mounted tanks to hanger brackets with bolts through the back of the tank. Assemble the large pipe between bowl and tank and tighten the couplings.)

Now you can attach the bowl to the floor permanently. Use a wrench to tighten the hold-down nuts at the base of the bowl, but don't overtighten them or you'll crack the bowl. Check to see that the bowl is still level and doesn't rock. Fill the caps with plumber's putty and place them over the nuts. Seal the joint between the base of the bowl and the floor with a bead of caulking compound.

Attach the toilet seat by inserting mounting bolts through the holes in the back of the bowl; then assemble the washers and nuts onto the bolts and tighten.

Connect the plumbing. Connect the water supply line to the underside of the tank. If your old plumbing had no fixture shutoff valve, install one now (consult a professional plumber for help). Finally, turn on the water and check for leaks.

BIDETS

A bidet—a one-piece fixture—is usually installed next to the toilet. Unlike a toilet, a bidet has a sink-type drain and trap and is plumbed for hot and cold water. (For product information, see page 60.)

Removing a bidet

A bidet is usually not difficult to remove. You just disconnect two water supply lines, a drainpipe, and the hold-down bolts.

Disconnect the plumbing. Before doing any work, turn off the

water at the fixture shutoff valves or main shutoff valve. Open all faucets; then unfasten the coupling nuts on the hot and cold water supply lines, so that all remaining water will be completely drained. These lines are either freestanding or attached to the wall behind the bidet. (Some bidets may be plumbed with mixing valves in the wall and a single water supply line running to the fixture.)

Behind and under the back of the bidet, you'll find the drainpipe connection and usually a pop-up drain assembly. First, loosen the clevis screw (see illustration on page 93) and disconnect this assembly. Then loosen the slip nuts on the trap and remove it.

Remove the bidet. Pry the caps off the flange at the base of the bidet and remove the nuts underneath them. If the nuts are rusted, soak them with penetrating oil or cut the bolts with a hacksaw.

Lift the bidet straight up off the hold-down bolts that secure it to the floor. You may need to rock the fixture gently first to break the caulk seal (if there is one) around the base.

Stuff a rag into the drainpipe to prevent debris from falling into the opening.

Installing a bidet

A bidet must be mounted to the floor with hold-down bolts. If you're hooking up a new bidet in an existing location and want to use the existing floor bolts, the distance between bolt holes must be the same as for the original fixture. Also make sure the fittings on the new model are compatible with the existing water supply and drain lines.

If you're installing a bidet in a new location, you'll need to extend supply pipes and drainpipes (see pages 72–75). Unless you're experienced in home plumbing, you'll probably want to hire a professional for this part of the job.

Position the bidet. Remove all packing material from the bidet and

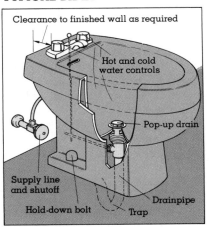

Clearance to finished wall as required — Hot and cold water controls — Pop-up drain — Supply line and shutoff — Hold-down bolt — Drainpipe — Trap

place the fixture so that its drain opening is directly over the drainpipe. If it's a new installation rather than a replacement, mark the locations for the hold-down bolts on the floor, using the holes in the bidet's flange as guides; then remove the bidet, drill holes sized for the bolts, and screw the bolts through the floor. Turn the bidet upside down onto a cushioned surface and apply plumber's putty around the bottom edge.

Remove the rag from the drainpipe and set the bidet back in position, using the bolts as guides.

Level the bidet, from side to side and from front to back, using copper or brass washers to shim beneath the bottom edge, if necessary. If you do shim, you may need to reseal the fixture to the floor. Hand tighten washers and nuts onto the hold-down bolts; you'll tighten them further after the plumbing connections are made. Connect the pop-up drain assembly, if there is one.

Connect the plumbing. Connect the drain and the two water supply lines. Once all connections are made, use a wrench to tighten the nuts on these lines, as well as the nuts on the hold-down bolts. (Don't overtighten the hold-down bolts or you'll crack the fixture.) Fill the caps with plumber's putty and place them over the nuts on the bidet flange. Turn on the water and check for leaks.

Walls & ceilings

A new moisture-resistant wall or ceiling can improve the bathroom's appearance and make the room easier to maintain at the same time.

This section will show you how to remove and apply the most popular wall treatments in today's bathrooms—gypsum wallboard, wallpaper, and ceramic tile. (For information on painting, see the special feature on page 101.)

GYPSUM WALLBOARD

This versatile wall covering has a gypsum core faced with thick paper. You can use it as finish material, putting paint or wallpaper over it, or you can use it as a backing for other materials, such as tile, wood, or panels of plastic-coated hardboard.

A special water-resistant grade is available for use around tubs, showers, and other damp areas. This wallboard is usually identified by a blue or green paper cover. It's best not to use it where you plan to paint or wallpaper, though—the compound you must use to finish joints between panels of water-resistant wallboard is nearly impossible to sand, so every imperfection will show through.

Panels are generally 4 feet wide and 8 feet long. (Lengths over 8 feet can be specially ordered.) Common thicknesses are ⅜ inch for wallboard used as a backing, ½ inch for wallboard used as finish wall covering.

INSTALLING WALLBOARD ON A WALL

Lift each wallboard panel into position and center the edges over wall studs. Then nail the panel to the studs, dimpling the wallboard surface slightly with the hammer. Stagger panels in adjacent rows so that ends don't line up.

Removing gypsum wallboard

If your bathroom's existing wallboard has only minor cracks or holes, you can probably repair it by filling in the cracks with ready-mixed spackling compound, then sanding smooth. But if it's wet, mildewed, or badly damaged, you'll have to remove it before installing other wall covering.

Use a broad-bladed prybar and a claw hammer to remove wallboard. Wear a dust mask to avoid inhaling gypsum dust, and cover all fixtures and the floor with drop cloths. Finally, be sure to turn off electrical power to the bathroom by flipping a circuit breaker or removing a fuse, so you won't risk hitting a live wire with the prybar.

Your wallboard may be nailed at intervals along the wall studs, or nailed only around the outside edges and sealed to the studs with adhesive. In either case, the removal procedure is the same.

Break through a taped seam between panels with the prybar. Then pry up the panel, using the stud for leverage, until you loosen a large piece. With both hands, pull the piece of wallboard off the studs. (Some of the nails will probably come off with it.) If the wallboard is attached with adhesive, you can leave the backing paper on the studs.

Once you've completely stripped the wallboard away from the studs, work through the area a second time and pull out any remaining nails.

CUTTING GYPSUM WALLBOARD

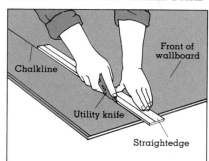

Cut wallboard along pencil or chalk line marked on front face, using utility knife guided by straightedge.

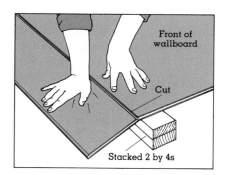

Break gypsum core by placing edges of stacked 2 by 4s under cut and pressing down on panel.

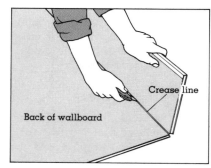

Complete cut by turning panel over, bending wallboard back, and cutting through back paper with utility knife.

INSTALLING WALLBOARD ON A CEILING

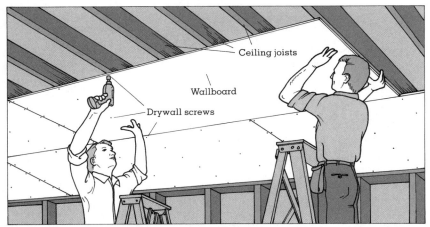

Ceiling joists

Wallboard

Drywall screws

It takes two to install a wallboard ceiling. Prop each panel in place with your heads; screw or nail first in the center and then where it will take the weight off your heads.

Installing gypsum wallboard

Installing gypsum wallboard is a three-step procedure. You measure and cut panels to size, hang them, and finish the seams and corners with wallboard compound and tape. Handle bulky panels carefully as you work; take care not to bend or break the corners or tear the paper covers.

Cut the wallboard. Though you'll use some full-size panels, you'll also need to cut pieces to fit around obstacles such as doors, windows, fixtures, and cabinets.

To make a straight, simple cut, first mark a line on the front of the panel with a pencil and straightedge, or snap a chalkline. Cut through the front paper with a utility knife; use a straightedge to guide the knife. Break the gypsum core by bending the board toward the back, as shown in the drawing on page 98. Finally, cut the paper on the back along the bend. Smooth the cut edge with a perforated rasp.

To fit wallboard around doors, windows, and other openings, measure and mark carefully. Measure from vertical edges of the opening to the edge of the nearest panel or a corner; measure from horizontal edges to the floor. Transfer the measurements to the wallboard and

make the cutout with a keyhole saw. For mid-panel cutouts, drill a pilot hole, then use a keyhole saw to make the cutout.

Basic wall application. Wall panels may be positioned either vertically or horizontally—that is, with the long edges either parallel or perpendicular to wall studs. Most professionals prefer the latter method because it helps bridge irregularities between studs and results in a stronger wall. But if your wall is higher than 8 feet, you may not want to use this method, since the extra height requires more cutting and creates too many joints.

Before installing wall panels, mark the stud locations on the floor and ceiling.

Starting at a corner, place the first panel tight against the ceiling and secure it with nails, drywall screws, or construction adhesive supplemented by nails. Drive in nails with a hammer, dimpling the wallboard surface without puncturing the paper. Fastener spacings are subject to local codes, but typical nail spacing is every 8 inches along panel ends and edges and along intermediate supports (called "in the field").

Apply additional panels in the same manner. If you're applying wallboard horizontally, stagger the end

joints in the bottom row so they don't line up with the joints in the top row.

Basic ceiling application. Methods for installing a wallboard ceiling are basically the same as those for walls. If you're covering both walls and ceiling, do the ceiling first.

Fasten panels perpendicular to joists with annular ring nails, drywall screws, or a combination of nails and construction adhesive. Screws are quick and strong, but you'll need a power screw gun or drill with adjustable clutch to drive them. Typical fastener spacing is every 7 inches along panel ends and at intermediate joists.

Because you'll need to support the heavy panels while fastening them, installing a wallboard ceiling is a two-person job. First, secure each panel at the center with nails or screws; then place the next few fasteners where they'll take the weight off your heads (see drawing above left).

Tape the joints and corners. If your wallboard will be a backing for paneling, you won't need to tape and conceal joints or corners. But if you're painting, wallpapering, or installing tile, you must finish the wallboard carefully. You'll need these basic tools and materials: 6 and 10-inch taping knives, a corner tool, sandpaper, wallboard tape, and taping compound (water-resistant wallboard requires water-resistant compound). See NOTE, page 100, for special instructions on taping water-resistant wallboard.

Finishing is done in stages over a period of days. To tape a joint between panels, first apply a smooth layer of taping compound over the joint with a 6-inch taping knife (see drawing on page 100). Before the compound dries, use the knife to embed wallboard tape into it, and apply another thin coat of compound over the tape, smoothing it gently with the knife.

Tape and finish all joints between panels in the same manner. Then, with smooth, even strokes of

■ Walls & ceilings

TAPING WALLBOARD JOINTS

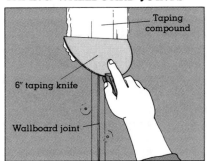

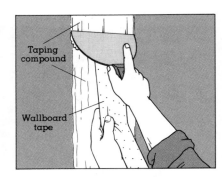

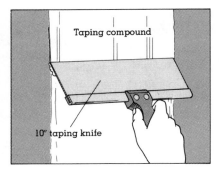

Apply a smooth layer of taping compound over wallboard joint, using a 6-inch taping knife.

Embed wallboard tape into the compound before it dries, and apply another thin layer of compound.

Apply a second coat a few inches on each side of joint, feathering compound out to edges.

the 6-inch knife, cover the nail dimples in the field with compound.

Allow the taping compound to dry for at least 24 hours; then sand lightly until the surface is smooth. Wear a face mask and goggles while sanding, and make sure the room is well ventilated.

Now use a 10-inch knife to apply a second coat of compound, extending it a few inches on each side of the taped joint. Feather the compound out toward the edges.

Let the second coat dry, sand it, then apply a final coat. Use the 10-inch knife to smooth out and feather the edges, covering all dimples and joints. Once the compound dries, sand it again to remove even minor imperfections.

NOTE: To finish water-resistant wallboard that will be backing for ceramic tile, first embed the tape in water-resistant taping compound along panel joints; then remove all excess compound with a taping knife. Apply a second thin coat over the wet taping coat and fill any nail dimples. Do not leave excess compound—it can't be sanded dry.

To tape an inside corner, it's easiest to use precreased tape. Apply a smooth layer of compound to the wallboard on either side of the corner. Measure and tear the tape, fold it in half vertically along the prepared crease, and press it into the corner with a taping knife or corner tool. Apply a thin layer of compound over the tape and smooth it out; then finish as you did the other joints.

Nail metal cornerbeads to all exterior corners to protect them. Apply compound to each side of the corner with a 6-inch knife. When it's dry, sand it smooth. With a 10-inch knife, apply a second coat of compound, feathering it. Allow to dry, then sand away imperfections.

Textured versus smooth finish. Though many people prefer the smooth look, texture can hide a less-than-perfect taping job—and add some visual interest to an uninterrupted wall. Some joint compounds double as texturing compounds; other effects may require special texturing materials. Ask your dealer for recommendations.

Professionals often apply texturing with a spray gun, but others produce good results by daubing, swirling, or splattering the compound with a sponge, paint roller, or stiff brush—whatever tool produces the desired appearance.

Let the compound set up until slightly stiff; then even it out as required with a wide float or trowel. Allow the finished surface to dry for at least 24 hours before painting.

Hanging new wallpaper

Next to paint, wallpaper is the most popular covering for bathroom walls. Easier than ever to install, wallpaper is available in a kaleidoscope of colors and patterns.

Choices for the bathroom. A wallpaper for the bathroom should be scrubbable, durable, and stain-resistant. Solid vinyl wallpapers, available in a wide variety of colors and textures, fit the bill. Vinyl coatings also give wallpaper a washable surface but aren't notably durable or grease-resistant.

If you're a beginner, you may want to consider prepasted and pre-trimmed paper.

To find an adhesive suitable for your material, check the manufacturer's instructions or ask your dealer.

Preparing the surface. To prepare for papering, you'll need to remove all light fixtures and faceplates. Thoroughly clean and rinse the surface. Most manufacturers recommend that you completely remove any old wallpaper before hanging a nonporous covering like solid vinyl.

If the existing paper is strippable, it will come off easily when you pull it up at a corner or seam. To remove nonstrippable wallpaper, use either a steamer (available for rent from your dealer) or a spray bottle filled with very hot water. Before steaming, break the surface of the old paper by sanding it with very coarse sandpaper or by pulling a sawblade sideways across the wall.

Within a few minutes of steaming (wait longer if it's a nonporous material), you can begin to remove the old paper. Using a broad knife, work down from the top of the wall, scraping off the old wallpaper.

If yours is a new gypsum wallboard surface, tape all joints between panels before papering. When

PAINTING: TIPS FOR A PROFESSIONAL FINISH

A fresh coat of paint is the fastest way to brighten up your bathroom. Here are some guidelines to help you do a professional-looking job.

Selecting tools & materials

One key to a good paint job is to choose the right materials.

Paint. Your basic choices in paint are water-base, or latex, paint and oil-base, or alkyd, paint. Latex is easy to work with, and best of all, you can clean up wet paint with soap and water. Alkyd paint provides high gloss and will hang on a little harder than latex; however, alkyds are harder to apply and require cleanup with mineral spirits.

In general, high resin content is the mark of durable, abrasion-resistant, flexible paint—the kind you need in a bathroom. Usually, the higher the resin content, the higher the gloss; so look for products labeled gloss or semigloss if you want a tough, washable finish.

An excellent choice for bathroom cabinets and woodwork is quick-drying alkyd enamel. It has a brilliant, tilelike finish that's extremely durable.

Tools. Natural bristle brushes are traditionally used to apply oil-base alkyd enamel paints; synthetic bristles are best for latex products. For window sashes and trim, choose a 1½ or 2-inch angled sash brush. A 2 or 3-inch brush or a paint pad is best for woodwork, doors, and cabinets.

Preparing the surface

To prevent cracking and peeling after the new paint dries, you must begin with surfaces that are smooth and clean.

It's possible to paint over wallpaper that's smooth and attached firmly to the wall. Apply a sealing primer such as pigmented shellac or a flat oil-base enamel undercoat. Let the sealer dry completely before you paint. It's often safer, though, to remove the wallpaper, especially if it's tearing and flaking.

Repairing the finish. For an old painted finish, sanding is sufficient if the surface is flaking lightly. Wash dirty areas on wood surfaces before sanding.

Roughen glossy paint surfaces with sandpaper so the new paint will adhere. (Rough, bare wood also needs sanding, as do patched areas.)

When a wood finish is in such bad condition that painting over it is impossible, you'll have to strip it. You can use an electric paint softener or heat gun, or a commercial liquid paint remover. With either method, you take off the softened paint with a broad knife or scraper, then sand the surface lightly until it's clean and smooth.

Once you've prepared the surface, carefully inspect it for small holes and cracks.

To repair small holes in wallboard, use spackling compound. For details on repairing other surfaces, consult a wall covering specialist.

Finally, dust everything in the bathroom, then vacuum the floor. With an abrasive cleaner, sponge the areas you plan to paint, then rinse. Allow about 24 hours for all washed areas to dry completely.

Prime the surface. Before doing any finish painting, be sure to prime the surface. Use the primer recommended by the paint manufacturer for the type of surface you'll be painting.

Applying the paint

To avoid painting yourself into a corner, you'll want to follow the working sequence outlined below.

Ceiling. If you're painting both ceiling and walls, begin with the ceiling. Paint the entire surface in one session. It's best to paint in 2 by 3-foot rectangles, starting in a corner and working across the shortest dimension of the ceiling.

On the first section, use a brush or special corner pad to paint a narrow strip next to the wall line and around any fixtures. Then finish the section with a roller, overlapping any brush marks. Work your way back and forth across the ceiling, painting one section at a time. Then go on to the walls.

Walls. Mentally divide a wall into 3-foot-square sections, starting from a corner at the ceiling line and working down the wall. As with ceilings, paint the edges of each section first with a brush or corner roller. Paint along the ceiling line and corners, and around fixtures and edges of doors or windows. Finish each section with a roller or brush, overlapping any brush marks.

At the bottom of the walls above the floor or baseboard, and along the edges of vanities and medicine cabinets, use a brush and painting guide to get a neat, even edge. Be sure to overlap any remaining brush marks with your roller.

As a final step, return to the ceiling line and again work down in 3-foot sections.

◾ Walls & ceilings

dry, sand the wall smooth and apply a coat of flat, oil-base primer-sealer.

To apply wallpaper over previously painted surfaces that are in good condition, clean off all the dirt, grease, and oil, and let it dry. If latex paint was used, or if you can't determine the type, apply an oil-base undercoat over the old paint.

Ready to start? Plan the best place to hang your first strip. If you're papering all four walls with a patterned paper, the last strip you hang probably won't match the first, so plan to start and finish in the least conspicuous place—usually a corner, door casing, or window casing.

Most house walls are not straight and plumb, so you'll need to establish a plumb line. Figure the width of your first strip of wallpaper minus ½ inch (which will overlap the corner or casing); measure that distance from your starting point, and mark the wall. Using a carpenter's level as a straightedge, draw a line through your mark that's perfectly plumb. Extend the line until it reaches from floor to ceiling.

It's a good idea to measure the wall height before cutting each strip of wallpaper. Allow 2 inches extra at the top and bottom. Be sure also to allow for pattern match.

Using a razor knife, cut the strips. Number them on the back at the top edge so you can apply them in the proper sequence.

With some wallpapers, you'll need to spread adhesive on the backing with a wide, soft paint roller or pasting brush; other papers are prepasted—all you have to do is soak them in water before hanging.

After pasting or soaking, strips should be "booked" (see below).

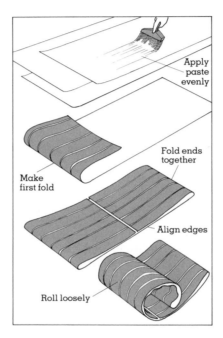

Apply paste evenly

Make first fold

Fold ends together

Align edges

Roll loosely

Trim the edges of the wallpaper at this stage, if necessary.

Hanging the wallpaper. First, position a stepladder next to the plumb line you've marked. Open the top fold of the first booked strip, raising it so that it overlaps the ceiling line by 2 inches. Carefully align the strip's edge with the plumb line.

Using a smoothing brush, press the strip against the wall. Smooth out all wrinkles and air bubbles. Then release the lower portion of the strip and smooth it into place.

Carefully roll the edges flat, if necessary, with a seam roller. To trim along the ceiling and baseboard, use a broad knife and a very sharp razor knife. With a sponge dipped in lukewarm water, remove any excess adhesive before it dries.

Unfold your second strip on the wall in the same way you did the first. Gently butt the second strip against the first, aligning the pattern as you move down the wall. Continue around the room.

Dealing with corners. Because few rooms have perfectly straight corners, you'll have to measure from the edge of the preceding strip to the corner; do this at three heights. Cut a strip ½ inch wider than the widest measurement. Butting the strip to the

HANGING THE FIRST STRIP

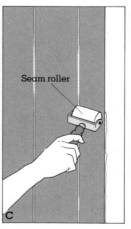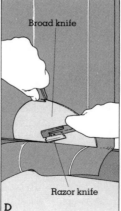

To hang wallpaper, first open the top fold of the strip, overlap the ceiling line, and align the strip's edge with the plumb line (A); press the strip against the wall with a smoothing brush (B). Release the lower fold and smooth into place; roll the edges flat with a seam roller (C). Trim the strip along the ceiling and baseboard with a broad knife and a razor knife (D). Remove excess adhesive with a sponge dipped in lukewarm water (E).

preceding strip, brush it firmly into and around the corner. At the top and bottom corners, cut the overlap so the strip will lie flat.

Next, measure the width of the leftover piece of wallpaper. On the adjacent wall, measure the same distance from the corner and make a plumb line at that point.

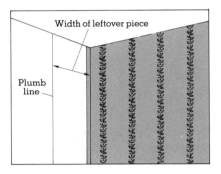

Position one edge of the strip along the plumb line; the other edge will cover the ½-inch overlap. (If you're hanging vinyl wallpaper, you should apply a vinyl-to-vinyl adhesive on top of the overlap.)

Cutouts. It's easy to cut around switches and outlets. Remove all faceplates before hanging the wallpaper; then, before making the cutout, shut off the electricity.

Hang the paper as described above. Then use a razor knife to make an X-shaped cut over the opening, extending the cuts to each corner. Trim the excess along the edges of the opening with the razor knife and a broad knife.

CERAMIC TILE

Few wall coverings have the decorative impact and durability of ceramic tile. It's a natural choice for any wall that might be sprayed or splashed—water, dirt, and soap film clean away in seconds.

On these pages you'll learn how to remove and install ceramic tile. For information on various types of wall tile, see page 63. If your plans call for a ceramic tile floor, install the floor tiles before setting tiles on the wall (see page 108).

Removing ceramic tile

Removing wall tile set in mortar is a tough job. If possible, replace only those tiles that are damaged. If tiles are clean and smooth and the wall surface is flat, consider installing the new tiles directly over them.

If you must remove old tile, proceed with caution (see "Removing the wall covering" on page 89). You may prefer to have a professional remove tile that is set in mortar.

If your wall tile is set on gypsum wallboard, you can more easily remove it yourself. Wearing goggles and a dust mask, use a cold chisel and soft-headed steel hammer to chip through the tile and backing. Once you've removed small sections, insert a prybar and pry off large sections until the wall studs are exposed.

Next, inspect the exposed wall framing for any water damage, and replace framing members if necessary. Then you can install backing for your new tile or for another wall covering of your choice.

Installing ceramic tile

Plan and prepare carefully before you install tile. First measure your bathroom and sketch your walls on graph paper. Choose and plan the placement of special trim pieces, such as bullnose, cove, and quarter-round edging tiles, as well as ceramic accessories—soap dishes, paper holders, and toothbrush holders. Your dealer can help you to select trim pieces.

Once you've designed your walls and selected tile, you're ready to begin. Described below are the steps you'll follow to install your tile, from backing to finished wall. (If you're installing pregrouted tile panels, follow the manufacturer's instructions.)

Before you start, remove baseboards and window and door trim, wall-mounted accessories and lights, and, if necessary, the toilet, bidet, and sink.

Prepare the backing surface. This is probably the most important step in installing wall tile successfully. Backing must be solid, flat, clean, and dry.

You can use existing gypsum wallboard or even existing wood or tile as backing if it's in good condition. You may need to clean, smooth out, or prime these surfaces before you're ready for new tile; ask your tile dealer for recommendations.

You may also opt for new wallboard backing. But for wet areas, it's safest to install cement backer board, available in 3-foot widths and various lengths. Standard panel thickness for new installations is ½ inch; fasten panels to wall studs with 1½-inch galvanized roofing nails. Fill joints between panels and at edges with thin-set adhesive or mortar. Though it's not strictly necessary, a waterproof membrane behind the backer board helps ensure a watertight wall.

For setting tiles on bathroom walls, choose either thin-set (cement-base) or epoxy adhesive. Thin-set adhesive, when mixed with a latex additive, is adequate for most jobs; epoxy is slightly more difficult to work with and more expensive. The same distinctions apply to cement-base and epoxy grouts. Read the labels and consult your tile dealer to determine which adhesive and grout are best for your situation.

Once your backing is prepared, you're ready to mark working lines.

Mark working lines. Accurate horizontal and vertical working lines help you keep tiles properly aligned so that your finished wall will look level and even. The horizontal working line should be near the bottom of the wall, because tiling up a wall is easier than tiling down.

If you're tiling around a tub, establish working lines there first. This way, you can plan for a row of full (uncut) tiles just above the tub, at bathers' eye level. This works out best if the tub is level to within ⅛ inch. Locate the high point of the tub lip with your level, and measure up one tile width plus ⅛ inch. Mark a level line on the wall through this point; then extend it carefully across

■ Walls & ceilings

all adjoining walls. This will give you a bottom row of full tiles around the tub. (You can fill in any small gaps below them with caulking later.)

If your tub is not level to within ⅛ inch, locate the horizontal working line from the low point of the tub lip, and follow the above method. You'll have to cut the bottom row of tiles to fit.

Then, on walls adjoining the tub, establish a line close to the floor. Start at the working line you extended from the tub wall and measure down a full number of tiles, including grout joints. Leave a space at least one full tile high above the floor. Mark the horizontal working line for this wall through this point with a straightedge and level (see illustration below).

To establish a line on a wall not adjoining a tub, find the lowest point by setting a level on the floor at various locations against the walls to be tiled. At the lowest point, place a tile against the wall and mark its top edge on the wall. If you're installing a cove base, set a cove tile on the floor and a wall tile above it (allow for grout joint); then mark the top of the wall tile. Using a level and straightedge, draw a horizontal line through the mark across the wall. Extend this line onto other walls to be tiled.

After marking your horizontal working lines, nail battens (1 by 2-

PATTERNS FOR SETTING TILE

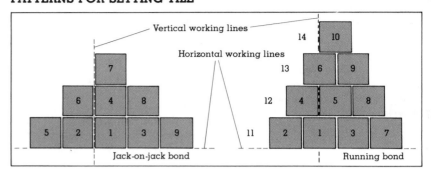

inch wood strips) all along the walls with their top edges on the lines. These will be your horizontal guides.

To establish a vertical working line, locate the midpoint of a wall and mark it on the horizontal working line. Starting at this point, set up a row of loose tiles on the batten to see how they'll fit at the ends of the wall.

If you'll end up with less than half a tile on both ends, move your mark one-half a tile to the right or left to avoid ending the rows with narrow pieces. Then extend the vertical working line through your mark and up the wall with a straightedge and level (see illustration below).

If you don't plan to tile to the ceiling line, mark the point where the highest tile will be set. Using a level, draw a horizontal line through this point across the wall.

Finally, be sure to mark locations of ceramic towel bars, soap dishes, and other accessories.

Set the tile. First, prepare the tile adhesive according to the manufacturer's directions. (Be sure to keep your working area well ventilated.)

To determine how large an area to cover at one time, consult the adhesive container label for the open time—the length of time you have to work with the adhesive after spreading. Comb the adhesive with a notched trowel to form ridges.

When you set the tiles, place each one with a slight twist—don't slide it. Keep spacing for grout joints uniform. Some tiles have small ceramic spacing lugs molded onto their edges; if your tiles don't have them, drive 6-penny finishing nails into the wallboard to act as temporary spacing guides (see illustration on facing page).

The way you'll begin setting tiles depends on which bond you use—jack-on-jack (with joints lined up) or running bond (with staggered joints).

For jack-on-jack, set the first tile on the batten so that one side is aligned exactly with the vertical working line. Set additional tiles as shown in the illustration above, forming a pyramid pattern. For running bond, *center* the first tile on the vertical working line, then follow the pyramid pattern (illustrated above), as you set the tile.

With either bond, continue setting tiles upward and toward the ends of the wall in the pattern illustrated. After laying several tiles, set

WORKING LINES FOR TILE

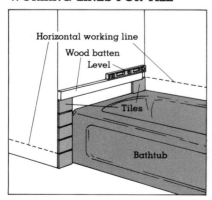

Extend horizontal working line around tub to adjoining walls, then measure to floor. Extend lines along adjoining walls.

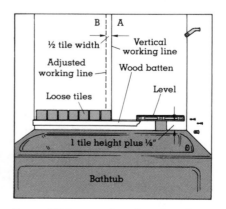

To establish vertical working line, locate midpoint of wall (A), then adjust (B) according to size of end tiles.

them into the adhesive by sliding a carpet-wrapped piece of plywood across the tiles as you tap it gently with a hammer.

Cut tiles to fit at the end of each horizontal row and at the top near the ceiling. (Use a rented tile cutter to cut straight pieces; use tile nippers to cut out irregular shapes.) For the top row of a wainscoting or other installation that doesn't reach the ceiling, set bullnose or cap tiles.

When you come to a wall where there are electrical outlets or switches, turn off the power to them. Remove the cover plates, if installed, and pull the outlets and switches from their boxes, but don't disconnect them. Cut and fit tiles around the boxes, then remount the outlets and switches.

On inside corners, butt tiles together. On outside corners, set one column of bullnose tiles to cover the unfinished edges of the tiles on each adjoining wall.

Around windows, finish off the sides and sill with bullnose tiles cut to fit.

Install ceramic accessories such as soap dishes in spaces you left open when tiling. Tape the accessories in place while the adhesive sets.

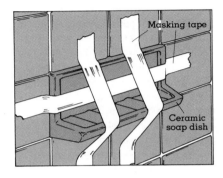

Now check your work. If anything is out of alignment, wiggle it into position before the adhesive sets. Clean adhesive from the face of tiles and accessories, and from joint spaces.

When the adhesive has set, carefully remove the battens. Twist nail spacers as you pull them out from the wall.

Spread adhesive at the bottom of the wall where the battens were, and set the remaining tiles, cutting them as needed.

Grout the tile. Before grouting, allow the adhesive to set properly—usually, you must allow 16 hours for epoxy-base adhesive and 48 hours for the cement-base type.

Remove any excess adhesive from the tile joints. Then mix the grout recommended for your tile, and spread it on the surface of the tile with a rubber-faced float or a squeegee, forcing it into the tile joints until they're completely filled. Scrape off excess grout from the tile, working diagonally across the surface.

Wipe the tiles with a wet sponge to remove any remaining grout. Rinse and wring out the sponge frequently, wiping until the grout joints are smooth and level with the tile surface. When the tiles are as clean as you can get them, let the grout dry until a haze appears over the surface. Then polish the haze off the tiles with a soft cloth. Finish (tool) the joints with the end of a toothbrush handle.

Seal tile and grout. Installations with unglazed tile or with cement-based grouts need to be protected by a grout and tile sealer. Most sealers for bathroom tile have a silicone base.

Follow manufacturer's instructions for applying these sealers. Both tiles and grout should be dry. On new tile, wait at least 2 weeks—this will give the grout a chance to cure completely. Apply a moderate amount of sealer, and wipe off any excess to prevent the tile from discoloring.

Finally, use caulking to seal all openings or gaps between pipes or fixtures and tile. Replace all trim, accessories, and fixtures.

INSTALLING WALL TILE

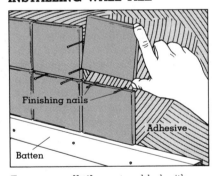

To **space wall tiles** not molded with spacing lugs, place 6-penny finishing nails between tiles.

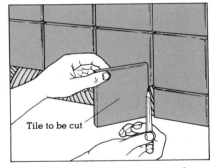

To **set bottom row of tiles,** remove batten on working line, mark tile and cut. Set in adhesive as for other tiles.

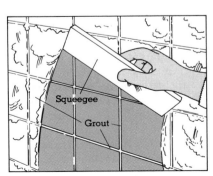

Spread grout on tile, forcing it into joints with a float or squeegee until they're full. Remove excess.

Use bathtub caulk to seal all openings between fixtures or pipes and tile.

Flooring

Two requirements for bathroom floors are moisture resistance and durability. Resilient flooring and ceramic tile are ideal choices on both counts. If you're completely remodeling your bathroom, it's a good time to put in ceramic tile, since it's ideally installed with cabinets, doors, and fixtures removed from the room. If you're replacing only the floor, resilient flooring is a good choice; it can be installed around most fixtures and cabinets.

The information in this section assumes that your floor is supported by a standard subfloor, with joists or beams below (see drawing on page 67). If your home is built on a concrete slab and your flooring will be installed over it, you need to make sure that the slab is dry, level, and clean before you begin any work.

RESILIENT SHEET FLOORING

Resilient sheet flooring is available with smooth or textured surfaces, in plain colors or in patterns. Though a few types are available in widths up to 12 feet, most sheet flooring is only 6 feet wide; seams may be necessary.

Plan the new floor. Take exact measurements of the floor and make a scale drawing on graph paper. If your room is very irregular, you may want to make a full-size paper pattern of the floor instead of the scale drawing.

Prepare the subfloor. Both old resilient and wood flooring make acceptable bases for new resilient sheets, provided their surfaces are completely smooth and level. Old resilient flooring must be solid, not cushioned, and firmly bonded to the subfloor. Uneven wood floors may need a rough sanding. Both types must be thoroughly cleaned, and any loose pieces must be secured.

If the old floor is cushioned or in poor condition, it should be removed down to the subfloor, if possible. If the old flooring is impossible to remove without damaging the sub-floor, or if the subfloor is in poor condition, cover the old flooring with ¼-inch underlayment-grade plywood or untempered hardboard. (If there are signs of water damage or insect infestation, consult a professional.)

Cut the flooring. The most critical step in laying sheet flooring is making the first rough cuts accurately. You may want your flooring dealer to make these first cuts for you; if so, you'll need to supply a floor plan.

To cut the flooring to size yourself, unroll the material in a large room. Transfer the floor plan directly onto the new flooring, using chalk or a water-soluble felt-tip pen, a carpenter's square, and a straightedge.

If your flooring will have a seam, be sure to allow for overlap or for matching the pattern (if any) on adjoining sheets. If your flooring has simulated grout or mortar joints, plan to cut the seam along the midpoint of the joint.

Using a linoleum or utility knife, cut the flooring so it's roughly 3 inches oversize on all sides (the excess will be trimmed away after the flooring has been put in place).

Cut 3" extra

Actual room size

If a seam is necessary, cut and install the piece of flooring that requires the most intricate fitting first; then cut and install the second sheet.

Install the flooring. Following are instructions for laying resilient sheet flooring using adhesive. Some types of sheet flooring can be laid *without* adhesive. In this case, you simply roll out the flooring and shift it until it's in the proper position, then apply adhesive around the edges or staple the edges in place. If you're considering this easy installation method, check with your flooring dealer to be sure the material you've selected doesn't require adhesive.

If you're installing a single piece of flooring, you can spread adhesive over the entire subfloor at once, or spread adhesive in steps as the flooring is unrolled. Check the adhesive's open time (the time you have to work with the adhesive while it's still tacky); follow the directions of the adhesive manufacturer.

If the entire floor has been covered with adhesive, slowly roll the flooring out across the floor, taking care to set the flooring firmly into the adhesive as you go. If you're working a section at a time, spread adhesive and unroll the flooring as you go.

If you're installing flooring with seams, spread the adhesive on the subfloor as directed by the adhesive manufacturer, but stop 8 or 9 inches from the seam. Then position the first sheet on the floor.

Next, position the second sheet of flooring carefully so that it overlaps the first sheet by at least 2 inches; make sure the design is perfectly aligned. Then roll up the flooring and spread adhesive over the remainder of the floor, stopping 8 or 9 inches from the edge of the first sheet of flooring. Reposition the second sheet of flooring, starting at the seam; again, take care to align the design perfectly. Then roll the flooring out, setting it into the adhesive.

When the flooring is in position, trim away excess flooring at each end of the seam in a half-moon shape so ends butt against the wall.

Using a steel straightedge and a sharp utility knife, make a straight cut (about ½ or ⅝ inch from the edge of the top sheet) down through both sheets. Lift up the flooring on either side of the seam, remove the two overlap strips, and spread adhesive on the subfloor under the seam.

Use the recommended solvent to clean adhesive from around the seam. When the seam is dry and

TRIMMING RESILIENT SHEETS

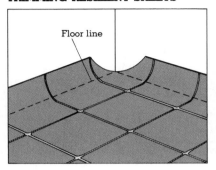

To trim inside corners, cut excess flooring away a little at a time until flooring lies flat in corner.

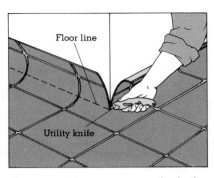

To trim outside corners, use utility knife to cut straight down to where wall and floor meet.

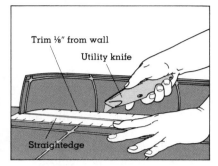

To trim along walls, cut flooring with a utility knife and straightedge, leaving a ⅛-inch gap for expansion.

clean, use the recommended seam sealer to fuse the two pieces.

Trim to fit. When the flooring has been positioned, you'll need to make a series of relief cuts at all corners so the flooring will lie flat (see above).

At outside corners, start at the top of the excess flooring and cut straight down to the point where the wall and floor meet. At inside corners, cut the excess flooring away a little at a time until it lies flat.

To remove the excess flooring along a wall, press the flooring into a right angle where the floor and wall join, using an 18 to 24-inch-long piece of 2 by 4. Then lay a heavy metal straightedge along the wall and trim the flooring with a utility knife, leaving a gap of about ⅛ inch between the edge of the flooring and the wall to allow the material to expand without buckling.

RESILIENT TILE FLOORING

Resilient tiles come in two standard sizes, 9-inch and 12-inch square. Other sizes and shapes are available by special order.

To find the amount of tile you need, find the area of the floor, subtracting for any large protrusions. Add 5 percent so you'll have extra tiles for cutting and later repairs. If your design uses more than one color, estimate how many tiles of

each kind you'll need by drawing your design with colored pencils.

Place the tiles. Laying resilient tiles involves three steps: marking the working lines, spreading the adhesive (unless you're using self-stick tiles), and placing the tiles. These steps are similar to those for ceramic tile (for details, see page 108). But unlike ceramic units, resilient tiles are laid tightly against each other, and, because they're made with machine precision, they must be laid out in perfectly straight lines.

Once a tile is in position, press it firmly in place. Lay half a dozen or so, setting them by going over them with a rolling pin. If you're using self-stick tiles, take extra care

to position them exactly before you press them into place (they're hard to remove once they're fixed to the floor). Also note the arrows on the back of self-stick tiles—lay the tiles with the arrows going the same way.

Cut the tile. To cut tiles, score them along the mark with a utility knife; then snap the tile along the line. For intricate cuts, use heavy scissors. (The tiles will cut more easily if warmed in sunlight or over a furnace vent.)

To mark border and corner tiles for cutting, position a loose tile exactly over one of the tiles in the last row closest to the wall (see below). Place another loose tile on top of the first, butting it against the wall. Using this tile as a guide, mark the tile beneath for cutting.

TRIMMING RESILIENT TILES

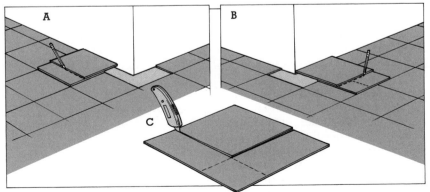

To lay out a border tile, first place a loose tile on top of the last full tile nearest the wall; then place a second tile over the first, butting it against the wall, and mark it for cutting (A). This same technique can be used to mark L-shaped tiles for outside corners (B). Score tiles with a utility knife (C).

■Flooring

CERAMIC TILE FLOORING

Installing a new floor of ceramic tile can be a very satisfying do-it-yourself project. New, easy-to-install tiles and improved adhesives and grouts make it possible for a careful, patient do-it-yourselfer to create a floor of professional quality.

Because it's usually possible to use existing ceramic tile as a subfloor (see "Prepare the subfloor," below), this section covers installation only—not removal. It's not easy to remove an old tile floor, particularly if the tiles were laid in mortar. So if removal is necessary, it's best to consult a professional.

Installing a ceramic tile floor is essentially a three-step operation: you lay evenly spaced tiles in a bed of adhesive atop a properly prepared subfloor, fill the joint spaces between tiles with grout, and seal the floor for durability and easy cleaning. In this section you'll find basic instructions for laying tile flooring; if you need more detailed information, turn to a contractor or your tile supplier.

Prepare the subfloor. Ceramic tile, masonry, wood, and resilient (except the cushion type) floors can be successfully covered with ceramic tile—provided the old floor is well-bonded, level, clean, and dry.

If the existing flooring is in poor condition, you'll need to repair, cover, or remove it before you can proceed. Fasten loose ceramic, masonry, or resilient flooring with adhesive; nail down loose wood flooring; fill gouges in resilient flooring; and sand wood floors smooth.

If the existing flooring is so badly damaged that it's beyond repair—or if a cushioned resilient flooring has been used—it will need to be removed down to the subfloor, if possible. If the old flooring is impossible to remove without damaging the subfloor underneath, or if the subfloor is in poor condition, you can cover the old flooring with ¼-inch underlayment-grade plywood or untempered hardboard.

Your tile dealer can recommend the best adhesive for your new tile floor (the type of adhesive depends on the type of flooring you'll be covering). Follow your dealer's instructions for preparing the subfloor, and be sure to check the directions on the adhesive container, as well.

Establish working lines. The key to laying straight rows of tile is to first establish accurate working lines. Following are instructions for laying out working lines starting from the center of the room. This method makes it easy to keep rows even and is the best method to use if the room is out of square or if you've chosen a tile with a definite pattern or design.

Locate the center point on each of two opposite walls, and snap a chalk line on the floor between the two points. Then find the centers of the other two walls and stretch your chalk line at right angles to the first line; snap this line only after you've used a carpenter's square to determine that the two lines cross at a precise right angle. If they don't, adjust the lines until they do.

Make a dry run before you actually set the tiles in adhesive. Lay one row of tiles along each working line, from the center of the room to each of two adjoining walls. Be sure to allow proper spacing for grout joints. Adjust your working lines as necessary to avoid very narrow border tiles.

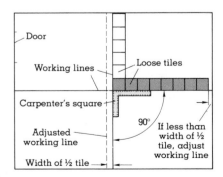

If you're working over a wood subfloor, temporarily nail batten boards along the two working lines that outline the quarter of the room farthest from the door; the battens

will provide a rigid guide for the first row of tiles. (If you're working over a masonry subfloor, you'll have to use the chalk lines as your guides.) You'll set tiles using the sequence shown below, completing the floor quarter by quarter. Work on the quarter by the doorway last.

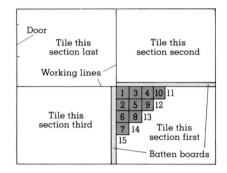

Set the tiles. Using a notched trowel, start spreading adhesive. Cover about a square yard at first, or the area you can comfortably tile before the adhesive begins to set.

Using a gentle twisting motion, place the first tile in the corner formed by the two battens (or chalk lines). With the same motion, place a second tile alongside the first. Continue laying tiles, following the sequence illustrated. Use molded plastic spacers to establish the proper width for the grout joints.

As the tiles are laid, set a piece of carpet-wrapped wood over them, and gently tap the wood with a mallet or hammer to "beat in" the tiles. Keep checking with a carpenter's square or straightedge to make sure each row is straight. Wiggle any stray tiles back into position.

To fit border tiles, measure each space carefully, subtract the width of two grout joints, and mark each tile for any necessary cuts.

When you complete the first quarter of the floor, remove the batten boards, then proceed with the next quarter. After all the tiles are placed, remove the spacers and clean the tile surface so it's completely free of adhesive.

Grout and seal the tile according to the instructions for wall tile on page 105.

Cabinets & countertops

In many homes, the need for bathroom storage has increased as people have collected more and more paraphernalia—bulky electric grooming appliances, children's bath toys, and cleaning supplies. For many families, a medicine cabinet just doesn't provide enough space.

This section will show you how to gain space by installing floor-mounted vanity cabinets, then topping them with countertops of plastic laminate or ceramic tile.

VANITY CABINETS

You can select a vanity cabinet to complement almost any style of bathroom. The vanity may be fitted with various types of countertops and sinks (see pages 54–56).

No matter what countertop and sink you prefer, the methods for removing and installing a prefabricated vanity cabinet in your bathroom are the same.

If a vanity cabinet higher than standard height is more comfortable, add a frame of suitable height underneath the bottom before installing the cabinet.

Removing a vanity cabinet

To remove a plumbed vanity, you'll need to disconnect the plumbing and remove the sink and countertop (see pages 82–83).

Pry away any vinyl wall base, floor covering, or molding from the base cabinet's kickspace or sides.

Old vanity cabinets are usually attached to wall studs with screws or nails through nailing strips at the back of each unit. Sometimes they're also fastened to the floor. Screws are easy to remove unless they're old and stripped. To remove nails, you may need to pry the cabinet away from the wall or floor with a prybar. To prevent damage, use a wood scrap between the prybar and the wall or floor. For a vanity with a solid back, you may have to first shut off the water at the main valve and remove the sink shutoff valves to pull the vanity away from the wall.

Installing a vanity cabinet

Before you begin, remove any baseboard, moldings, or wall base that might interfere. From the floor, measure up 34½ inches—the height of a standard vanity cabinet. Take several measurements and use the highest mark for your reference point. Draw a level line through the mark and across the wall.

If the vanity has a solid back, measure, mark, and cut the holes for the drain and water supply pipes, using a keyhole or saber saw.

For both solid and open-back vanities, locate and mark all wall studs (see page 68) in the wall above where the vanity will be installed. Move the vanity into place.

Level the top of the vanity side-to-side and front-to-back, shimming between the vanity and floor as needed. Both shims and irregularities in the floor can be hidden by baseboard trim.

Some cabinets are designed with "scribing strips" along the sides. Other manufacturers offer decorative panels to "finish" the end of a cabinet run. Both designs include extra material you can shave down to achieve a perfect fit between the cabinet and an irregular wall.

To scribe a cabinet, first position it; then run a length of masking tape down the side to be scribed. Setting the points of a compass with pencil to the widest gap between the scribing strip and the wall, run the compass pivot down the wall next to the strip, as illustrated below. The wall's irregularities will be marked on the tape. Remove the vanity from the wall and use a block plane, file, or power belt sander to trim the scribing strip to the line. Then reinstall the cabinet.

If your cabinet doesn't have scribing strips, you can cover any large irregularities between the wall and cabinet with decorative molding. Scribe the molding as required.

When the cabinet is aligned with your reference marks on the wall, extend the stud location marks down to the hanger strip on the back of the vanity, drill pilot holes through the strip into the wall studs, and secure the vanity to the studs with woodscrews or drywall screws. If the studs aren't accessible, fasten the vanity with wall anchors.

Once the vanity cabinet is secure, install the countertop and sink, then connect the water supply lines, the trap, and the pop-up drain (see pages 83–85).

INSTALLING A VANITY CABINET

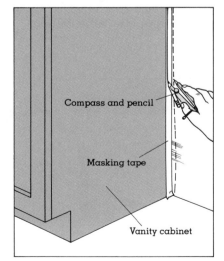

Compass and pencil

Masking tape

Vanity cabinet

Scribe and trim sides of vanity to make a snug fit when wall is out of plumb or is uneven.

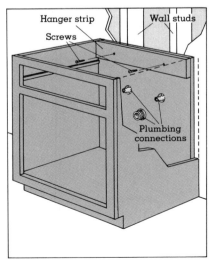

Hanger strip   Wall studs

Screws

Plumbing connections

Secure vanity cabinet to studs by screwing through hanger strip across the back. Drill pilot holes first.

■ Cabinets & countertops

POST-FORMED LAMINATE COUNTERTOP

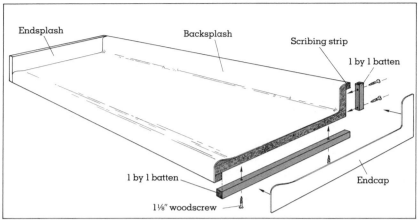

Countertops, like cabinets, rarely fit uniformly against walls. Usually, the back edge of a post-formed countertop comes with a scribing strip that can be trimmed to follow the exact contours of the wall. Follow the instructions for scribing cabinets on page 109.

Fasten the countertop to the cabinets by running screws from below through the cabinet corner gussets or top frame and through any shims or wood blocks. Use woodscrews just long enough to penetrate ½ inch into the countertop core. Run a bead of silicone sealant along all exposed seams between the countertop and walls.

COUNTERTOPS

Plastic laminate and tile are two popular materials for countertops. Both are durable, water-resistant, and straightforward to install.

Installing a plastic laminate countertop

Laminate countertops are divided into two types: post-formed and self-rimmed. Post-formed countertops are premolded one-piece tops, from curved backsplash to bullnosed front. The term "self-rimmed" means that you apply the laminate of your choice over a core material.

Post-formed countertop. Since post-formed countertops come only in standard sizes, you'll normally need to buy one slightly larger than you need and cut it to length. To cut the countertop with a handsaw, mark the cut line on the face. Mark the back if you're using a power saw. Use masking tape to protect the cutting line against chipping (you'll probably have to redraw the line, this time on the tape). Smooth the edge of the cut with a file or sandpaper. Plan to cover that end with an endsplash or endcap (a preshaped strip of matching laminate).

Endsplashes are screwed into the edge of the countertop or into "built-down" wood battens attached to the edge, as shown above. Endcaps are glued to an open end with contact cement or, in some cases, pressed into place with a hot iron.

Self-rimmed countertop. To build your own laminate countertop, you'll need to choose the laminate (¹⁄₁₆-inch thickness is the standard) and cut the core material to size from ¾-inch plywood or high-density particle board.

Build down the edges of the core with 1 by 3 battens (see drawing below). Then you can laminate the countertop (do sides and front strips first and then the top surface).

Measure each surface to be laminated, adding at least ¼ inch to all dimensions as a margin for error. Mark the cutting line. Score the line with a sharp utility knife; then cut with a fine-toothed saw (face up with a handsaw or table saw, face down with a circular saw or saber saw).

Apply contact cement to both the laminate back and the core surface to be joined, and allow the cement to dry for 20 to 30 minutes. Carefully check alignment before joining the two; once joined, the laminate can't be moved. Press the laminate into place, using a roller or a rolling pin to ensure even contact.

Use a block plane to trim the laminate flush with the core's edges; then dress it with a file. Or trim with an electric router equipped with a laminate-trimming bit.

Backsplashes or endsplashes should be cut from the same core material as the main countertop, then butt-joined to the countertop with sealant and woodscrews.

SELF-RIMMED LAMINATE COUNTERTOP

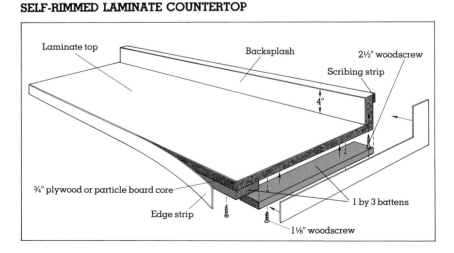

Installing a ceramic tile countertop

Wall tiles, lighter and thinner than floor tiles, are the normal choice for countertops and backsplashes. Standard sizes range from 3 inches by 3 inches to 4½ inches by 8½ inches, with thicknesses varying from ¼ inch to ⅜ inch. Another choice, mosaic tiles (see page 63), makes your job easier, especially in backsplash areas.

Prepare the base. Before laying tile, remove any old countertops; then install ¾-inch exterior plywood cut flush with the cabinet top, screwing it to the cabinet frame from below. For moisture-tight results, add a waterproof membrane, followed by a layer of cement backer board on top.

Surfaces may need to be primed or sealed before tile is applied. To determine the best base and preparation for your job, read the information on the adhesive container or ask your tile supplier.

Plan the layout. Before you start laying tile, you must decide how you want to trim the countertop edge and the sink. For ideas, see the drawing below.

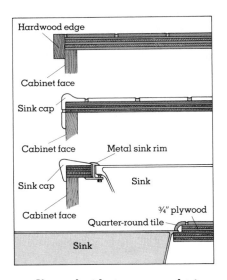

If you decide to use wood trim, seal the wood and attach it to the cabinet face with finishing nails. When in place, the wood strip's top edge should be positioned at the

HOW TO SET COUNTERTOP TILES

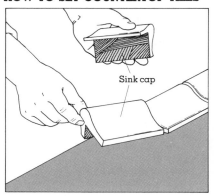

First, set edge tiles in place, starting from the center line, after buttering the backs with adhesive.

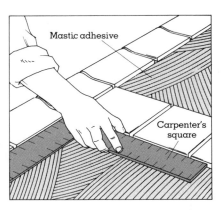

Next, install field tiles. Use a square to keep the tiles perpendicular to the edge trim.

same height as the finished tile. A recessed sink, commonly used with tile countertops, is also installed at this time (see page 85).

On the front edge of your plywood base, locate and mark the point where the center of the sink or midpoint of a blank countertop will be. Lay the edge tiles out on the countertop, starting from your mark. Some tiles have small ceramic lugs molded onto their edges to keep spacing equal; if your tiles don't, use plastic spacers, available from your tile supplier.

Carefully position the rest of the "field" tiles on the countertop. Observing the layout, make any necessary adjustments to eliminate narrow cuts or difficult fits.

If the countertop will have a backsplash or will turn a corner, be sure to figure the cove or corner tiles into your layout.

Mark reference points of your layout on the plywood base to help you re-create it later; then remove the tile.

Set the tiles. Set all trim tiles before spreading adhesive for the field tiles. Thin-set adhesive, mixed with latex additive, is water-resistant and easy to use.

Butter the back of each front-edge tile and press it into place, aligning it with the reference marks. If your edge trim consists of two tile rows, set the vertical piece first.

Next, butter any back cove tiles and set them against the wall. If you've installed a recessed sink, lay the sink trim next. Be sure to caulk between the sink and the base before setting the trim. If you're using quarter-round trim, you can either miter the corners or use special corner pieces available with some patterns.

Spread adhesive over a section of the countertop. Begin laying the field tiles, working from front to back (see illustration, above). Cut tiles to fit as necessary. As you lay the tiles, check the alignment frequently with a carpenter's square.

To set the tiles and level their faces, slide a 1-foot-square scrap of cloth-covered plywood over them and tap the scrap with a hammer.

Unless you're tiling up to an overhead cabinet or window sill, use bullnose tiles for the last row. If a wall contains electrical switches or plug-in outlets, you can cut tiles in two and use tile nippers to nip out a hole.

Apply the grout. Remove any spacers and clean the tile surface and grout joints until they're free of adhesive. Allow thin-set adhesive to set for 24 hours before grouting the joints. For details on grouting tools and techniques, see page 105.

After grouting, wait at least 2 weeks for the grout to cure; then apply a recommended sealer.

Index

Content Chemistry
An Illustrated Handbook for Content Marketing

by Andy Crestodina

ISBN: Paperback: 978-0-9883364-0-7
ISBN EPUB: 978-0-9883364-1-4
ISBN Kindle: 978-0-9883364-2-1

Table of Contents

Introduction

Part One: Lecture

Part Two: Lab

Introduction

Welcome to Content Chemistry

This book is the result of thousands of conversations with hundreds of companies over the last 12 years. On January 1, 2000, I started the new century with a new career on the web. Since that day, I've immersed myself in nearly every aspect of digital marketing. In April 2001, I co-founded a web design company called Orbit Media Studios with my great friend Barrett Lombardo. Today, Orbit is an award-winning team of 30 specialists with hundreds of happy clients and nearly 1,000 successful projects.

Through all of that experience, I've learned many things about digital marketing. The book you're reading now is a compilation of the most important and effective lessons I've learned.

The simplest way to summarize all of it goes something like this...

To be successful, websites must do two things: 1. Attract visitors, and 2. Convert those visitors into leads and customers. In order to do this, web marketers must do two things: 1. Create content, and 2. Promote it. I've learned that content makes the difference between success and failure on the web.

The structure of this book is based on those four aspects, broken into two sections: Lecture and Lab. The Lecture section includes the theory of web marketing, which consists of attracting visitors (traffic) and getting them to take action (conversions). The Lab section covers web marketing in practice, which is creating content and promoting it.

By the time you finish reading this book, you should have a solid foundation of all the main topics as well as a good understanding of the specific actions you'll need to take to succeed on your own. You'll know which actions lead to which outcomes. You'll know where you're going and how to get there.

Beyond this, my hope is that your new insights into web marketing will motivate you to get started and stay active. I hope you realize that web marketing is enjoyable because it's creative, something both social and analytical. There's nothing intimidating about it. You may discover that, yes, web marketing is critical to modern business, but it's also a lot of fun.

Andy Crestodina
Strategic Director, Orbit Media Studios
@crestodina | Google+ | LinkedIn

Who This Book is For

This book is for people who are interested in improving their marketing, increasing sales and growing their business. You don't need to be a social media celebrity or a best-selling author. You do need to be yourself. And regardless of who you are, it's almost certain that you're well suited for content marketing.

If you are a thoughtful and detail-oriented person who enjoys researching and writing well-considered articles, content marketing is for you. If you're a fast, informal writer who can produce quick posts based on today's news, content marketing is for you.

If you are analytical and prefer digging through data over chatting with people, content marketing is for you. If you're a social person who would rather connect with people than analyze numbers, content marketing is for you.

Introverts and extroverts, number-crunching researchers and big-picture thinkers, content marketing has something for everyone. However, **you must write**. All content marketers have this in common.

How to Use This Book: Experiment and Measure

This book is called "Content Chemistry" for a reason. As in chemistry, content marketing is about experimentation and measurement. Like a chemist, we'll mix chemicals (content), add energy (promotional activity), and observe and measure the reactions (analytics). Then we'll repeat or try something new.

- **Experimentation**: These practices will continue to evolve. Techniques should be adapted to suit your business. It's an ongoing process of trial and error, and gradual improvement.

- **Measurement**: Virtually every aspect of web marketing is measurable, much more so than with traditional advertising. This is part of the fun but also a necessary part of the work. *If you're not measuring results, you're not doing content marketing.*

Results will often be unexpected, but the purpose remains constant: we seek awareness, relevance and trust.

There is no need to read this book cover to cover, so feel free to jump around. Each page has insights and ideas for you to try. Depending on your skill level, you may skim the lecture (Chapters 2 and 3) and go straight to the lab (Chapters 4 and 5).

The techniques in this book are intended to demonstrate the concepts. I have tried them all and found each to be successful. Once you understand both the theory and practice, I invite you to try a little chemistry of your own!

What is Content Marketing?

Content marketing is the art and science of pulling your audience toward your business. It is based on the concept that there are relevant prospects looking for your product or service right now. If you can connect with them, if you can help them and teach them, some of them will become loyal customers.

> *Content Marketers create and promote useful, relevant information with the goal of attracting and engaging website visitors, and then converting those visitors into leads and customers.*

We do this by creating, publishing and promoting content that is relevant to our clients and prospects. We use blogs, search engine optimization (SEO), social media and email marketing.

Content marketing is sensitive to the behaviors and psychology of potential buyers. Whether we're looking for jet engines or consulting services, a wedding DJ or a local florist, we are more likely than ever to look to the Internet before making a decision to act. Every day we search, we research, we read recommendations and we seek advice from experts.

Where traditional marketing aims to interrupt and distract, content marketing aims to attract and assist.

The Evolution of Marketing

To understand the future of marketing, we must first understand the past. Let's take a brief look at the history of marketing.

**1950–1994
Traditional Marketing**

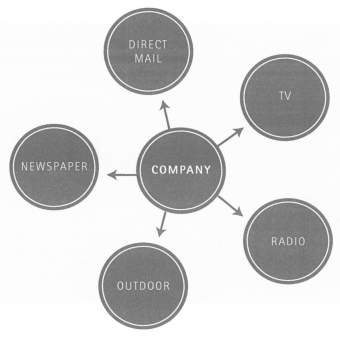

In the beginning...

Marketing was dominated by advertising and that meant buying media. It meant *buying space* in newspapers and hoping consumers would notice before they turned the page. It meant *buying time* on TV and hoping consumers would keep watching when the show cut to a commercial break.

Businesses sent postcards and letters to our homes and called us during dinner, pushing out their messages with whatever budget they could muster. They hoped that consistent, repeated distractions and interruptions would convince us to buy. Some businesses still do.

But that magazine ad had limited space and the TV commercial had precious little time. If the ad budget was cut, the message disappeared completely.

And it was always so hard to tell what was actually bringing in sales. There was an old saying among marketing executives: "I know I'm wasting half of my advertising budget, I just don't know which half."

Content marketing is a slow process. Although the techniques in this book are things you can (and should) start doing today, the impact on sales and revenue may be months or years away. Many of the tactics are cumulative, such as increasing email subscribers, growing social followings and building links. Building up your content and audience takes time. Don't expect to get rich (or be relevant) overnight.

**1950–2004
Traditional Marketing
+ Web**

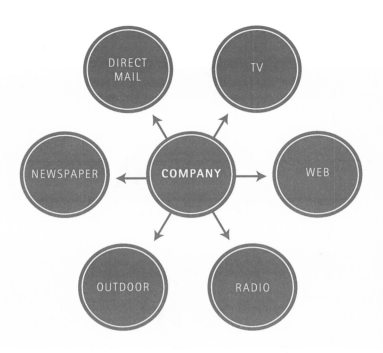

Then the web came along and, like magic, advertising wasn't limited by space and time. Once online your brochure could be a hundred pages, but printing and postage wouldn't cost you a penny. So the web became another channel to push out those ads. "Brochureware" websites were born and the sales copy was simply pasted in from other advertisements. Little, if any, effort was made to treat the web as a unique channel with new opportunities.

But unlike traditional marketing, web traffic was measurable. People began to talk about how many "hits" their online brochures were getting.

**2005–2009
Web-Centric Marketing**

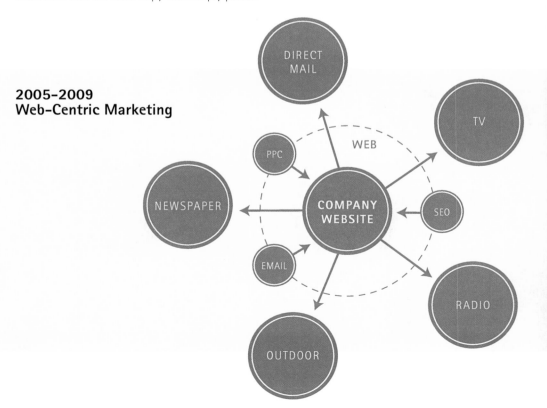

Then, a shift...

Slow, steady changes in technology and consumer behavior reached a tipping point. Suddenly the website was the center of all marketing efforts. The push of the traditional ad campaigns directed consumers to the web. Every billboard, TV commercial, radio spot and magazine insert had a web address at the bottom.

As people began to see the value of web marketing, billions in marketing budgets were moved toward search engine optimization, pay-per-click advertising and email marketing.

Also during this time, traditional advertising became less effective. Consumers had more ways than ever to dodge the interruptions of advertising. Spam filters blocked unwelcome email. DVRs skipped distracting TV ads. Banner blockers cleaned the blinking boxes off websites. "Do not call" lists helped keep the telemarketers away.

2010
Modern Marketing

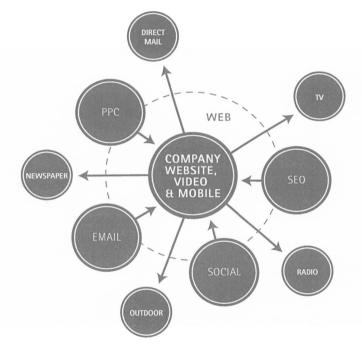

Welcome to modern marketing! It's new and improved, with more creative ways to connect with the people who matter to you. And the best part is that if you create meaningful content, those people will come to you.

The barriers have been removed and, rather than advertise on television, you can be your own TV station. Rather than seek publicity through PR, you can start your own online newsroom and grow your readership. You'll spend less money on printing and postage, and more time teaching something useful. You are on the web, and the web is in people's pockets.

We are in a golden era of social, video and mobile marketing, and it's built on content. The simple act of reading this book means you are likely to take advantage of these combined mega-trends.

Ready? Let's go.

Content Marketing vs. Advertising

Content marketing (also known as inbound marketing) is nothing new. It is simply using content to connect with potential buyers and partners. The content earns the interest and trust of the audience by being entertaining or informative.

Content marketing is not only different from advertising, it's the opposite of it. Content marketers attract their audience by being relevant. Advertisers inject themselves into other relevant media, hoping to be noticed. It's pull versus push.

CONTENT MARKETING (INBOUND)	ADVERTISING (OUTBOUND)
teach, help	sell
attract, interact, connect	distract, interrupt
brains	budget
the magnet	the hammer

You're probably like me.

You probably don't like to be interrupted by TV or magazines ads. You probably don't click on many banner ads. You probably use a spam filter.

You probably like to look for things on your own terms, research the options and read reviews. You probably listen to input from friends and you may even share recommendations with them.

This explains why content marketing is emerging as a winner. It's a friendlier, more credible and more sensitive way for us to connect with information, including the information that drives our purchasing decisions. Dollar-for-dollar and hour-for-hour, inbound is beating outbound.

Let's start by looking at how websites make money...

Web Strategy and Website ROI

Whether you're spending cash out of pocket or just investing your time, the return on investment in web marketing comes down to three main factors:

- Traffic (number of visitors)
- Conversion Rate (percentage of visitors taking action, becoming leads or subscribers, etc.)
- Maintenance Costs

That's it! Generally speaking, traffic times the conversion rate equals leads. Subtract from that the time and cost of managing and promoting the site, and you have your ROI. Simple, right?

Everything a content chemist does should increase traffic and conversions while minimizing the cost and time in any way possible.

Going one level deeper, we can see how the variables are determined. Let's look at a fictional case study and show how ROI can be calculated. This example will be an imaginary business that seeks to generate leads from visitors who find the site through search engines.

Case Study: Libby's Laboratory Services

Like a lot of businesses, Libby's business provides a service that people look for online.

Libby offers laboratory services, including staffing and testing, to research facilities. She's been doing this for a while and she's good at it. But Libby needs more leads if she's going to grow her business, and it's hard to connect with researchers looking for lab services.

So how much money will Libby make from her website and content marketing? How much new business will she get? How many leads would the site need to generate in order to pay for itself? What is the return on this investment? Let's figure it out.

Traffic...

Well, Libby won't have any leads if she doesn't get any traffic. She has a relatively unknown brand. She's in a small niche and wants search engines to help people find her business.

To estimate search engine traffic, she'll need to investigate the "search volume" of her top keyphrases. She needs to know how many monthly searches there are for "laboratory staffing." If the new site ranks high for these phrases, people will see Libby's site in the search engine listings.

Each time the site appears in a search results page is an "impression." Of course, the more phrases Libby's site ranks for, the more impressions she'll get. So she'll want to target a range of phrases.

But how high she ranks is also a big factor. A higher rank means exponentially more clicks (see Figure 2.2c). All other things being equal, the top ranking site gets a LOT more traffic than number two, and so on down the line. The effect of rank on traffic is exponential, so Libby plans to target some phrases that aren't too competitive.

Two factors determine the total number of impressions: the number of keyphrases a site ranks for and the rank for each keyphrase. Therefore...

$$\text{(Number of Keyphrases)(Search Volume}^{\text{Rank}}) = \text{Impressions}$$

When the site ranks, it attracts an audience and some of them will click. The percentage of searchers that click on Libby's listing is the "clickthrough rate" or CTR. Each click is a visit.

$$\text{Impressions x CTR = Visits}$$

So the more phrases, the higher the rank, the more popular the phrases, the more impressions and ultimately, more visits. Sound complicated?

Fortunately for Libby, her cousin Dale is a web strategist. Together, they research keyphrases and check search volume in Wordtracker and Google Adwords (see Chapter 4 for details). They check the competition using Google, OpenSiteExplorer and Alexa. Then they estimate clickthrough rates by looking at similar sites in Google Analytics and Google Webmaster Tools. They make an educated guess and estimate that with a well-optimized site *they can eventually expect 1,000 targeted visitors per month from search engines.*

...times conversions...

Getting traffic from search engines is great, but it's not the same as leads. If a researcher looking for lab services finds Libby's website, he's not a lead yet. He is just a visitor. When a lead calls or fills out Libby's contact form, he is officially a "conversion." The better the site, the higher the "conversion rate." There are many factors that determine the conversion rate, including design quality (brand loyalty and overall appeal), content format (text, images and video), the content itself (compelling, informative and relevant), and usability (navigation and an easy-to-use form).

$$\text{Visits x Conversion Rate = Leads}$$

Libby meets with Dale again to do more research. They study industry benchmarks and look at other laboratory services sites. They assume Libby's new site will be excellent – or at least good – in all of the conversion factors listed above. In the end, *they figure a 2% conversion rate is attainable.* Thanks again, Dale!

This formula is for illustrative purposes only. Here, a higher rank in search engines would mean a larger "rank" number in the formula. Also, in reality, search volume and rank are per keyphrase, and not simply multiplied by the number of keyphrases. Unlike the other formulas in this book, you can't simply plug numbers into this one!

...equals leads...

Now all they have to do is multiply the projected visits by the estimated conversion rate. They calculate that *the site should generate 20 leads per month.*

...times closing rate...

Now they need to convert the leads into actual customers. Dale can't help here, but Libby has a pretty good sales process in place and she can close around 50% of her leads. Each time she does this, she sells $1,000 worth of lab services. It costs her about $500 in time and overhead each time she provides this service. So generally speaking, the value of a lead to Libby is about $250.

Now that we have all the pieces, we can put them together in a (very cumbersome but comprehensive) set of formulas for estimating the return on the investment for a marketing website*.

(Leads x Closing Rate)(Price – Time and Materials) = Profit

$$K \times (S^R) = I$$ $$I \times CTR = V$$ $$V \times CR = L$$ $$(L \times CL)(P - Dc) = \$$$	**K** = number of keyphrases **S** = search volume **R** = rank **V** = visits **L** = leads **p** = price **$** = profit!	**CTR** = clickthrough rate (search engines) **CR** = conversion rate (website) **CL** = closing rate (sales) **Dc** = delivery costs or cost of goods and services sold (time and materials)

*There are other many other variables that could have been incorporated into this formula (including other sources of traffic, etc.) but to add them all here would have made the forumula more confusing than useful.

...equals profit.

Now it's time to do the math. Let's plug in Libby's estimates.

(20 leads x 0.5 closing rate)($1,000 lab service price – $500 time & materials)=$5,000 profit

If Libby can meet all of the targets above, *her website and marketing efforts will bring in up to $5,000 in profitable leads per month. In other words, if she invests $15,000 and ranks well and converts visitors, the website will pay for itself in 3 months. After that, it will be profitable.* Over its lifetime, the new site will likely generate tens of thousands of visitors, thousands of leads, and hundreds of thousands of dollars in revenue and profit.

But Libby isn't expecting instant results. She knows something very important...

A great site is not enough

Libby knows that launching the site is just the beginning. There is still is a lot of work to do, but she's committed to content marketing.

- She's going to do the ongoing work to get results in search engines. She knows that search engine marketing takes time.

- She's going to consistently create and promote relevant content.

- She's going to boost traffic with a new email newsletter called *Laboratory Services Monthly.*

- She's committed to following up on her web leads and tracking them using a database like Highrise or SalesForce.

And most of all, Libby is committed to providing the best possible laboratory services. She plans to have a visible presence and a good reputation, both online and off.

What You'll Need

Now you should have a sense of what content marketing really is and how it differs from advertising. We saw how marketing has evolved and where the big-picture trends are going. And we looked briefly at the end results and how they're measured.

To take advantage of the techniques in this book, you'll need a website. You'll also need tools to go along with it. Here are the basic tools for content marketing:

1. **Blog**
    The blog should share the same domain as your main website, so the address of the blog is http://blog.website.com or http://www.website.com/blog (preferably, the latter).

    If you do not have a blog, you will still be able to use many of these techniques with web pages, rather than blog posts, assuming you can easily update your website using a Content Management System (CMS) such as WordPress, Mighty-Site or Drupal.

2. **Contact Form for Lead Generation**
    A contact page with an email link is insufficient since it will not allow you to easily measure results. If your business sells products on an ecommerce site, the shopping cart will be more important than this contact form.

3. **Email Service Provider (ESP)**
    ESPs such as MailChimp, Constant Contact and Emma provide an email marketing template and service for sending mass emails, and offer reporting tools.

4. **Web Analytics**
    Google Analytics or Hubspot is necessary for measuring activity on the website. Without measurement, there is no data from which to make iterative improvements.

5. **Social Media Presence**
    For the more advanced techniques found in this book, you will need a basic presence in the social networks. This generally means thoughtful, complete profiles on Twitter, Google+, LinkedIn and/or Facebook, with enough activity and followers to make you and your business look credible.

If you have these tools, and the motivation to embrace content marketing principles, you're ready to go.

Part One: Lecture

1 Traffic Sources

When you look at your website analytics (Google Analytics, Hubspot, etc.) you'll see that traffic is generally categorized into three groups:

- Search traffic - visitors who found you by searching for a keyphrase in a search engine

- Referring traffic - visitors who clicked a link on a website and landed at your site

- Direct traffic - visitors who typed your web address into their browser

Although it's interesting, this breakdown of traffic is not all that accurate or meaningful. For example, you might think search traffic is new people who found you out of the blue. But some of that traffic is likely old friends who searched for your business name, so that number is often misleading.

Although direct traffic is supposedly from visitors who typed the address into a browser or clicked on a bookmark, it actually includes many other types of traffic. Any visits that are not from referring websites or search engines is lumped into direct traffic. This includes visitors who clicked on links that weren't in browsers, such as Twitter apps and email programs. Not all direct traffic is truly direct.

Here's an example: Suppose you send an email newsletter to two subscribers, one of whom uses Outlook and the other uses Yahoo! mail. Since Outlook is installed software and Yahoo! mail is used in a web browser, the subscriber who clicks from Outlook will be recorded as direct traffic. The other, who clicked from within a browser while using Yahoo!, may be recorded as referring traffic. In fact, both visitors were from an email campaign, which isn't really what direct or referring traffic is supposed to be. More about tracking email traffic soon.

There are advanced ways to set up Google Analytics to minimize these tracking issues. But first let's focus on driving results rather than tweaking how results are measured.

As a content marketer, you must plan to generate traffic *through activity*. Let's re-categorize the traffic sources to align them with our three main content marketing techniques: Search Engine Marketing, Social Media and Email Marketing.

Search Engine Optimization (SEO)

Search engines are a critical source of traffic for almost every site. Watch your own behavior online for a few hours and you'll find yourself entering keyphrases and searching Google or one of the other search engines.

Since two thirds of all searches happen within Google, we'll focus there. But the principles of ranking in Google are fundamentally similar to all search engines.

Ultimately, all SEO efforts have one focus: **to indicate that your site is relevant**. Every time you see or hear the phrase "search engine optimization," substitute the words "indicating relevance" and you'll have the right mindset to do good SEO work.

Your goal is simply to help Google help people find you. Cooperate with Google and stay on their good side. The key to SEO is to have valuable content and confirm this to Google with great links from relevant sites.

The outcomes of successful SEO efforts can be impressive:

An individual post may be initially promoted through email, but if it also ranks well in search engines it will continue to get traffic for years.

Ranking high in search engine results is exponentially better than ranking low. Potential visitors tend to trust that Google delivers relevant results, so the top ranking sites get a disproportionate share of the glory.

According to a study by Optify, the first three spots in Google get 58.4% of all clicks. The top spot gets more than 36% of clicks and second place gets 12.5%. Everyone knows that page two is no-man's-land, but not everyone realizes that *ranking first drives almost three times as much traffic as ranking second.*

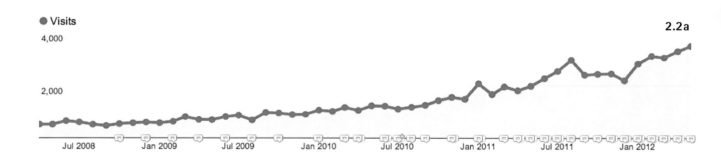

As a site gradually ranks higher and ranks for a wider range of phrases, traffic climbs.

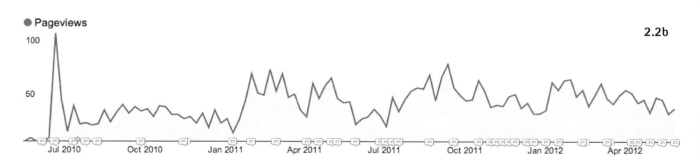

Organic Click Thru Rate by Search
Position *Figure 2.2c*

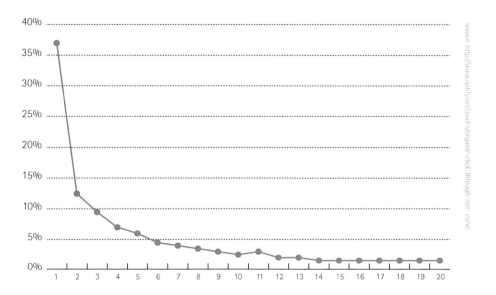

Black Hat vs. White Hat SEO Some search optimizers try to trick Google by using techniques that go beyond indicating relevance. They stuff pages full of keyphrases, hide keyphrases behind images or use the same color for text and backgrounds. Some even program their websites to show different versions of content depending on whether the visitor is Google or human. They also buy, rent and trade with people to get more links to their sites.

These are all considered "Black Hat" techniques; they can be destructive and are not recommended. Remember, Google has a small army of math Ph.D.s led by Matt Cutts, Google's head of web spam. These people are smarter than you and I. If they catch you using Black Hat tricks, they have every right to put you on their blacklist. Once blacklisted, your domain will never rank again, even when people search for the business name. This is a devastating outcome for a content marketer.

Stick to the usual "White Hat" techniques and focus on indicating your relevance. Provide valuable content that is focused on topics (keyphrases) relevant to your audience. Build genuine connections (links) with relevant websites

Search engine marketing is typically a slow, long-term form of marketing. It can take years of work to rank for an important phrase. It's called "optimization" because it's an iterative, ongoing process. SEO is evolutionary, not revolutionary. Be patient.

Why do sites rank in search engines?

This is an important question. Google's secret formula is far more valuable than the recipe for Coke. Although we'll never know for sure what the algorithm is, there are thousands of people researching it every day. They work tirelessly to better understand the criteria Google uses to determine who ranks for which phrases.

One of my favorite search engine research companies is SEOmoz. Every two years, they send a survey to some of the top search engine optimizers around the world. The results are published as the Search Ranking Factors and may be one of the best publicly available sources of information about how Google works.

The SEOmoz 2011 Search Ranking Factors surveyed 132 optimizers, and the aggregate of their expert opinions looks like this:

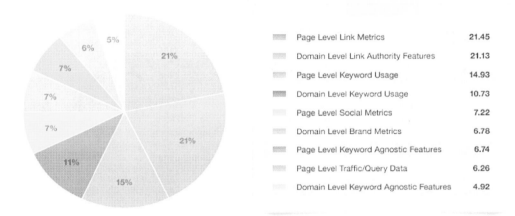

	Page Level Link Metrics	21.45
	Domain Level Link Authority Features	21.13
	Page Level Keyword Usage	14.93
	Domain Level Keyword Usage	10.73
	Page Level Social Metrics	7.22
	Domain Level Brand Metrics	6.78
	Page Level Keyword Agnostic Features	6.74
	Page Level Traffic/Query Data	6.26
	Domain Level Keyword Agnostic Features	4.92

NOTE!

To avoid going into the technical details of things like "page level keyword agnostic features," I'm simplifying this chart by breaking down these factors into five groups and redrawing the chart as follows:

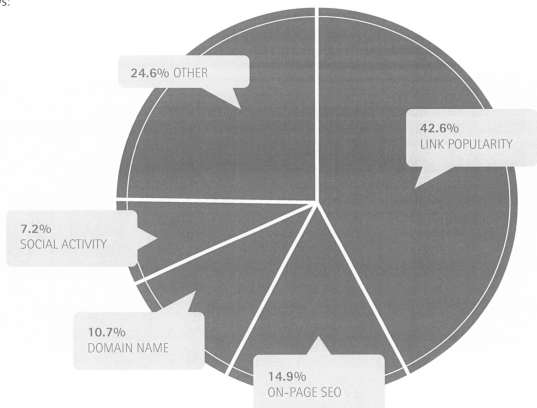

Link Popularity: Links from other websites to your website.

On-Page SEO: Attributes of your website, such as the use of keywords on your pages.

Domain Name: This includes use of keywords in your domain.

Social Activity: This includes sharing on Facebook and Twitter. Note: At the time of this survey, Google+ had not been launched.

Other: This includes factors such as the time it takes pages to load, the number of errors, content freshness, the number of searches for the company name, clickthrough rates from search engines, bounce rates, etc.

Suddenly it's clear that a big factor in how high you rank in search engines is links on other people's websites. If you're serious about SEO, getting good links has to be part of your content marketing efforts (more about link building in Chapter 4).

Search + Social: Google's AuthorRank

Google is clearly committed to social media. Google+ already has 170+ million users. But it's more than just a social network; it's tightly connected with the search engine. Users who are logged in are seeing changes in their search results. Activity on Google+ is affecting the rank of websites. It generally works like this:

Jack is friends with Jill so he adds her to one of his Google+ circles. Jill likes Bucket Co. so she clicks +1 on this website. Now, when Jack searches for "water pails," the Bucket Co. website ranks higher in search results. Jack can see that Jill likes this brand.

This is a big change for Google and it's probably just the beginning. The important question is: *How will Google+ and social activity affect search results for everybody?* This may be the biggest question in all of web marketing.

Here's the answer: Google will improve search results by connecting content to authors and rating authors based on their credibility. Links will still be important, but the credibility will be supported by social activity. The evidence for this can already be found in search results, and not just for people who are logged in to Google+. There is also significant supporting evidence on the Official Google Webmaster Central Blog, Google's patents and in statements from Amit Singhal, the head of Google's core ranking team.

It's now important to do a few things differently. Whenever possible, content should be connected to a credible Google+ profile. This means having a digital signature that links directly to the profile or links to a bio page on the website that links to the Google+ profile.

Once Google can make this connection, they can make sure they're posting the original version of an article. This helps them solve the problem of duplicate content. Imagine being a librarian in a library where most of the books are photocopies. How would you determine which is the original? This is what Google deals with as they try to sort out the Internet (more on duplicate content in Chapter 4).

More importantly, Google can now begin to use the credibility of authors to affect how high something should rank. According to their patent on this technology, "The identity of individual agents responsible for content can be used to influence search ratings." The metric given to the credibility of authors is right there in the name on the patent: Agent Rank. (You'll learn how to take credit as the author using digital signatures and author boxes in Chapter 4.)

This is also the premise behind Content Chemistry. It is another example of the convergence of web marketing practices that were once distinct: Social media and search engine optimization. Link building alone will be less effective if content isn't connected to a credible author, and author credibility will be cultivated using the skills of the social media marketer.

Now that we have a general idea of how search engines work, let's introduce the three key SEO-related activities that a content marketer should focus on:

- Keyphrase research
- On-Page search optimization
- Link popularity

"A good product can only be built where we understand who's who and who is related to whom. Relationships are also important alongside content. To build a good product, we have to do all types of processing. But fundamentally, it's not just about content. It's about identity, relationships and content." -Amit Singhal, Jan 28, 2012

source: Search Engine Land, emphasis added

Keyphrase Research

The first step in search marketing is always the same: picking your keyphrases. If you do everything else right but get this wrong, you won't see any results. As a content marketer, you must carefully choose phrases that meet three criteria:

- **Search volume**: How many people are searching for this phrase?
- **Competition**: How many websites are relevant for this phrase? Are they powerful sites?
- **Relevance**: If someone found your site while searching for this phrase, would they be happy? Would you be happy they found you?

The ideal keyphrase has high volume, low competition and is highly relevant to your business. Specific techniques for researching keyphrases are found in Chapter 4.

On-Page SEO

There are many ways to indicate on your pages that your content is relevant. As a writer of web content, you have multiple opportunities to indicate your pages' relevance for the target keyphrase. It often requires some small compromises to the writing, but if done well the page will rank much higher and be seen by many more people. It's worth the compromise. Trust me.

Here's a list of the most important places to use your target phrase to help Google understand that you are relevant. They are listed in order of importance.

- Title: Between <title> and </title>.
- Headers: Between <h1> and </h1> as well as <h2> and so on.
- Body Text: This is all the text on the page that isn't within links.

- Meta Description: Although it doesn't actually appear on the web page, the meta description often appears in search results as the snippet.

Chapter 4 has more detail on the specific ways you should use keyphrases in your writing.

Link Building

This is the most important ranking factor. I've seen web pages with little or no text rank high for popular phrases. This is possible because other websites indicate that the page is relevant for the phrase. This evidence is in the links.

Think about it: If 1,000 websites link to a page about the U-505 Submarine and each of those 1,000 links have text such as "learn more about the U-505 Submarine," then the page must be relevant for that topic. The links are a powerful indicator of relevance. This is especially true if those 1,000 sites are also about submarines and those sites have many inbound links themselves.

This is why link popularity is an excellent way for search engines to see what sites are really about. As we saw from the SEOmoz research above, link popularity is a heavily weighted ranking factor. Why? Because it's hard to fake. If SEO was only about which page uses the phrase most often, anyone could put "U-505 Submarine" on the page a hundred times and rank high. Google would then be full of spam. This is why links matter so much.

So, link text (also known as anchor text) is very important. If you're hoping to rank for "kids jet packs" then it's a very good thing if there are many links to your site with this phrase in the text of the links.

In the early days of SEO, search engines paid attention to another tag called "meta keywords," however this was abused by spammers and is no longer a ranking factor. You can still add meta keywords to a page, but it's not recommended. They're not useful for anything, except telling your competitors what phrases you're trying to rank for.

CAUTION!

Not all links are created equal

Some links to your site will be much more valuable than others. These are the characteristics of an ideal link:

- It's from a website that has many incoming links itself (high link popularity).

- It's from a page that doesn't have many outgoing links.

- It includes one of your target keyphrases in the link text.

- It's from a site that is relevant to your industry (more on that later).

Follow vs. Nofollow: As Google crawls the zillions of pages of the Internet, it follows links from one site to the next. Commenting on blogs often creates a link back to the website of the commenter. When SEOs realized they could generate links just by commenting, blogs were flooded with low value comments. Website owners can tell Google **not** to follow certain links by adding a tiny code that says "nofollow." Google skips these links, which then have much less value (if any) to the website on the other end. Today, most popular blogs have links within comments set to "nofollow," so blog commenting is not considered an important SEO tactic.

When you're looking at websites as possible linking opportunities, it's important to make sure that the link isn't designated "nofollow." It would be frustrating to spend hours writing and editing a high-quality guest blog post, give it to a relevant site, see it go live...and then realize that the link to your site is tagged "nofollow" (more on guest blogging in Chapter 5).

SEO summary

In the end, ranking in search engines and indicating your relevance comes down to great content written by a credible author and supported by great links. In other words, if you want to rank high, be good. Build and maintain a great online presence. If you are the best site on the Internet for that topic, Google will try hard to help people find you.

Target good keyphrases, use them in appropriate ways and look for opportunities to get high quality links to your site. But above all, strive to be truly relevant.

In the lab section, you'll learn the specific techniques for researching keyphrases.

CAUTION!

NOTE!

The factors that lead to high rankings (content and links) are cumulative. If 100 sites link to you, those links aren't likely to go away. If you post 10 pages of search-friendly content, you can keep that content live for years. For this reason, search engine advantages tend to be durable.

Social Media Marketing

Traffic from social media is the direct result of activity. Unlike traffic from search engines, where one page may rank well for years, messages within social media tend to be short-lived because the stream of posts and Tweets flows on with time. If you're active in social channels and you stop, so does the traffic.

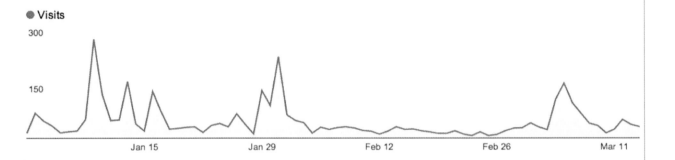

● **Visits**

The good news is that by being active in social channels you can drive traffic relatively quickly, especially if your social network is already developed. If you post or Tweet today, you'll get traffic today.

Social media is a skill like anything else. An expert knows ways to dramatically increase the odds of good things happening. A novice or someone who understands social media but not marketing is not as likely to drive results. Well, they might drive somewhere, but not toward a measurable goal.

A developed social media network is an important tool for every content marketer. Here is a quick list of specific activities in which a social network is valuable:

- Find and connect with people who are likely to share your content.

- Say thank you to people who have helped you.

- Increase your chances of getting press, speaking engagements and guest blogging opportunities by offering to help with promotion.

- Monitor trends by following experts.

- Test out possible email subject lines.

- Promote your content and the content of others in your network.

If you're not familiar with the differing features of the major social networks, here is a **social media network comparison chart**:

FACEBOOK	GOOGLE+	TWITTER	LINKEDIN
Two-way connecting	One-way following	One-way following	Two-way connecting
Friends Lists	Circles for tracking	Lists	
Groups	Circles for limited sharing		Groups
Posts	Posts	Tweets	Updates
63,206 character maximum	100,000 character maximum	140 character maximum	700 characters
Facebook's "EdgeRank" determines which fans, followers see posts.	Post visible to any follower and the public, if desired	Tweets visible to any follower and the public	Posts visible to your connections
Posts can be edited but only within seconds of posting	Posts can be edited	No editing	No editing
Sharing	Re-sharing	Retweeting	
Post likes	+1 voting on posts	Favorites	Update likes
Comment on posts	Comment on posts	Tweets	Comment on posts
Comment likes	+1 on comments	Favorites	Comment likes
Name mentions	+Mentions	@Mentions	
Inline graphics and media	Inline graphics and media	Inline graphics and media	Inline graphics and media
Messages	Post to specific individuals	Direct messages	Direct messages
	Posts in web search results	Tweets in web search results	
1-to-1 video chat (Skype)	Group video chat (Hangout)		
IM Chat	Chat	TweetChat	
Unfriend	Block Users	Block Users	Flag

(adapted from Hazen Carpenter's "Is Google+ More Facebook or More Twitter? Yes." and Guy Kawasaki's Why I Love Google+. LinkedIn column added by author)

FACEBOOK	GOOGLE+	TWITTER	LINKEDIN
B2C	B2C/B2B	B2C/B2B	B2B

Each network has its own pros and cons. Depending on your audience, some networks are more useful than others. Facebook is more relevant for business-to-consumer companies, whereas LinkedIn is better for business-to-business. Google+ and Twitter are so versatile that they are relevant to both B2B and B2C companies.

Twitter and Analytics

Traffic from Twitter is notoriously difficult to measure. Twitter is a platform-independent network and can be accessed from a huge range of mobile apps and tools, as well as from Twitter.com. But traffic from apps is tracked separately from traffic from websites.

This means that traffic from Twitter may be recorded as coming from a referring site if the click was on Twitter.com or websites like HootSuite.com, but will look like direct traffic if the click was on the Twitter app or HootSuite app.

In the lab section in Chapter 4, you'll learn to create content that's more likely to be shared and to promote it quickly using social media channels.

Email Marketing

Although it may now seem like traditional digital marketing, email marketing is a powerful traffic generator. We don't know any serious content marketers who don't use email marketing.

Email creates a pulse in your analytics. Do it regularly and it will look as steady as a heartbeat on an EKG.

Email is great for all kinds of businesses. For B2B service companies with long sales cycles, email is a way to keep in touch between purchases and build credibility for leads that are already in the pipeline. For B2C product companies with short decision cycles, a well-timed email can drive sales almost instantly.

Ethical email marketers keep the following principles in mind:

- List growth
- List cleanliness
- Email timing
- Subject lines
- Content and calls to action
- Testing and reporting

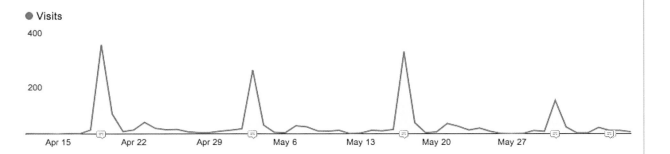

If you are actively driving traffic to your site through social media, be sure to keep an eye on your mobile stats. Traffic from social media sources is more likely to be from mobile devices. See Mobile in Chapter 3.

Email Service Providers

Your email service provider (ESP) is the tool you use to create emails and send them to your list. There are hundreds of ESP options to choose from. Some are very inexpensive and cost nothing until you have several thousand subscribers. Others provide a more personalized service, even offering creative design. Here are some general criteria for selecting an ESP:

- **Deliverability**
  One of the main functions of an email company is to make sure your emails get through. Unless there's something wrong with your list, you should expect at least 97% of emails to be delivered. These companies have full time staff dedicated to keeping your email server from getting "blacklisted" by the Hotmails and Gmails of the world. These people have titles like "ISP Relations" and "Director of Deliverability."

- **Easy to Use Interface**
  The tools you use to manage your list, and create and send an email newsletter, should be simple and require no more time or effort than necessary. None of them are perfect.

- **Reporting**
  Without reports, you can't get smarter. And with pretty charts that are easy to read, you're more likely to pay attention and get smarter faster. Reports should be meaningful and compelling. They should show delivery, open and clickthrough rates in ways that make you want to be a better marketer.

Other criteria for selecting an ESP can include the ability to segment lists, do A/B testing and integrate with a CRM (Customer Relationship Management) system or database of contacts. Of course, price is also relevant!

> "Send timely, targeted, relevant, valuable emails to people who have asked for them."
> - DJ Waldo (during an interview on Internet Radio for Smart People)

Tracking Traffic from Email Campaigns

The long term goal of email marketing is to always measure results and continually improve. But unless you add special tracking code, the traffic from your email campaigns will be mixed together with all your other traffic in Google Analytics, making it harder to measure what people are doing after they arrive.

To make the traffic from email appear separately in Google Analytics, use the Google URL Builder. Put each link from your email into this tool, then add the three main parameters into the form: Campaign Source, Campaign Medium and Campaign Name.

Example: You have a website located at www.site.com. You are sending an email newsletter promoting a summer sale. This email will have a link to your home page.

In the URL Builder, enter "newsletter" as the campaign source, "email" as the campaign medium and "summer_sale" as the campaign name.

TIP!

One useful email marketing metric that is rarely emphasized and isn't available within all ESPs is the "Click-to-Open Rate" (sometimes shown as CTOR or CTO). This is the number of unique clicks divided by the number of unique opens. It's useful because it shows how likely people are to engage with your emails after they open them. This removes the variability of open rates and lets you focus on engagement. A CTOR of 20-30% is considered good.

Website URL: *

http://www.site.com/page

(e.g. *http://www.urchin.com/download.html*)

Step 2: Fill in the fields below. **Campaign Source**, **Campaign Medium** and **Campaign Name** should always be used.

Campaign Source: *	newsletter	(referrer: google, citysearch, newsletter4)
Campaign Medium: *	email	(marketing medium: cpc, banner, email)
Campaign Term:		(identify the paid keywords)
Campaign Content:		(use to differentiate ads)
Campaign Name*:	summer_sale	(product, promo code or slogan)

Step 3

(Generate URL) (Clear)

http://www.site.com/page?utm_source=newsletter&utm_medium=email&utm_campaign=:

Click "Generate URL" and the link changes from http://www.site.com to http://www.site.com/page?utm_source=newsletter&utm_medium=email&utm_campaign=summer_sale.

Now, paste the new links generated by this tool into your email. Traffic from this email will appear as a separate source in traffic sources and within the Campaign section.

Traffic from links that were created using the URL Builder appear as a separate traffic source, shown on this chart in yellow.

In the lab section, you'll learn the specific aspects of email marketing campaigns that drive results.

■ **40.91%** Search Traffic
16,468 Visits

■ **30.73%** Referral Traffic
12,370 Visits

■ **21.12%** Direct Traffic
8,501 Visits

■ **7.23%** Campaigns
2,912 Visits

TIP!

The URL Builder can be used to track links from any source, not just email. Traffic from online ads and social media sources can also be tracked as campaigns. You could even track traffic from QR codes or links in your email signature this way.

2 Conversions

When a visitor takes action and becomes a lead or customer, the chain reaction is complete. Every form that is filled out and submitted, and every share button that is clicked, is a conversion that can be measured. First, let's look at why visitors convert.

All visitors - all of us - want our problems solved and our desires fulfilled. Maybe we were thinking of the problem or the desire when we came to the site, or maybe not. Either way, *visitors convert into customers when the hope for a solution is stronger than the fear that they'll be disappointed.*

So there are two factors at work: one is pulling them toward conversion and the other is friction that is pushing them away.

Which force is stronger?

MOTIVATION
compelling content,
easy to use site,
strong design, trust

FRICTION
weak or unclear content,
unanswered questions,
hard to use site,
lack of trust, confusion

VISITOR

GOAL

If the motivation is stronger than the friction, the visitor converts, meeting their goals and yours.

Types of Conversions

Generating leads and sales is the ultimate goal of most websites, but there are many types of conversions and all of them are good. The smaller successes are important steps toward turning visitors into fans and fans into customers.

Subscribers, followers and fans are some of the best conversions because *they allow you to connect with people when they're not on your site.* Now your content can reach farther to people who have asked to receive it, allowing you to drive greater traffic and higher conversions in the future.

CONVERSION TYPE	USED FOR	REVENUE	OPT-IN	CONTENT*
Lead	lead generation	$		
Customer	ecommerce	$		
Subscribers	newsletter, RSS		☑	
Event Registrant	events, webinars			
Donor	non-profit	$		
Follower / Fan	Social Media: Twitter (follower, Tweet) Facebook (fan, like) Google+ (follower, +1) LinkedIn (follower)		☑	
Member	account creation: community, directory, forum, ecommerce		☑	
Reviewer	products, movies, business			
Commenter	blog			
Register to download	eBooks, whitepapers			✳
Applicant	recruiting		☑	✳
Entrant	sweepstakes, promotions			

These conversions actually collect content from visitors, which can be repurposed. See Chapter 4 for details.

Conversion Factors

There are many factors that combine to determine what percentage of visitors convert.

- **Overall design appeal of the site**
  Does the site look professional?

- **Relevance**
  Are the products or services relevant to the visitor you attracted? How targeted is the website traffic?

- **Clarity of navigation**
  Will visitors understand the labeling of links and buttons? Does the navigation layout follow standard web conventions?

- **Content quality**
  Is the value proposition clear? Is the information useful to the visitor? Does it answer their most important questions? Does it use simple, natural language? Does the content seek first to help, and then to promote the business? (see Content Quality in Chapter 4)

- **Content format**
  Is the content presented in visual, compelling format, such as images and video? Is the text-based content legible and formatted for easy scanning and reading?

- **Trust**
  Is the website from a known brand? Is there "social proof" or third-party validation, such as lots of Facebook fans, prominent testimonials, positive reviews, BBB rating and industry/association credentials?

- **Compelling calls to action**
  Does the site give credible, relevant reasons to take action?

- **Simple, prominent forms**
  Are the conversion forms visually prominent? Are the forms short and easy to complete?

The more YESes to the above questions, the higher a site's conversion rate will be. Any NOs present obvious problems: distraction, confusion, distrust, annoyance and irrelevance.

TIP!

Typically, an overall conversion rate of 3% or more is considered high. If the conversion rate is 1% or lower, something is probably wrong.

The better you understand your target audience, the more likely you are to create an online experience that converts well. When possible, create personas, send surveys or do focus group testing. If nothing else, talk to the sales and customer service teams to learn what questions, concerns and objections your potential customers have.

If you can discover those things which pique visitors' interest; create urgency; and address any fears, uncertainties and doubts, you can more easily create a website and develop content that speaks to visitors directly. This is great for your conversion rate.

Short Forms

There is an inverse correlation between the length of forms and the percentage of visitors who fill them out and submit. The more form fields, the lower the conversion rate.

Resist the temptation to create a "warmer lead" by asking for too much information. Long forms are considered "greedy." Often the information you're looking for can be gathered when you follow up on the lead offline. For lead generation forms, include and require the minimum number of fields: name, phone number, email, and possibly company name and message.

Thank You Pages and Subsequent Conversions

In our experience designing and building websites at Orbit Media, we have found that the subsequent page after a first conversion is an excellent place to let the visitor take action again. If visitors had enough interest and trust to take action once, they may take action twice if offered the opportunity on the thank you page.

The trick is to first give visitors what they want. For example, many ecommerce shopping carts ask visitors to create an account before checking out. This isn't what the visitors were hoping for. They clicked "buy now" not "buy after I give you my email address and password."

In the analytics accounts of our clients, we've seen the lack of a "guest checkout" option *reduces sales by 30-50%*. Requiring visitors to first create accounts is simply greed for more information on the part of a self-centered website owner. This is counter to the principles of content marketing. First, give them what they want. Then, they may give you what you want.

On one website, we added the option to create an account after the checkout process. A simple sentence of benefit copy was right there next to it: "We'll remember your address for a faster checkout next time. We'll also store your order history and let you create a wishlist." The percentage of shoppers who created accounts increased by 40%.

TIP!

Create content that addresses the questions and concerns that are specific to various stages in the buying process and the conversion funnel. More about the sales funnel in Chapter 6.

NOTE!

In some cases, forms need to include questions that allow the website to automatically route the conversion to the right person within an organization. For example, a contact form may route job applicants to HR and leads to the sales team, provided it lets the submitter self-select.

Thank you pages are often missed opportunities to let the visitor become more engaged.

- A lead generation thank you page may offer a newsletter sign-up:
  "If you'd like to receive our best advice as a monthly email, sign up below."

- A job applicant thank you page may offer social media buttons:
  "To be the first to know about open positions, follow us on Facebook."

- An event registration or donation thank you page may offer to let the visitor share the news:
  "Share this on Twitter and let your friends know you're going / you donated."

Even if it doesn't offer a subsequent conversion, the thank you page can still guide the visitor toward more content with links to pages and posts, rather than be a complete dead end.

Converting Visitors into Email Subscribers

"Enter email address" next to a subscribe button isn't exactly a great pitch for your newsletter. On the other hand, if you include the right message next to that sign-up box, you may see a higher conversion rate for subscribers.

- State the Topic: If the visitor can't tell what the newsletter is going to be about, you aren't conveying the value of subscribing.

- Indicate Frequency: If the visitor can't tell how often the newsletter is coming, they may hesitate to subscribe.

- Social Proof: Show the number of subscribers or a testimonial to indicate that others appreciate the content.

Beyond these copy tips, the design of the sign-up box should be visually prominent through color, size and position on the page. We'll look take a closer look at email signup forms in Chapter 5.

Measure...

As explained in Chapter 1, the percentage of website visitors who take action is called the conversion rate. Conversion rates for each possible conversion on any website should be set up as separate goals within Google Analytics. This will allow you to measure the success of each and then optimize the site to better convert. This is called Conversion Rate Optimization (CRO).

Funnel Visualization

To optimize the site for conversions, you need to see where any problems are and what needs to be fine tuned. To help you see what's happening on and around the conversion pages, Analytics has a report called "funnel visualization."

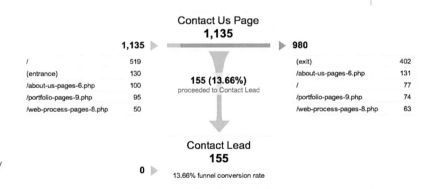

This report shows how many people came to the Orbit contact form, what pages they came from, how many and what percentage completed the form and, for those that didn't, what pages they visited next.

Note that some of the visitors who didn't convert by completing the form may still have met their own goals and possibly yours. This report doesn't show how many people called you, converting from a visitor to a lead over the phone. The report doesn't show how many people were just looking up your address to send you flowers and a giant check.

With Google Analytics, it's possible to create longer funnels, or rather, chains of successive funnels. This is useful for ecommerce sites (or any site with forms that take up multiple pages) and allows you track the shopping cart abandonment rate in a more visual report. You'll see how many and what percentage of people progress from the shopping cart to the checkout page to the thank you page.

...and Improve

Now that you can see this activity, you can begin to look for ways to improve the site to make it more compelling and easier to use. If the number is low, ask yourself the following questions:

- **Did the site answer enough of visitors' initial questions?**
  Talk to the sales team to learn the most common questions and objections. Add content that answers top questions and addresses top concerns.

- **Did the site connect with visitors as people?**
  The site should connect on a human level, through pictures of the team, videos from company leadership, photos of your offices, etc.

- **Does the site convey trust?**
  If not, add third-party credentials, badges for certifications, association memberships, testimonials, case studies, security information (ecommerce) and content that demonstrates experience and expertise.

- **Is the site easy to use?**
  Make sure the forms are short, and pages and sections are named properly. Any tiny bit of confusion between the website and the visitor is friction. The site should guide visitors effortlessly through the series of pages that teaches them, helps them and gently offers to let them take action.

- **Is the content compelling?**
  All the text and video on the top pages must be concise and compelling. When visitors leave the contact form and go to other pages, they're giving you another chance. Make sure those pages are strong. See Content Quality in Chapter 4."

Results are determined by two numbers: Traffic and conversions. Traffic times the conversion rate equals leads and revenue. Now that you have a balanced view of both halves of the equation, you can approach web marketing more efficiently. Always try to first diagnose and fix the biggest problems and grab the lowest-hanging fruit.

 **CAUTION!**

Special Section: Mobile

One of the biggest trends in web marketing is the trend toward mobile. Surprisingly, most marketers are not yet responding to the explosion of visits from mobile devices. According to a study by the mobile analytics company Flurry, there was a huge disconnect in 2011 between where advertisers are allocating budgets and where visitors are spending their time.

But don't rush out and build a mobile site just yet. "Everybody's doing it" is not good decision criteria. Good decisions are based on evidence, especially when those decisions have cost implications.

A great mobile site is basically a separate site, with simpler navigation, no rollovers, no Flash, a one-column layout, more concise content and features that work well with the phone, such as click-to-dial, maps and video. Even if it's not fancy, it's going to cost something. Mobile websites don't grow on trees!

There is another approach to mobile websites called "responsive design." The idea is to build one site that adapts itself to display well on screens big and small. A site like this automatically resizes itself depending on the size of the device. There can be design compromises with responsive websites, but recently there are some impressive examples of very responsive designs. These sites change layouts, image sizes and even navigation styles for several screen sizes. It's one website, but thanks to some elaborate programming, it displays very differently for phones, tablets and as a full site.

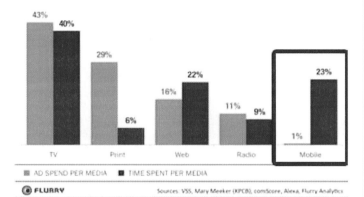

2011 U.S. Ad Spending vs. Consumer Time Spent by Media

Check your stats

Before you spend a dime on a mobile site, look at the data. Look at Google Analytics under **Audience > Mobile > Overview** and view the data as percentages (the pie chart view). Here are some examples of what you might find when you look at what percentage of your visitors are accessing the site from mobile devices:

Company A's Mobile Visitors

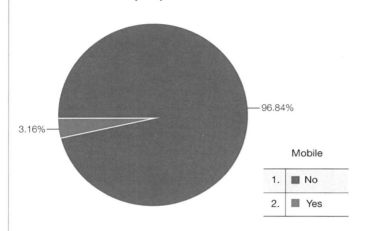

96.84%

3.16%

Mobile

1.	■ No
2.	■ Yes

Company B's Mobile Visitors

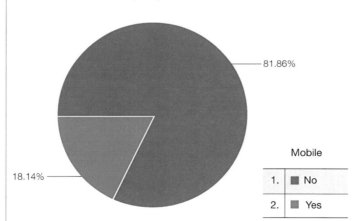

81.86%

18.14%

Mobile

1.	■ No
2.	■ Yes

Only 3% of Client A's visitors are using mobile devices, but 18% of Client B's visitors are. Obviously, Client B has a bigger need for a mobile site. But these are extreme examples. Most sites we see are in the 5-7% range for mobile device visitors. These numbers are always higher for companies that are actively involved in email marketing and social media.

Keep in mind that in Google Analytics, mobile visitors include people using tablets as well as phones. But the experience of using a site on a iPad (and almost all tablet users are on iPads) is often very similar to the experience on the full site, since even the first edition iPad had a screen resolution of 1024 x 768. This is a size and shape that is similar to the monitor settings on most desktops and laptops.

So look at **Audience > Mobile > Devices** and view the percentages. You'll see that a big chunk of your mobile visitors may be on iPads.

As long as the site doesn't contain Flash (which won't display on iPads and iPhones) or use rollover effects in navigation (there is no mouse cursor on tablets) it may work just fine for these visitors. It's more important that we find out how many visitors are using phones. It's these people who are more likely struggling to navigate and read on a really small screen. (pinch... zoom... scroll... click... oops!... back...)

Let's see what percentage of your visitors are using phones. Take the percentage of total mobile visitors and multiply it by the percentage of non-tablet mobile visitors and you'll see what percentage of your visitors are on phones. In the case of Company B, 18% of visitors are mobile and 60% of those visitors are not on iPads, so around 11% of visitors are using phones.

It's also important to consider the experience our mobile visitors are having. Check to see if these people are sticking around. The "bounce rate" is the percentage of visitors who leave the site after seeing just one page. If the bounce rate for mobile visitors is very high, it's more important to become mobile-friendly sooner.

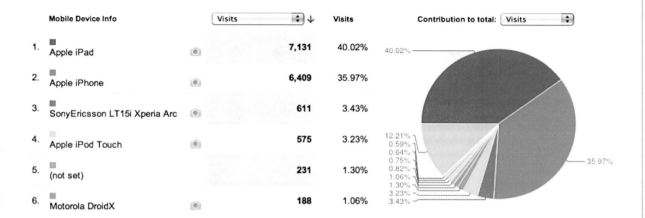

Mobile Device Info	Visits	Visits
1. Apple iPad	7,131	40.02%
2. Apple iPhone	6,409	35.97%
3. SonyEricsson LT15i Xperia Arc	611	3.43%
4. Apple iPod Touch	575	3.23%
5. (not set)	231	1.30%
6. Motorola DroidX	188	1.06%

Here's a general benchmark for deciding when to build a mobile site...

Mobile	Avg. Time on Site	% New Visits	Bounce Rate
No	00:05:23	63.73%	41.58%
Yes	00:02:13	60.80%	63.80%

If not now, when?

Even if you have a low percentage of mobile visitors today, these numbers will change. Check back every few months. Look at the trend in Google Analytics over the last few years and extrapolate. You'll be able to predict the month and year that you will reach that 8% threshold.

Yes, mobile websites are popular, but if you do it, do it right and do it for the right reasons. Check your stats to see if the small screen is a big priority.

MOBILE rule of thumb!

When 8% of visitors are on mobile devices, start planning your mobile site. It's even more important when the bounce rate for these visitors is higher.

Part Two: Lab

3 Content

The following is a guide to virtually all the types of content on the Internet. It also explains how to quickly create new content by repurposing content you already have.

Atomize Your Content: The Periodic Table of Content

Content is made up of pieces. And pieces can be broken down into smaller pieces or combined into larger pieces, just like the elements on the Periodic Table. Thinking about content as particles will give you ideas on how to quickly create new content by "atomizing" your existing content into smaller pieces or combining content into larger compounds.

But before you turn your articles into particles, let's look at what the content universe is made of. Once we know what's on the Periodic Table of Content, we'll be ready to start smashing particles in the content accelerator.

 NOTE!

This section is itself an example of repurposed content; it was originally a very popular blog post on the Orbit site. It's been viewed and shared thousands of times and was translated into French and German.

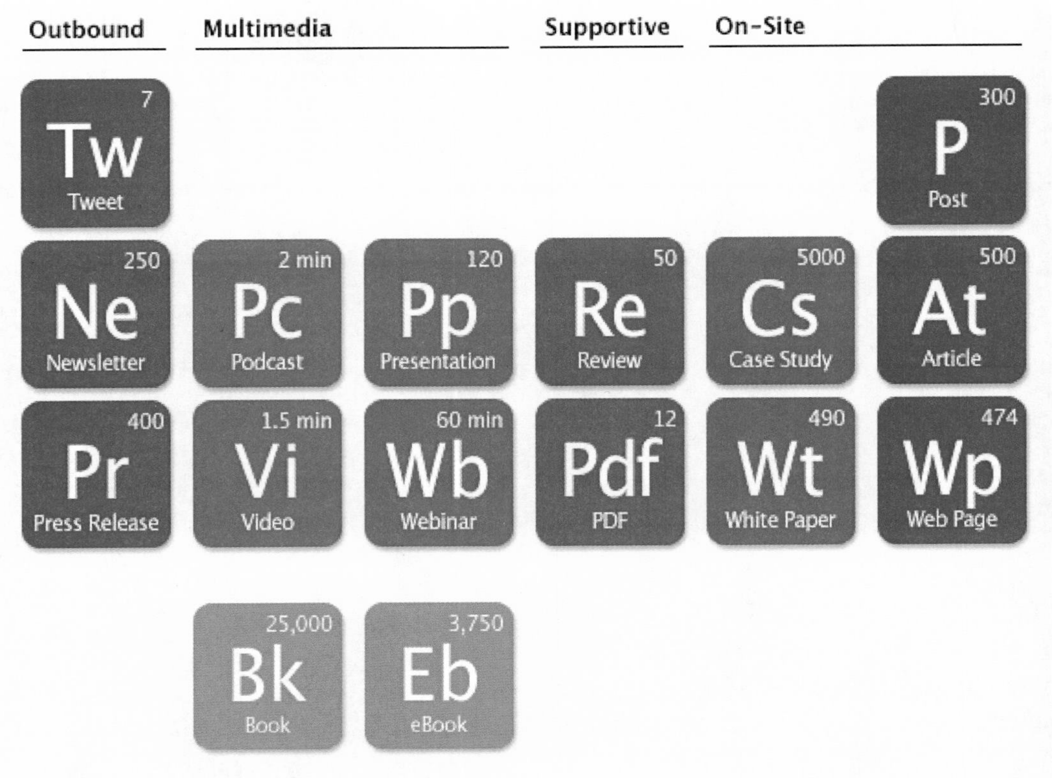

Outbound	Multimedia			Supportive	On-Site	

Tw 7 — Tweet

P 300 — Post

Ne 250 — Newsletter

Pc 2 min — Podcast

Pp 120 — Presentation

Re 50 — Review

Cs 5000 — Case Study

At 500 — Article

Pr 400 — Press Release

Vi 1.5 min — Video

Wb 60 min — Webinar

Pdf 12 — PDF

Wt 490 — White Paper

Wp 474 — Web Page

Bk 25,000 — Book

Eb 3,750 — eBook

Elements at the top of the chart are small and tend to have a shorter half-life. Elements at the bottom are larger, slower to create and last longer.

Elements to the left appear everywhere, on billions of sites and various devices. Elements on the right are more likely to be on your site.

The number in the top right indicates the typical length or number of words for that Element.

What follows is a description of each particle and examples of how to break it down or combine it with others. If you don't want to read them all, just look at the ones you already have and the ones you want to create.

Tw (Tweet) a tiny particle, which survives in nature only a short time. Tweets are known for traveling far and in many directions, and they may be comprised of subatomic links, mentions, hashtags and quotes.

- *Any content can be atomized into Tweets.* Doing so can lead to small chain reactions of shares and clicks. Quotes, stats, captions and headlines can all be made into Tweets.

- Tweets can be combined into a post. For example, use three Tweets and add your own commentary, or simply list 12 related Tweets.

P (Post) One of the primary building blocks of web content, Posts can be seen as updates on social media sites (Facebook, G+) or in corporate blogs or other streams. They tend to be timely, short-lived and date-stamped. Posts are informal, highly shareable and may include images.

- Since Posts are already small, they can only be broken down into Tweets.

- Posts are strongest in compounds with other elements: Link to posts from Tweets and Newsletters. Link from Posts to Web Pages.

Ne (Newsletter) an outbound particle that lives slightly longer than the Tweet. It has more properties, including subject lines and link tracking, so it requires careful handling.

- Newsletters should always link to Posts and Articles. Their energy is lower unless this bond is created. If a Newsletter gives the full text and doesn't link to something else, the visitor doesn't click and no traffic is generated. Never put the full text into a newsletter. Always combine!

Pc (Podcast) The Podcast is pure, distilled audio and has no visual energy. Podcasts are typically less powerful than Video, but more powerful than text because of their ability to convey tone. Create them using radio frequency microphone technology.

- Podcasts are easy to create by recording readings of Articles and Case Studies.

- Podcasts may be byproducts of the Presentation creation process. Simply pull the audio track out of a Video or Webinar, or record the presentation using a smartphone and edit later.

Pp (Presentation) No longer viewed only on projectors during speeches, today Presentations can be found across the web, ranking in searches and shared through social media. They are most powerful when charged with visual content like charts and images.

- Post Presentations to Slideshare and embed them in Web Pages, including LinkedIn.
- Record the audio track to create a Podcast.
- If possible, use social media coverage to live Tweet those juicy sound bites during the presentation. Use a predetermined hashtag sub-particle.

Cs (Case Study) Sometimes known as "success stories," Case Studies increase credibility and are useful when trust is critical and the sales process is long. The problem-solution-result structure is easy to spot. Case Studies are powerful because they can be atomized into almost anything.

- Break them down into outbound Newsletters, less formal Articles and two or three Tweets to increase traffic.
- Combine with Reviews (use the Testimonial isotope) and link to Web Pages to increase conversions.

Re (Reviews) (aka recommendations or testimonials) Since the recent explosion of these particles, Reviews can be found everywhere. Find them on your Yelp page, LinkedIn, Google+ Local Page or free-roaming emails.

- Combine them with your Web Pages through testimonial chemistry, but never create a Web Page of testimonials. Reviews are supportive content that increase the credibility of other Particles. When they stand alone (on a testimonials page) they are weaker, since reading reviews is typically not the main reason why people visit websites. They go to get information and learn.
- Add reviews to Case Studies, Newsletters and Press Releases.

At (Article) An extremely versatile element, Articles are slightly larger and more structured than Posts. They are less self-serving than Web Pages. Articles are created to inform and entertain, not just market and promote.

- Atomize Articles into Posts and Tweets.
- Transform into Web Pages (add product/ service information) or Case Studies (restructure, add example).
- Combine 5 articles into an eBook or 20 articles into a Book.

TIP!

When Webinars require registration/subscription, subsequent Newsletter particles have greater energy and reach.

Pr (Press Release) This targeted, highly-charged particle travels quickly. Although it was once directed specifically at media, today it can be found ranking in search engines and reaching a wider spectrum.

- Press Releases are easy to convert into Web Pages and Articles, but be careful. Rewrite the Press Release before posting it on your site to avoid the duplicate content penalty. Each Web Page particle on your site should be original and unique on the web.

Vi (Video) Although the content and messaging may overlap with surrounding particles, the format stands alone as one of the most compelling and powerful formats for content.

- Most content can be atomized into Video in any properly equipped lab.

- Video becomes more powerful when bonded to a Web Page (a process known as "embedding"), which improves the page's conversion rate (visitors into leads).

Wb (Webinar) Similar to a Presentation, but always with audio and sometimes with video. When viewed in real time and given a hashtag, Webinars often generate Tweets.

- Create Video or Podcast particles through recording technology.

- If the Webinar requires registration, be sure to atomize a summary or transcription. Make it viewable as an Article for people who weren't able to attend the live version.

Pdf (PDF files) These are supportive particles that should never stand alone. Any valuable content that is currently within a PDF but not on a Web Page should be atomized immediately, since PDFs are not search friendly and lack Analytics.

- Best when bonded to Web Pages as alternate (print-friendly, downloadable) versions of Articles, White Papers, Press Releases, etc.

- There are only a few specific environments where PDFs can stand alone and still have value: Scribt and Slideshare.

Wt (White Paper) Also referred to as a Research Report, Technical Brief, or Guide, White Papers tend to be formal, text heavy and a bit boring. Historically common, many White Papers still exist in legacy content and sometimes they are relevant for years. *These are prime candidates for atomization.*

- One White Paper can often be broken down into three or more Article or Posts.
- If the White Paper is available only as a PDF, make it into a set of Web Pages.
- Post on Scribd.
- If there is an Executive Summary, this may be broken off into a Case Study or Web Page.
- Subatomic quotes and stats can become Tweets.

Wp (Web Page) A stable particle that's clear, direct and easy to control. Its effectiveness is also easy to measure. Web Pages are powerful in both search engine marketing and at converting visitors into leads and customers. They are not frequently shared on their own, however.

Case Studies, Articles and White Papers should all be atomized into Web Pages.

Marketing PDFs should always be converted into web pages.

Reviews should not be combined into a Web Page since "testimonial" pages generate disproportionately low visits. Reviews should be added to various pre-existing web pages.

Bk (Book) Offline particle with a history of endurance. No particle is older except the ancient Scroll (Sc) and Slab (Sl).

- Books can be created by combining many Article particles through editing fusion. This process releases large amounts of credibility.
- Books can be atomized into Articles and White Papers.

Eb (eBook) Similar to the Book but shorter. Similar to the White Paper, but less formal and text-heavy. eBooks typically feature more design elements (charts and images) and can be created easily using presentation software such as Powerpoint or Keynote.

- Convert White Papers into eBooks.
- Combine Articles with a similar theme into an eBook.

TIP!

When eBook downloads require registration/subscription, subsequent Newsletter particles have greater energy and reach.

Atom Smashing Examples (good and bad)

Multiplying Video (good): Brad Farris of EnMast made a one hour Webinar interview of three experts. Later, he atomized the video into three shorter Videos, each of which was of an expert answering a specific question.

Atomic Meltdown (bad): A biomedical company hired a PR firm that used the company's home Web Page as a press release and submitted it to online news wires. The explosion in duplicate content caused Google to blacklist the domain. *The company no longer ranked, even for its own name.* Hazmat suits and a Reconsideration Request were needed to clean up.

Final Thesis

Content marketing is exactly like high energy physics. Well, not really. But you can accelerate your publishing if you look at the content around you and think about combining things and breaking things down...a webinar becomes a podcast...the podcast becomes a blog post... combine the blog post with a newsletter...etc.

Create an inventory to see what you have. Group your content into topics and elements. See if anything is missing or if anything can be atomized quickly.

Be a web marketing scientist, find something to atomize, and make your marketing go boom.

Content Development: How to Write

Yes, video and audio content are wonderful, but we're going to focus on text content here. Writing is absolutely essential in web marketing. You must write to be a content marketer.

"Before you create any more "great content," figure out how you are going to market it first." -Joe Pulizzi & Newt Barrett

Channels

Start by considering where and how the content will be published. You have four main options:

1. Web page
2. Blog post
3. Blog post and newsletter
4. Guest post

Here is a summary of the differences between these channels and how they relate to publishing:

1. **Web Page**: If you don't have a blog, this may be your only option for publishing content. If you do have a blog, this may still be a good choice. If the piece you're writing is focused on a key product or service, or if it contains critical information for anyone making a purchasing decision, it probably should be an actual web page on your site rather than a post within the blog.

   Although web pages should be informative and useful to readers, they are typically more marketing focused. Here's where you're selling as much as teaching.

2. **Blog Post**: These are similar to web pages, but are date stamped and associated with an author. The tone may be more informal. If your website is a newspaper, the blog is where Op-Ed pieces will go. They should be useful and informative, not salesy or marketing-focused. Here's where you're teaching, more than selling.

   Unlike web pages, blog posts should have a conversational tone that invites comments. Great blog posts are the starting point for a conversation that continues in the comments beneath.

 NOTE!

Although web pages and blog posts are listed separately, the blog should be embedded in a website within the same domain. The ideal place for a blog is www.website.com/blog. Hosting a blog using a subdomain is also good, such as blog.website.com. I do not recommend blogging on a separate domain such as myblog.blogspot.com since your website will not get a link popularity (search marketing) benefit from any inbound links to your blog posts.

are promoted using email marketing. These should contain your best content and be on a topic that your subscribers find interesting. Newsletters should include an excerpt from the article or a short summary, and then link to the full text on your website with a compelling call to action. This will allow you to measure clickthrough rates, solicit comments, encourage sharing and convert subscribers into leads and customers.

4. **Guest Post / External Website**: Same as any blog post, but published on a website other than your own. Guests posts may not be as tightly focused on your usual topics. If you write something that you find interesting but your typical visitors may not, consider finding a home for it on another site. Guest blogging is a powerful link building tactic that will be discussed in more detail in Chapter 5.

At Orbit, one of our clients launched a site and simultaneously hired a PR firm to promote it. Rather than write an original press release, the PR firm simply copied the text from the website homepage and submitted it to the online newswires. Within minutes, there were more than 1,000 instances of that home page content on the web.

Google flagged this as likely spam and

blacklisted the domain. Suddenly, the website disappeared from search results, even for searches for the business name. Imagine not ranking for the name of your business. Devastating.

The client blamed Orbit and, although we hadn't caused the problem, we were able to repair it by filing a reconsideration request that explained what happened. The Google web spam team manually removed the domain from the blacklist.

To avoid a possible duplicate content penalty, be sure that all of the content on your website is original.

How original is original? The threshold for "original" is likely around 25%. In other words, no web pages or posts on your site should be more than 25% the same as other pages and posts on the web or you may risk a penalty. If you are ever tempted to summarize another post on your site (or write a summary of one of your posts when guest blogging) don't use an excerpt of more than one fourth of the original article.

Keyphrase Research

Believe it or not, I research keyphrases before writing almost anything. Since it's not difficult or time consuming, it's foolish not to align your content with a keyphrase people are searching for. Rather than simply writing content on a topic you find interesting, you can write content on a topic you find interesting and people are looking for.

Investigating keyphrases is like reading the minds of millions of people. It may sound strange, but I look up the popularity of words and phrases almost every day. It's truly amazing the things you can learn within minutes:

- You'll find out what people really call your products or services, helping you to avoid using jargon and to talk about your business using top-of-mind phrases for your audience.

- You'll discover which related services and products people are looking for, helping you to consider expanding your offerings (or at least your content).

- You'll know where people are looking for your services and products, helping you to understand where the demand is and whether you should expand or adapt.

With two minutes of research, I can tell which cities in the U.S. have the most people looking for Botox treatments. I can tell you what questions people have about tree trimming. I can tell which times of year people are looking for math tutors. I can tell you whether interest in vegetarian dog treats is increasing or decreasing. I've seen clients decide to add new products and open stores in new locations based on this research.

As a content marketer, the two primary uses for keyphrase research are to find phrases to include in your content and to get ideas for new content. By doing keyphrase research, you'll create content that is more friendly for search engines and more relevant to your audience.

The ideal keyphrases are those that meet three criteria: Many people are searching for them (high search volume), the website has a realistic chance of ranking relative to other sites (low competition) and the page that would rank is relevant to your business.

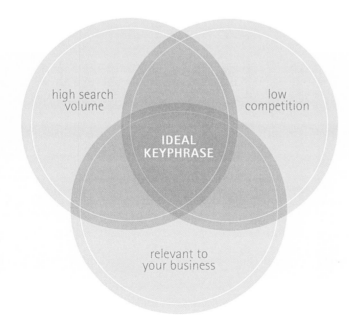

Let's look at the specific tools and actions that uncover the keyphrases that meet all three criteria.

How to Research Keyphrases

Although there are many tools that show how popular various keyphrases are, I recommend the Google tools because they have the most data. The two tools we'll use here are Google AdWords Keyword Tool and Google Trends. They're very different but they compliment each other. Let's compare.

- **Google AdWords Keyword Tool**
  Suggests many phrases and shows estimated numbers for monthly search volume (how many people are searching for the phrase) in the U.S. and around the world.

- **Google Trends**
  Shows trending for specific phrases over time. Allows comparison of phrases and also suggests a few phrases.

The Keyword Tool is your bread and butter for research, but Google Trends is a great compliment.

Google AdWords Keyword Tool

Here's where we narrow down a universe of possible phrases to the one or two you'll eventually focus on. The goal is to disqualify the phrases with too few searches (the invisible) or too much competition (the impossible).

1. Start Wide

Enter several possible phrases into the box at the top of the page and click Search. Here's an example of the results for the phrase "HVAC repair."

At the top of the list, you'll see the specific phrase you entered, along with the average number of monthly searches over the last year. This is the "search volume." These are listed in two columns: Global (everywhere) and Local (your country, which is indicated at the top of the page). For most businesses, the local column is the one that matters most.

	GOOGLE KEYWORD TOOL	GOOGLE INSIGHTS
suggested phrases	up to 100	10
search volume displayed as	specific numbers (estimates)	trending (line graph)
geography	U.S. (local) and world (global)	countries, states, metro areas

 **NOTE!**

This tool is known to leave out some data in the suggested keyphrases, so if you have a good feeling about a phrase, enter it manually if you don't see it suggested.

Keyword	Competition	Global Monthly Searches ?	Local Monthly Searches ?
hvac repair ▾	High	40,500	40,500

| ✓ Save all **Keyword ideas (100)** | | 1 - 50 of 100 ▾ | ‹ › |

Keyword	Competition	Global Monthly Searches ?	Local Monthly Searches ?
hvac repair atlanta ▾	High	480	390
hvac repair chicago ▾	High	590	480
hvac repair costs ▾	High	590	590
hvac repairs ▾	High	2,900	2,400
hvac ▾	High	1,830,000	1,220,000
service experts ▾	Medium	40,500	27,100
heating and air ▾	High	823,000	673,000
air conditioning units ▾	High	673,000	550,000

As you review the wide range of related phrases, you're looking for two things: Phrases that more specifically relate to your topic and completely new phrases that have a similar meaning, especially those with high search volume. Add these to your original list.

2. Narrow In

As you try more phrases and find some you like, try checking the box labeled "Only show ideas closely related to my search terms" at the top of the page, then click Search again. This narrows the results to help you focus on more specific phrases.

So far, you've been reviewing the search volume for the "broad" use of each phrase. This includes related keyphrases due to synonyms and related grammatical forms. When you get close to a few

phrases you like, select "[Exact]" in the Match Types box. Now you're seeing the search volume for the specific phrase, just as if it was typed into Google.

▾ Match Types ⑦
- ☑ Broad
- ☐ [Exact]
- ☐ "Phrase"

If you are researching many phrases or collaborating with others, it may help to download the possible phrases from the Keyword Tool into a spreadsheet. But for most blog posts and articles, this research can be done quickly.

⚠ CAUTION!

The "competition" column on this list is not competition within the organic Google search results, but rather competition within Google AdWords. That's because this tool was originally intended to be a tool for AdWords advertisers. In many cases, keyphrases listed as "Low" may have little competition in AdWords Pay-Per-Click advertising, but are actually highly competitive and would be difficult to rank for in organic SEO.

How many searches are enough?

For most businesses, it's ideal if the main keyphrase for your site has thousands of searches per month. The home page should be optimized for this phrase. Interior pages, such as product and service pages, should be optimized for more specific phrases. Those phrases may have hundreds of searches per month. Search volume for a blog post's target keyphrase may be even lower, with fewer than 100 searches per month.

For businesses where the value of a potential transaction is high, such as a B2B service company, it may be useful to target very specific phrases with very few searches. If only 30 people search for a phrase each month, that's still a potential visitor every day. Long, very specific search phrases, such as entire questions, are referred to as "long tail" keyphrases.

These phrases may have little, if any, competition. If you target a long tail phrase with six or seven words, it's possible that you'll have the only page on the Internet with that combination of those words together in that order. You may rank high within days of posting the content and the visitors may be highly targeted. A few hours of content marketing today may lead to a steady trickle of traffic and a handful of qualified leads for years to come.

Secondary Keyphrases

It's unlikely that a single page will rank high for many phrases, especially a blog post. For this reason, it's best to target one keyphrase. You may have success targeting more than one phrase, if the phrases have words in common. This is easier if the phrases share the first word or two, rather than the last. If the primary and secondary keyphrases are completely dissimilar, the page is less likely to rank for both.

3. Check Competition

Now that you have a few phrases you think you like, let's see how competitive they are.

The only way to really gauge the competition for a given phrase is to search for it. As you do this, keep in mind that search results are personalized for you and may not be similar to what someone else sees. Here are three tips get a better sense for what "typical" search results might be for a given phrase when you're checking competition in Google:

1. Make sure you're logged out of Google+.

2. Set the location to the location for your target audience. Leave it set for your city if your audience is local. Set it to "United States" for a national audience.

3. If you're really skepical of the search results you're seeing, visit www.google.com/adpreview to search Google with fewer of the signals that are specific to you and your computer.

Search Results May Vary

Now you should be looking at a search engine results page (or "SERP" as the SEOs like to say). The last few years have brought much more diversity in the types of content in search results, so there's a good chance you're seeing images, news, video, local listings and, of course, ads. All of these are in addition to the usual organic listings. They are called "blended" or "universal" search results.

> For most businesses, it's ideal if the main keyphrase for your site has thousands of searches per month. The home page should be optimized for this phrase. Interior pages, such as product and service pages, should be optimized for more specific phrases.

⚠ CAUTION!

Searching for some phrases will return local search results. If there's a map in the top right corner and the search results page is dominated by a group of local listings (usually in a group of seven or three), the usual search engine optimization efforts aren't going to be enough. You'll need to do Local SEO, which is not based on content marketing.

Your local listing in Google is a Google+ Local page. To improve the ranking of this page in the local listings, make sure that your business information is up to date on all of the Internet Yellow Pages websites (IYPs) and anywhere else where you have a business listing. Sites that show your business name and address are called "citations." Submit your business to IYPs and directories to create more citations and improve the rank of your Google+ Local page. Consider everything from Yelp and Merchant Circle to local directory sites and chambers of commerce. Positive reviews may also affect the rank of a Google+ Local page.

Here are some criteria for determining whether a phrase is competitive:

- There are 10 pay-per-click ads on the page, three at the top and seven down the side. This means others have already determined the keyphrase is valuable.

- There are tens of millions of results. This means there are many pages on the web that are relevant for this phrase.

- The top ranking sites have the target keyphrase at the beginning of the link. This means those sites have the keyphrases at the beginning of their page titles, which indicates the owners of these sites know a bit of SEO.

- The top ranking sites are popular, well-known sites. Unless you invent a time machine, you're not going to outrank Wikipedia. If the top three or five sites are trusted, reputable websites, they'll have loads of link popularity and therefore powerful domains. You're not likely to compete without focusing serious time and resources. More information on how to estimate the authority of a domain in Chapter 5: Guest Blogging.

Relevance

It should go without saying that there is a third criteria for choosing keyphrases: Relevance. It's pointless to target a phrase that is completely irrelevant to your business.

The ideal phrase is highly relevant to a problem your business solves for people. This phrase brings them to content that teaches something about the problem or solution. The more relevant the

phrase and valuable the content, the higher the conversion rate from these visitors will be.

But phrases and content that are only indirectly related to your business can also drive traffic and eventually leads. It just has to be useful to the visitor and somehow related to what you offer.

- Bad indirect targeting: Real estate company targets the name of a nearby college.

- Good indirect targeting: Real estate company targets phrase with the community name and education-related phrases.

Even "low quality" visitors can be valuable. They may share your content, subscribe to your newsletter, follow you on Twitter, comment on a post or link to you from their blog. Every visit is a chance for something good to happen.

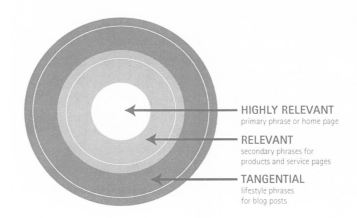

HIGHLY RELEVANT
primary phrase or home page

RELEVANT
secondary phrases for
products and service pages

TANGENTIAL
lifestyle phrases
for blog posts

Case Study: Graphic Design vs. Web Design

In June 2010, Nick Haas, Orbit's web design team leader, had an idea for an article. He wanted to describe the difference between traditional graphic design and the kind of web design done at Orbit.

Rather than simply write a great blog post, we took a few minutes to do the research using the Keyword Tool. We discovered that the phrase "graphic design vs. web design" is searched 58 times per month.

When checking competition in Google, there didn't seem to be any popular domains ranking high. The sites that were ranking didn't seem to be well optimized (i.e., they didn't have the phrase at the beginning of their title). It seemed we had found a very specific phrase with relatively low search volume but with very low competition. Bingo.

So Nick wrote the article with the phrase in mind. The article is just as informative and well written as it would have been without this research, but now it was destined to rank. For details on exactly how to include the phrase on the page in the appropriate places, see the Article Checklist section later in this chapter.

Nick's article, Graphic Design vs. Web Design: Separate And Not Equal, went live on June 22, 2010. In less than a week, it was ranking like a champion. It's been in the first or second position for that phrase ever since. For the first few months, it was visited once or twice a day. Then a few sites began linking to it and traffic increased. When a high profile blog linked to it, it jumped again.

Since the post went live, it's been visited more than 3,100 times. Recently, it has received 6-7 visits per day, and 25% of that traffic comes from social sharing and referring sites.

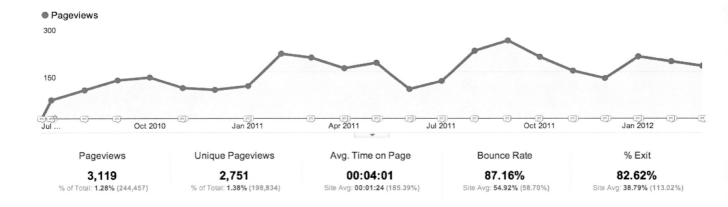

A bit of keyphrase research goes a long way.

 NOTE!

The boost in link popularity to this individual blog post benefits the trust and authority of the entire orbitmedia.com domain, and potentially helps the rank of all the pages on the site.

Google Trends

When you have a sense of what phrases you plan to target, take a minute to validate those phrases using Google Trends. Here is an example of the two main ways to use it.

Suppose you're a web design company (just imagine!) and you're creating a page about a new service for marketing your clients' websites. But should you call it web marketing, digital marketing or internet marketing?

1. Visit Google Trends.

2. Enter those three phrases.

3. Choose "United States" as a filter.

4. Click "search."

Here's what you'll see...

Keyphrase Trending: Ohh! Charts!

Yellow line: "internet marketing"

Red line: "digital marketing"

Blue line: "web marketing"

Although "internet marketing" is the more popular phrase, you can see that sometime during the summer of 2011, "digital marketing" became a more popular phrase than "web marketing." Had you researched these phrases in early 2011 using only the Google Keyword Tool, you may have concluded that "web marketing" is a better phrase than "digital marketing." Not so today!

Seeing this trend, especially with the forecast, it's clear which of the two is the more popular phrase. I have often been surprised by keyphrase trending.

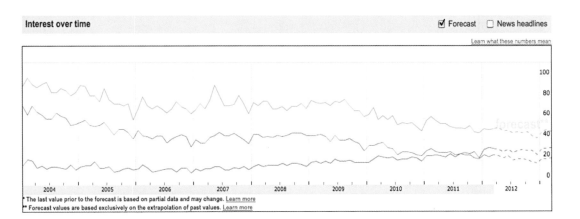

Interest over time — ☑ Forecast ☐ News headlines

* The last value prior to the forecast is based on partial data and may change. Learn more
** Forecast values are based exclusively on the extrapolation of past values. Learn more

TIP!

Seasonality. Since the data goes back to 2004, you can see seasonal trends for various phrases. You'll notice that most phrases have seasonality. With some phrases, it's dramatic.

Geographic Differences: Nice maps!

- **"Web Marketing"**
  "Web Marketing" search popularity across
  the U.S.: Search volume is distributed
  relatively evenly.

- "Digital Marketing"
  "Digital Marketing" search popularity
  across the U.S.: Mostly in states with major
  metropolises.

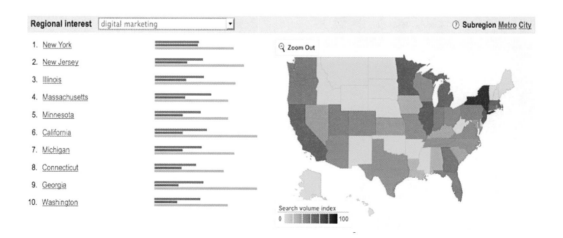

- "Internet Marketing"
  "Internet Marketing" search popularity across the U.S.: Usage of this keyphrase is much stronger in Florida and Nevada than in other states.

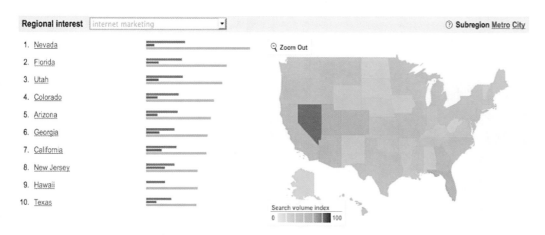

Conclusion? Start an internet marketing company in Nevada.

I'm kidding. Going back to the page you're planning to write, consider using the target keyphrase "internet marketing." But if the phrase is too competitive, or if you're looking for a secondary phrase, target "digital marketing." Adjust based on your state or metro area.

You may not have time to check all your target phrases this way, but always check your main phrases. Should you check a keyphrase for a blog post? Maybe not. But a phrase for your home page, services pages, or product pages? Absolutely!

- Target phrases that are trending up whenever possible.
- Target phrases that are popular in your region whenever possible.

Now that you're an expert at keyphrase research, it's time to learn how to incorporate target phrases into your content.

Article checklist

Before you click the publish button, make sure you've included these properties and that you're doing them all in the right way. Incorporating them into your content will make the next step, content promotion, far easier and more effective.

ASPECT	PROPERTIES
Title	☑ Includes the target keyphrase once, at the beginning of the title if possible. ☑ Max 66 characters
Meta Description	☑ Includes the target keyphrase ☑ Max 155 characters
Keyphrase Usage	☑ Keyphrase used four to six times in the article
Formatting	☑ Headers and subheads ☑ Short paragraphs ☑ Bullet lists
Links	☑ Link to product or service page ☑ Links to related Posts or Pages
Images	☑ Minimum one image (copyright and possibly attribution)
Mention	☑ Mentions: Experts and/or someone active on social media (optional)
Call to Action	☑ Invites reader to comment, subscribe, etc.
Length	☑ 400 - 600 words for Articles, Posts and Pages
Author Box	☑ Several sentences about the author's relevance ☑ Link to full on-site bio or Google+ Profile (see Google Authorship below) ☑ Link to Twitter and LinkedIn accounts

Title

It's the text at the top of the browser, above the address bar, for any web page. Depending on your browser, it may also be in the tab. In the code, it's whatever text is inside the <title> tags. It is very important.

The title becomes the link when the page or post ranks in search engines. If it's too long, it gets truncated. 66 characters is the limit. Be brief.

Titles are strong indicators to search engines what the page is about, so use your target keyphrase, use it once, and if possible, use it at the beginning of the title. The prominence of the keyphrase (in other words, how close it appears to the beginning) is very important.

It might be tempting to put your business name at the front of the title. Don't. Search engine marketers have a saying: "brand last." Start with your keyphrase, end with your business name. Remember, your first goal is to help people. Promoting yourself comes second.

Meta Description

Although Meta Keywords are almost totally useless, the Meta Description remains important. It doesn't appear in the content of the page, but it is highly visible in search results. Below each link in a search results page is a "snippet" of text. In Google this snippet is either an excerpt from the body text or, more often, the meta description. So make it good.

Write it as a single-sentence, plain English summary of the content. Don't just use the title or headline. Use your target keyphrase at least once, but not more than twice. Limit the number of characters to 155 to be sure the description will fit within the snippet.

Chicago Ecommerce Web Site Design & Development | Orbit Media ⬅— **Link**: title of the page
www.orbitmedia.com/**ecommerce-web-design-pages-47**.php
Orbit creates **E-commerce** sites that are visually striking, easy to navigate and ⬅— **Snippet**: meta description of the page
designed with SEO best practices in mind to help your online business thrive.　　　　　　　　　　　　(or occasionally, a page excerpt)

 NOTE!

Rich Snippets: Big changes in Google are leading to much more interesting snippets. You might have already noticed movie times, product reviews and author information appearing as snippets. These are called "rich snippets" and are possible when specific tags are added to page elements. They may include reviews when product pages rank, ingredients when recipe pages rank and movie times when your local theater ranks. Google is gradually adding all kinds of information to search results pages.

To see how to have your picture appear in search results as a rich snippet, see the Google Authorship section below.

Keyphase Usage

We recommend including the target keyphrase in the body of the article at least twice, but not more than five times. In each instance, all the words in the phrase should appear together as a "bonded" phrase. This should come naturally if the phrase is relevant to the topic. During editing, go back to make sure it's used but not overused.

Formatting

People tend not to read online; we tend to scan. Content marketers must accept this and adapt by adding formatting to their content. Big, blocky, dense paragraphs are less likely to be read. Content with more formatting is more likely to engage the reader.

- **Headers and subheads**: Breaking up the article into short sections makes it much more accessible to busy readers. Each section should begin with a header that serves as a mini headline for the paragraphs that follow.

- **Short paragraphs**: Generally no paragraph should include more than three or four sentences. Very short paragraphs of one sentence or even one word can be used to add emphasis.

- **Bullet lists and numbered lists**: These are very easy to scan and work well within almost any post. Some very successful posts are nothing more than lists. Some blogs, such as 12most.com, are based entirely on list formatted content.

- **Bold and italics**: Excellent ways to add emphasis and make content more easily scanned, but don't overdo it.

Formatting is good for search engines as well as humans. If you leave out the formatting, you miss opportunities to use your keyphrase in more ways. Subheaders and bullet lists are opportunities to use words from a target phrase and indicate relevance a bit more.

TIP!

It's likely that punctuation is dropped in Google, so if you're having trouble incorporating the phrase, consider ending one sentence with the beginning of the phrase, and beginning the next sentence with the end of the phrase. For example, if you're targeting "Tampa telephone repair," the following sentences include one instance of the phrase: We're located in north Tampa. Telephone repair services include dial tone tuning and button replacement.

CAUTION!

Don't overdo it on the keyphrase usage. If you compromise your writing to the extent that it makes no sense to your human reader, you're probably guilty of "keyword stuffing." Using the phrase over and over in unnatural ways is both terrible for your readers and bad for search engine optimization. Google can see right through this and there's a chance you'll be penalized. So don't do it!

Links

Your goal as a content marketer is to eventually convert visitors into leads and customers. As Barry Feldman put it, "Your site is the mousetrap, your content is the cheese." If you don't help make those connections between the cheese and the trap, you catch fewer mice.

Look for opportunities within articles to link to web pages about your products and services, and to other content. Doing so creates a benefit for conversions and a visible impact on the "average pages per visit" metric in Analytics.

There is also an SEO benefit to this. Internal linking is an easy opportunity to use keyphrases within the link text. When linking to other content, use the target keyphrase in the links. Although these links have far less importance on rank than links from other websites, they are still helpful in indicating relevance to search engines.

Example: Consider which of the two following links does a better job of indicating relevance:

1. Learn more about hedgehog shampoo.
2. Click here to learn more about hedgehog shampoo.

The first example tells the search engines what's behind the click and what the subsequent page is about. The second example does not.

Images

Posts with images are more interesting to look at and more likely to be shared. Some posts are dominated by images. A post called "10 Great Uses of Typography on Home Pages" may consist mostly of screenshots. These types of posts are often very successful in social media.

Infographics are another great example. They are nothing more than a giant image with little or no text surrounding the image on the page. And they frequently go viral. Infographics are typically highly visual representations of data and statistics, but often they are simply cleverly reformatted lists.

The following infographic is a list of the relative effectiveness of various SEO link building strategies, formatted to look like a popular board game. Brilliant!

TIP!

Every few months, go back and look at older posts. Try to find opportunities to add links to your more recent content and vice versa.

Adding images to posts is also important because when content is shared in social networks, an image from the page is generally pulled in and appears within the post. This makes the content more prominent in that social stream. Shared posts without images are not as prominent and have a visual disadvantage.

"Data shows that posts with images get more views, shares, and time on page. There's something about making content visually interesting that gets people to bounce less."

-Shane Snow, Co-Founder, Contently

Some sites have a policy of never publishing a post without at least one image. If you guest post on these sites, they may reject your post unless you add an image, or they may add images for you. They may use a lot of bad stock photos and it might not be pretty. Plan ahead and find an image at a site like http://www.istockphoto.com/ or http://www.flickr.com/creativecommons/.

Mentions

Don't hesitate to mention other people within your content. Input from experts adds credibility and makes your content more interesting. For promotional reasons, it can be effective to deliberately mention those who are active in social media. They may share your content once it's posted.

Some content was made to be shared. Here are some examples:

- Event Recap: Short event summary that mentions attendees and presenters.
- Ask the Experts: Send a few questions to five or more experts.
- Response Articles: Refer to something recently published. Act quickly to make it part of the conversation.

In each case, the article is likely to be shared by the people you mentioned. It's useful to mention those who have social followings.

Call to Action

Now that you have provided friendly, helpful advice to your readers, it's time to ask for a little bit in return. Every great post has a call to action that invites the visitor to become more engaged with your content or your business.

For Blog Posts, the call to action might simply be an invitation to leave a comment. Ask a question that the reader can answer with a comment, solicit other ideas that would complement the suggestions made in the post or even invite the reader to disagree with you.

Beyond comments, a call to action may be a one sentence pitch to subscribe to the newsletter. If the content was truly useful, the moment they finish reading the post is the high point of their appreciation and the most likely time for readers to subscribe.

For web pages, a call to action may be a link directing visitors to read more on another page. Or best of all, it's an offer to start a conversation. The call to action could be a polite invitation to fill out a short form...and become a lead.

TIP!

Calls to action should use the same compelling language that you use while authoring subject lines, headers, Tweets and anything else that you want a reader to act on. "Contact Us" is not a call to action. "Ask Andy for more advice on web marketing" is.

Length

If you write a very long article, you might get a comment that says "TLDR" (too long, didn't read)...if they leave a comment at all.

There's a time and place for epic 2,500 word blog posts, but don't do it too often. Generally, work within the length recommendations on the Periodic Table of Content. Make an exception when you're truly inspired to write something longer and it's not practical to break it into two parts. Also, if your standard length is longer and your readers expect and enjoy the format, keep it up!

Author Box

Some blog software makes creating an author box very easy. Easy or difficult, it's worth the effort, since it has social, search and conversion benefits. The ideal author box includes the following:

- Profile picture
- Brief biography (no more than a few sentences)
- Link to bio and/or link to Google+ profile, with rel=author code (see Google Authorship below)
- Link to Twitter and LinkedIn profiles

TIP!

Create a semi-standard HTML code for your author box. This will make it easy to add to posts on your site or share with other sites when you're guest blogging. Here is one that I often use:

Andy Crestodina is a 12-year veteran in web marketing and the strategic director of Orbit Media, a <a href="http://www.orbitmedia.com">Chicago web development firm</a>where he collaborates on content marketing with anyone who is interested. You can find Andy on <a title="Author: Andy Crestodina on Google+" rel="author" href="https://plus.google.com/113272929328812128697?rel=author" target="_blank">Google+</a> and <a title="Andy Crestodina on Twitter" href="http://www.twitter.com/crestodina" target="_blank">Twitter</a>.

This is how it might look on a web page:

Andy Crestodina is a 12-year veteran in web marketing and the strategic director of Orbit Media, a Chicago web development firm where he collaborates on content marketing with anyone who is interested. You can find Andy on Google+ and Twitter.

Google Authorship:
How to Get Your Picture in
Google Search Results

Ever wonder why some people's faces are showing up in search results? How do they do that?

They do it by adding a bit of code to a link in their author box. It's the rel="author" code mentioned above and it's added to the Google+ link. It allows Google to create a "rich snippet" in the search results page whenever that page ranks.

Stands out, doesn't it? It is more prominent and more credible. It's all possible through the magic of Google authorship and the rel=author tag.

If the value of this isn't obvious, consider this: According to one study on the impact of rich snippets on traffic, **the number of clicks increased by 150% once the rich snippet was added**. This is one of those opportunities to give yourself a significant advantage in Google.

rich snippet!

SEO Zombie Hunt | Search Engine People | Toronto
www.searchenginepeople.com/blog/**seo-zombie**-hunt.html

 by Andy Crestodina · in 2,102 Google+ circles · More by Andy Crestodina
The dead are out there, lurking in your site, your links and your keywords. Get out there into the woods and hunt the **zombies** that wander through your **SEO**.

normal, boring snippet...

Seo Zombie | Adsense - Make Money Online
www.adsensemakemoneyonline.com/tag/**seo-zombie**/
Jun 21, 2009 – Justin over at **SEO Zombie** designs wordpress themes which he happens to be damn good at and when I was looking for a theme for this site a ...

 TIP!

Even if you're not active in Google+, Google Authorship will still work, but you do have to set up your Google+ profile. At the very least, take 15 minutes to go through the Google+ Jumpstart Guide.

Step One: Verify your email address on Google+

Google wants to know that your account is legit. Make sure you're using an email address with the same domain as the domain of your blog.

According to Google, as long as you're posting on that domain, and the posts have the same byline as the name on your G+ account, this is enough to make the connection. But don't hold your breath...

Step Two: Link from your Google+ profile to your content

On the right side of the "About" page of your Google+ profile, there is a place to add "Contributor to" links. Link to your content from here.

- If you have a bio page on your blog, link to this bio.

- If you don't have a bio page, link directly to the post itself.

Step Three: Link from your content to your Google+ profile

From the byline or author box at the bottom of your post, link to your Google+ profile, adding "rel=author" in the link.

- If you have a bio page on your site, link to the bio with "rel=me" in the link.

- If you don't have a bio page on your site (or if you're having trouble getting authorship to work), link directly to your Google+ profile with "rel=author" in the link. See the sample code at right.

Work Phone   773.353.8301
      Email   andy@orbitmedia.com ✓ ← **STEP 1:** Verify email

Contributor to ← Bio on Orbit site   **STEP 2:** Link to the host blog from here
   Blog: Content Chem
   Blog: Plagiarism
   Blog: Profile Pics
   Search Engine People
   Entrepreneurs Unpluggd
   SpinSucks.com
   Straight North
   Kuno Creative
   Crains Chicago Business
   Marketing Profs
   ICIC

Written by Andy Crestodina

Andy Crestodina is the Strategic Director and co-founder of Orbit Media Studios, an award-winning 30-person Chicago web development company. You can find him on Google+ and Twitter. Over the past 12 years, Andy has provided web strategy and advice to more than 1000 businesses. He's kinda like the Bruce Willis of web marketing.
Orbit Media's Blog | ⬛ | ⬛ | ⬛ |

STEP 3: Link to Google+ Profile in the post
`<a rel="author" href="https://plus.google.com/u/0/PROFILE_ID?rel=author">`

TIP!

What about for guest blog posts?

When you guest blog, make sure that you give the host blog the proper HTML with a link to your Google+ profile and rel=author in the link. If the host doesn't add the markup, you don't get the rich snippet.

Then add a link to the guest blog post itself in your Google+ "Contributor to" links. Unfortunately, linking to the homepage of the host site probably won't work. You may end up with a very long list of links as time goes on, but the SEO benefits make it worthwhile.

Troubleshooting

Not working? Try these steps.

1. **Check to make sure you're verified.**
   Put the link to the post into Google's rich snippet testing tool and see how it should display in search engines.

2. **Make the connection more directly.**
   If you were linking from your Google+ profile to a bio on your site, try linking to the specific posts instead. Forget rel=me and go with rel=author.

3. **Add more tags.**
   Add ?rel=author to the end of the destination URL, like so:

Find Andy on <a title="Author: Andy Crestodina on Google+" rel="author" href="https://plus.google.com/113272929328812128697?**rel=auth or**" target="_blank">Google+</a>

There you have it. Search meets social, coming soon to a keyword near you. Now go connect all the content you publish anywhere online, and your smiling face will be there next to it when it ranks.

Sample Article

The following article includes all the properties that make up a good piece of web content. An edited version of this article ran as a guest post on Marketing Profs on April 12, 2012.

This is a good web marketing article: 7 reasons

Rather than just describing best practices for a web marketing article, let's wrap them all together in a self-referential post. It's so meta! Here are the seven reasons why this is a good web marketing article.

1. This article is optimized for search engines.

Before I started writing, I looked at Google Keyword Tool and discovered that 320 people search for "web marketing article" each month. So I decided to do a little SEO copywriting and included the phrase once in the title, once in the URL, and six times in the body of the article itself.

It's kind of a competitive phrase, but why not give it a shot? It doesn't take long. So this article is search optimized.

2. This article has an image.

Articles with images are more likely to be shared, so I'm putting in an image. Here it is:

Dr David Jefferies, Guildford, Surrey UK

This article is about itself. So is this image...
and this sentence.

Articles with images look good, partly because when they're shared in social networks (Facebook, Google+, LinkedIn, etc.) a thumbnail of the image appears.

3. This article mentions other people and blogs.

If you mention people in your posts, you might get their attention, and they just might share it through their networks. Copyblogger actually gives three reasons for this: credibility, promotion and networking.

Simply put, one of the fastest ways to grow a new blog is to mention other sites with big audiences in your guest post appearances.

If you drop a handy email or Tweet before the guest post goes live, you can harness the sheer awesomeness of their contact lists. Most of the time they will at least Tweet out your guest post and thus associate themselves with your content.

So mention a big blog and let them know about the post...just like that!

4. This article has lots of formatting.

A web marketing article should have plenty of formatting, making it scannable for visitors. Formatting makes articles much easier for visitors to read and a bit easier for search engines to rank. This article uses:

- Headers and subheaders
- Short paragraphs (no paragraph is longer than three sentences)
- Bullet lists, like this one

5. This article links to another page or post.

A good web marketer always looks for opportunities for internal linking. These links are an important part of *web strategy*. This is a good web marketing article, partly because of the link. The link is good for two reasons:

- It tells Google that the page you're linking to is relevant for the phrase within the link.

- It guides visitors from one page to the next through a "conversion funnel." Links pull visitors deeper into the site, toward the contact form, where they may become a lead.

6. This article doesn't take itself too seriously.

If it did, it wouldn't have been much fun to write and it probably would be no fun to read. This is web marketing, not a bone marrow transplant.

7. This article has a call to action for comments.

Here goes: If you can think of anything that would make this a great web marketing article, I would love to hear suggestions. Feel free to leave a comment below. I'm always learning and interested in any feedback.

Andy Crestodina is the strategic director of Orbit Media, a web development company in Chicago. You can find Andy on Google+ and Twitter.

Content Quality

Content chemistry is a science, but don't forget the art. If your writing is boring, salesy or irrelevant, no amount of chemistry will help. All the usual rules apply. Know your audience. Do your research. Tell a story. Find your voice.

These are all critically important, but they are not our focus here. Still, I can share with you a general structure and approach for writing, after the planning and research are complete. We're going to reconstruct a popular post from the Orbit Media Blog called Your Brand is Your Blog, Your Blog is Your Brand, originally written by our very own Mary Fran Wiley.

1. **Write the "takeaway," a single sentence summary.**
    First, Mary Fran determined the overall point of her post:

    You have to identify the voice of your brand; you need to figure out who the voice behind the blog is and to whom it is speaking.

2. **Write the outline and headers.**
   Then Mary Fran laid out the main points she wanted to make, in the order she wanted to make them:

   Your Brand is Your Blog,
   Your Blog is Your Brand

   1. Start by carving your niche.

   2. Embrace your personality
   (or your brand's personality).

   3 Go ahead, get out there and shine!

3. **Fill in the blanks with short, rough paragraphs.**
   Next, she added bullet points under the main points, then went back and added a sentence or two to explain each bullet point:

   Your Brand is Your Blog,
   Your Blog is Your Brand

   1. Start by carving your niche.
   Be different.
   Be awesome at just one thing.
   Always be improving.

   2. Embrace your personality
   (or your brand's personality).
   Put yourself out there.
   Share your opinions and views.
   Be consistent.

   3. Go ahead, get out there and shine!
   Join the conversation.
   Connect with people.
   Be humble.

4. **Edit, refine and polish.**
   And finally, Mary Fran spent some time editing and revising the post before asking a few colleagues to proofread it for her before it was published.

   See Mary Fran's completed post on the Orbit Media Blog: Your Brand Is Your Blog, Your Blog Is Your Brand.

Content Criteria: don't publish unless you meet one of these 3 criteria.

I read a lot of blogs - some good, some bad. A few weeks ago, I read something by Bill Sebald that stuck with me. He said:

> *I urge you to start writing content that actually is either 1) actionable, 2) a strong opinion, or 3) proven to some degree.*

These are great blog criteria. Basically, if it's not useful, if it's a weak opinion, or if it makes unsupported claims, it's probably not good. This makes sense.

Then I came across something in a book called *Elements of Content Strategy* by Erin Kissane. Erin explains how good content works by relating to the context of the reader. There are three elements: physical (doing), emotional (feeling), and cognitive (learning).

Sound familiar? The three blogging criteria recommended by Sebald align perfectly with the user contexts described by Kissane.

- **Actionable = Physical**
- **Proven = Cognitive**
- **Strong Opinion = Emotional**

Unless the post connects on one of these levels, it probably isn't worth the reader's time (and they're certainly not going to share it). We all need to make sure that our content meets one or more of these three criteria:

1. **The reader can DO something.**
   It's practical. There are steps they can take. Actionable posts lend themselves to list formats, which makes a post more scannable and reader-friendly.

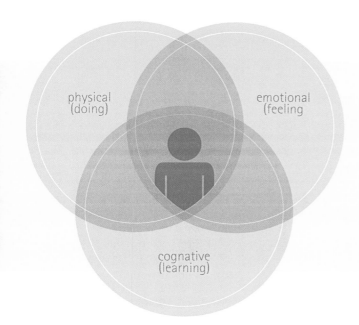

physical
(doing)

emotional
(feeling

cognative
(learning)

2. The reader LEARNS something.
If you want to teach something, you need supporting evidence. Facts, research, and expert input make your assertions more believable.

3. The reader FEELS something.
You felt something while you wrote it. It's your voice and your opinion. It means something to you, good or bad. If you don't care, why would your readers?

If your content doesn't meet at least one of these criteria for writing, try one of these tips:

Give instructions: The step-by-step instructions (such as this one), a list of action items, or 'How to' posts are extremely popular for a good reason: the goal is to help the reader.

Add examples: If you make assertions but don't give examples, you may be making unsupported claims. This is why Harvard Business School focuses on case studies. Without proof, it's just academic. Add examples, surveys, statistics, quotes, screenshots, and any other supportive content.

"The more informative your advertising, the more persuasive it will be." - David Ogilvy

Add some attitude: Don't hedge your bets. Edit that first draft and take out all those qualifying words. They take the directness and edge out of your writing. During editing you can tweak the tone and strengthen opinions. Do it right and a group of sentences like this:

"In many cases, blog posts are vague and may not be useful to readers. This is often because they do not provide enough actionable advice."

...becomes a sentence like this:

"Vague blog posts aren't useful, since they just aren't actionable for readers."

...or even this:

"If a blog post isn't actionable, it's useless."

A few words about quality...

There are hundreds of books and thousands of blog posts about writing great content. Many of these were written by true masters of the craft. Here are a few quotes from some of the greats. These should give you a bit more insight and maybe even some inspiration.

> *"On the average, five times as many people read the headline as read the body copy. When you have written your headline, you have spent eighty cents out of your dollar."*
> *-David Ogilvy*

> *"Clarity trumps persuasion" -Dr. Flint McGlaughlin*

> *"Make the customer the hero of your story"*
> *-Ann Handley*

"Either write something worth reading or do something worth writing about." -Benjamin Franklin

> *"Stop trying to write. Do more research."*
> *-Robert Bruce*

> *"Copy is never written. Copy is assembled."*
> *-Eugene Schwartz*

> *"Write a crappy first draft." -Brad Farris*

> *"The more informative your advertising, the more persuasive it will be." -David Ogilvy*

> *"Be a person." -Sonia Simone*

> *"The difference between the almost right word & the right word is really a large matter–it's the difference between the lightning bug and the lightning." -Mark Twain*

> *"In this age of microblogging and two-second sound bites, almost no one has the attention span, or time, to read more than a few sentences." -Tim Frick*

> *"Focus on the core problem your business solves and put out lots of content and enthusiasm, and ideas about how to solve that problem." -Laura Fitton*

> *"Authenticity, honesty, and personal voice underlie much of what's successful on the Web." -Rick Levine*

> *"I urge you to start writing content that actually is either 1) actionable, 2) a strong opinion, or 3) proven to some degree." -Bill Sebald*

> *"Remarkable social media content and great sales copy are pretty much the same - plain spoken words designed to focus on the needs of the reader, listener or viewer." -Brian Clark*

> *"Don't bunt. Aim out of the ball park. Aim for the company of immortals." -David Ogilvy*

> *"The secret to prolifically creating excellent content isn't inspiration or brilliance - it's found in structure, planning and research. Start with the audience and the angle"*
> *- Danny Iny*

That last quote is from an excellent post by Danny Iny on Copyblogger: A Fool-Proof Formula for Creating Compelling Content.

4 Promotion

In this chapter, we'll look at specific activities for promoting content. This isn't about the more passive approach of posting search optimized blog posts and then waiting to rank in Google and watching the traffic roll in. This is about taking specific, deliberate action to raise the visibility of your content.

We'll focus on three of the most effective techniques for promoting content:

- Email Marketing
- Social Media
- Guest Blogging

These are the basic activities that professional content marketers use in continuous cycles. Although each could be considered a separate skill, and there are specialized vendors that exclusively focus on one, these techniques are far more effective when used in combination.

If you don't promote your content, you won't get traffic.

Set your expectations for results at the same level as the effort, time and budget you put in.

Email Marketing

In Chapter 2, we looked at the traffic benefits of email marketing. Now let's look in detail at six specific aspects of a successful email marketing campaign:

1. Email Design

When your subscribers open the email, they'll decide within a split second if they want to invest the time to take a look. You need to hook them quickly, and the design of the email is critical. If the email looks like an advertisement with one big flashy graphic, that's generally bad. If the email looks like a page from a book with dense paragraphs and tiny text, that's also bad. You want to give them something in between.

Make a magazine

A few months ago, I was giving a seminar on email marketing. Before it began, I prepped the room by putting a few things on one of the tables: a book, an advertising insert and a magazine.

 TIP!

As a general rule, you should spend half as much time promoting content as you spend creating it. If you spend two hours writing something, you should spent an hour promoting it.

As the seminar began I watched people sit at the table and then casually interact with these materials. A few people glanced past the ad then pushed it out of the way. Someone picked up the book and looked at the cover, only to put it down again. But the magazine? The person sitting nearest to it picked it up, sat back in her chair, and began flipping through the pages.

Why did the magazine have the most pull? Because it was accessible. The images of the magazine pulled her in and invited her to look, then the words held her attention a bit longer. In less than a second, she was paying attention. Her hand moved, she flipped to a page, and she was invested.

The book didn't grab her as fast and looked like a bit more work. The ad may have caught her attention, but she knew what it was and didn't find it very interesting.

Great email marketing does the same thing. It is visual and the content isn't too dense. The content presumably has value and isn't just trying to sell you something. To make your email like a mini-magazine, include the following aspects:

- **Lots of links**
  Research results in Hubspot's Science of Email Marketing show that emails that include more links have a higher clickthrough rate than emails with fewer. Don't be shy about adding links.

- **Images**
  See the Images section of Chapter 4.

- **Compelling teasers**
  Include a short excerpt or summary of the article that gets the reader interested. The link to the full article appears after the teaser text. This link may include a call-to-action such as *Learn the secrets of email marketing* > or may simply say *Read more* >.

Mobile Friendly Emails

Email messages are very likely to be read on mobile devices. Use the following guidelines to make sure your email design is mobile friendly. See the Mobile section in Chapter 3.

- Left-aligned text.

- Readable and navigable even when images are off. If you use graphical buttons, also add text-based links.

- Small file sizes for quick load time. Avoid large, high resolution images.

- Test the email by viewing it on various phones. Don't forget to click the links to check the landing pages, which should also be mobile friendly, if possible.

2. Subject Lines

Competition inside an inbox is fierce and subject lines are critical. They are your hook. If they don't make the recipients curious enough to open your messages, they're not doing their job.

The email subject line is generally the article title, but not always. There is no need to include the target keyphrase since it has nothing to do with SEO. Use whatever will be most compelling to your audience. Be interesting, helpful, emotionally provocative or all three.

REMINDER

See the Inspiration section at the end of this book for a list of writing ideas and headlines, many of which would make excellent subject lines. Also, consider the following tips about specific words and numbers that can impact the results:

Use Words That Improve the Open Rate

The words you choose in your subject line have a direct impact on the percentage of people who open the email. When Hubspot partnered with MailChimp to analyze 9.5 billion emails, they discovered which words are most effective and published the data in a study called "The Science of Email Marketing."

Most Clicked Subject Line Words

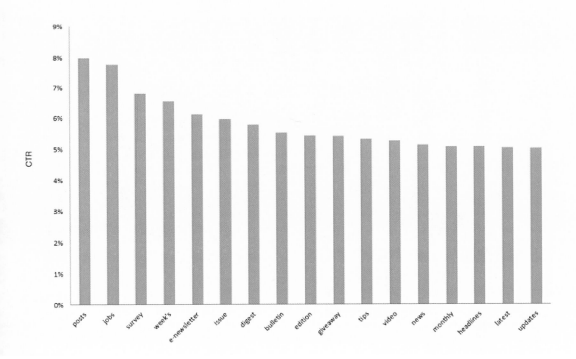

Consider these top-performing words: posts, week's, e-newsletter, digest, bulletin, edition, monthly, latest. They all have something in common: they all indicate that the email is part of a regular series. The recommendation from Dan Zarella, who presented these findings, is to use a subject line that indicates the email is part of a series.

Don't Use Words That Decrease Deliverability

Some words are more likely to be used in spam emails, so spam filters are looking for them. To make sure your emails get through, avoid using these words:

Most Abuse Report Subject Line Words

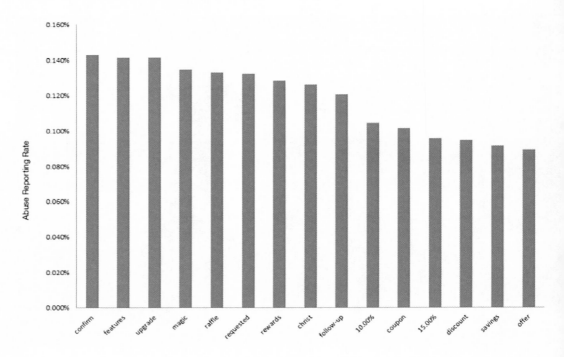

Consider the worst-performing words: raffle, rewards, 10%, coupon, 15%, discount, savings, offer. They all have something in common: They're frequently used in advertising. Emails with these words in the subject line are probably trying to sell you something, rather than inform or help you.

If you're even tempted to use these words in your subject lines, you haven't embraced the central principle of content marketing: To help your business by first helping others through useful content, not advertising.

Odd Numbers

Next time you find yourself in a store checkout aisle, notice the magazine headlines. See any numbers? Magazine publishers and content marketers seem to have a fondness for odd numbers. Perhaps odd numbers are perceived as more credible or scientific.

I'll admit, it's difficult to resist the temptation and I've used this technique many times. I suspect an email called "3 ways to get more 7 step articles in your top 10 lists" would have a nice clickthrough rate.

Odd or even, numerals stand out in lines of text. Using numeric characters can make an email subject line (and its blog post headline) more prominent in the recipient's inbox or Twitter stream.

3. Sender Name

The "sender name" is a huge factor in building trust and increasing open rates. Many marketers forget to check this, but no email recipients forget to look. Along with the subject line, it's all you've got. Use it to build enough trust to earn the click.

If the sender name includes a person's name in addition to the brand, the email is more likely to be opened. For example, an email from "Susan Clark | Zippy Accountants" will have a higher open rate than an email from "Zippy Accountants."

The sender name isn't the same as the "from" address. Don't use "sclark@zippycpa.com" as your sender name. And "Do Not Reply" isn't a friendly name to call yourself.

The sender name is easy to change from within your email service provider. Some even make it easy to test different sender names with an A/B test. Half of your list gets the email with one sender name, the other half receive it with a different sender name. Now you can see how various sender names can affect the open rate.

4. List Growth

The size and quality of your list outstrips all other factors in the success of email marketing efforts. Here are a few basic principles for growing a large and engaged readership. The key is to get permission but be aggressive.

Sales Activity = Subscriber Opportunities

If the sales person was friendly and helpful, and the content is good, the new subscribers will be likely to open and read your emails. Actual prospects are your most valuable subscribers!

Is it ok to add people to your list without asking for their permission?

Yes, but your standards should be very high. Seth Godin once wrote a blog post suggesting that you add anyone to the list who would complain if you didn't add them. For example, our job at Orbit Media is to help our clients with their web marketing. They would be unhappy if we didn't share our latest web marketing techniques with them, so we add our clients to the list.

Properties of a Good Email Signup Form

To succeed in email marketing you need to build a great list. To build a great list, your site needs a good email signup form. This post is about email signup forms and how they affect email subscriptions. This is very important to anyone doing email marketing.

There are four main factors in visitor subscriptions. Coincidentally, they all start with 'p'.

- **Prominence**
  The signup form is highly visible on the page; it's large, uses contrasting colors and appears in several places.

- **Promise**
  There is a description of the benefits to subscribing, what kind of information and how frequently. In other words, "What's in it for me?" (WIIFM)

- **Proof**
  There's evidence that it's legitimate, especially social proof, such as a testimonial or number of subscribers.

- **Privacy**
  Assure the subscriber that they won't receive spam and that you won't share their information with anyone else.

If you're in a business with an active sales team, they should be trained to share relevant content with prospects. If the prospects find it useful, offer to add them to the list. This is a long, slow process, but results in an ever-larger list of email subscribers.

It is illegal and inconsiderate to send unsolicited commercial email if the recipients have no way to unsubscribe. Although "spam" is any unsolicited email and generally a terrible idea, it is only illegal if recipients cannot remove themselves from the list. Make sure that every marketing email you send includes a link that allows the recipient to unsubscribe. These links are typically added automatically by the email service provider.

Here are five examples of email signup forms, good and bad.

Example: Marketing Profs

This form is doing everything right to maximize subscriptions. It's got all four p's.

It's *prominent* on the page. It's both large and a separate color.

The *promise* made is the content "tools and knowledge you need to market smarter."

The *proof* is in the header, "World's Largest Marketing Community." Sounds good!

Even *privacy* is addressed with a small link.

Example: Orbit Media

At Orbit, for years we had a link at the top of the blog that let visitors click to get to a page with a signup box. It looked like this: ⟶

Then one day, we made a change. We let people subscribe without leaving the page. So now the signup form looks like this: ⟶

And here's what happened. Look at the Google Analytics for weekly signups and conversion rates, this year and last year...

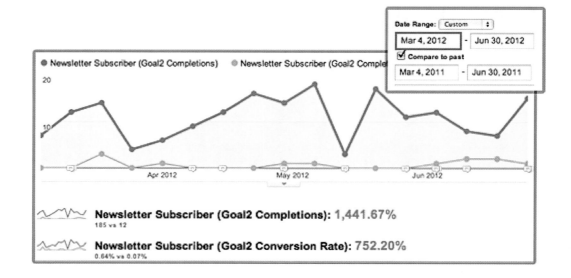

increase in the conversion rate leading to a 1400% increase in subscriptions. Aside from the change to the form, the only change we've made in our marketing is an increase in the frequency of publishing in May and June.

New subscribers from your site is an important metric to track in Analytics and should be set up as a separate goal. This will allow you to test and improve the sign-up form's prominence and call to action.

Stay Connected

For many B2B companies, a relatively small number of high-value connections is better than a large number of low-value connections. If you sell insurance or if you're an attorney, a lead is potentially very valuable and quality is more important than quantity. If you're a B2C company selling t-shirts or chocolate, an individual transaction isn't worth quite as much so quantity is likely more important than quality.

If you're in a B2B business, it's worth taking the time to keep an eye on which emails don't get through. Watch your "bounces." Emails often bounce when people move from one company to another. Every bounced email is an opportunity to keep in touch with people and connect with new businesses.

Find people on LinkedIn to see where they went, then connect with them and ask if they would like to stay subscribed. If so, you can get their new email addresses and re-subscribe them. If the connection with these people was real and they valued your content, they'll happily agree to stay on your list.

TIP!

Once visitors subscribe, they'll arrive at a thank you page and get a confirmation email. Take advantage of these additional touch points by gently inviting them to connect with you through other channels such as Facebook, Twitter, LinkedIn and Google+.

When you get new subscribers, you might want to email them to welcome them to the list. This email will thank them for signing up, give them a idea of what to expect and remind them to keep an eye out for the newsletter. Tell them to "Make sure you add us to your 'whitelist' to keep us out of your spam folder!" These welcome emails can be sent automatically by setting up an auto-responder. Contact your web designer or email service provider for details.

It's easier to maintain connections when you combine social media with email marketing. You may lose touch via email, but LinkedIn, Twitter, Facebook and Google+ connections remain in place.

5. When to Send...and How Often

Timing is everything. Let's look at Hubspot's research on the impact of timing and frequency of email marketing.

Timing

The day of the week makes a difference. Although most businesses wouldn't think of it, the research suggests that sending marketing emails on a weekend is a good thing. Saturdays and Sundays have higher clickthrough rates.

Effect of Day-of-Week on Clickthrough Rate

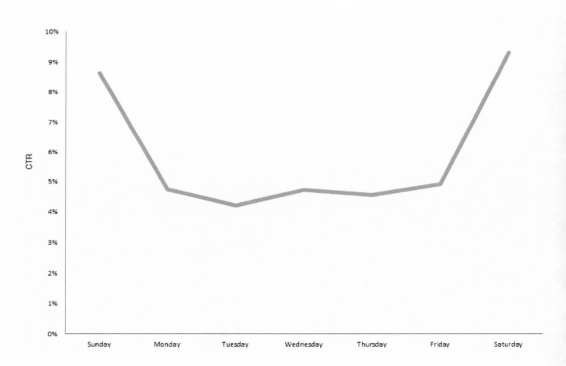

Effect of Day-of-Week on Unsub Rate

Impact on unsubscriptions supports the case for weekend emails. Subscribers are slightly more likely to unsubscribe earlier in the week.

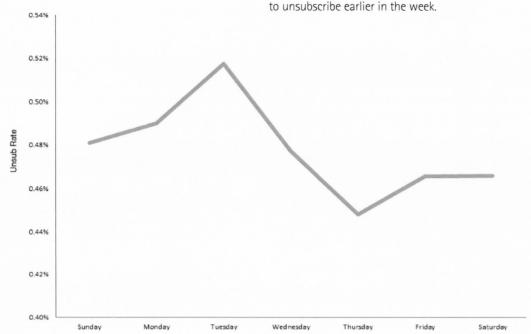

Effect of Time-of-Day on Clickthrough Rate

The time of day is another way to fine tune your email marketing. The research suggests that early morning is a better time to send email.

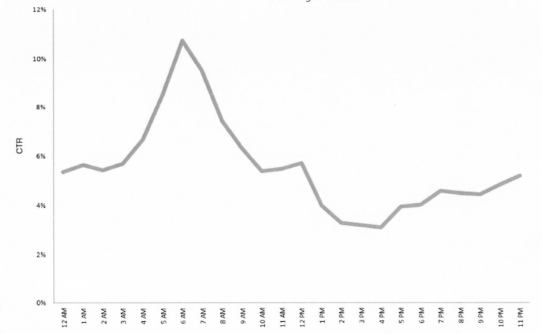

It's likely that your subscribers have set aside some time to read email in the morning, which can lead to dramatically higher clickthrough rates. In the late afternoon, most of us are in "clean up" mode and trying to process many things quickly before shutting down for the day.

Every list is different and success will depend on the preferences of your target audience. As always, it's important to experiment with timing. Try doing exactly what the research suggests, or assume that this is what everyone else is doing and try counter-competitive timing.

Once you find something that seems to work, stick with it for a while. This will help set the expectation that your email is coming. They might not rush to their inbox every Wednesday at 9:30 AM ready to click, but they won't be surprised to see your message then, either.

If the quality of the content is very high, the timing is less important. People will hold onto it and read it when they're ready. They may read it many times. If you check your email stats days or weeks later, and the clickthrough rates are still trickling upward, you will know you wrote something good.

Frequency

No one can open or click your emails if you don't send them. So far, we've looked at the factors that can increase the rate that people open and click emails, but the total amount of traffic you drive also depends on how frequently you send. This is a huge factor!

So how often should you send email newsletters? The answer: *as often as you can consistently produce relevant, useful content.*

- **Minimum Frequency**
  You should send often enough that you stay in people's minds. But also consider the length of the sales cycle of your product or service. If it takes one month for a prospect to meet a competitor and buy from them instead, your email frequency should be every two weeks at a minimum.

- **Maximum Frequency**
  Yes, there is a point at which you may actually annoy people by sending too frequently, but if your content is good, you might be surprised at how often you can send successful email campaigns. I've heard many people say "My subscribers don't want to get email that often," but when I dig deeper, I find they've never tested the limit or they got one or two negative comments and backed off completely.

Yes, if you send more frequently, the percentage of people who click on every email may drop, but your goal is traffic, not a high clickthrough rate. Consider this: Even if your clickthrough rates drop by half, sending email weekly rather than monthly will double your traffic. You'll get half the traffic from each email, but you're sending four times as often.

TIP!

The real maximum should be based on the upper limit of your company's ability to produce relevant, useful content. If many people within an organization can contribute, and if you have a guest blogger outreach program, the upper limit may be very high.

6. Measure and Improve

As with everything in content marketing, the key to successful email marketing is to experiment, measure, iterate and improve. Many email service providers make A/B testing easy by allowing you to try different times of day, days of the week, and designs and subject lines, all using the same list and isolating the other variables.

Watch the Analytics carefully and listen for feedback. If you think there is an opportunity to improve, don't be afraid to redesign your template, send at a different time or tweak your frequency. If it doesn't work out, you can try something else in the next email.

Final note on email: perhaps more than any other channel, *successful email marketing depends on the quality of the content.* To convince your subscribers that your next newsletter is worth opening and clicking, you must make *this* newsletter interesting and useful. Build trust through consistent quality in your email content, or watch your email stats degrade over time.

Create your publishing calendar, set the due dates for writing and editing, keep an eye toward list growth, and then send, test, measure and send again.

Social Promotion

It's true. Thanks to social media, there is no need to hope and wait for visitors to find you by searching, and no need to put all your eggs in one email marketing basket. With social media, there are actions you can take right now that will drive a bit of traffic within the hour.

Post on the Networks: Facebook, Google+, LinkedIn, etc.

The first step in social media promotion is posting on the networks. Generally speaking, all content should be posted on all networks. It's possible that some fans and followers will see the same post more than once, but don't worry about overwhelming them. It may prompt them to take a closer look and give them more options to share.

- Facebook
- Google+
- LinkedIn
- Secondary Networks
  StumbleUpon, Delicious, Pinterest, Reddit, Digg, etc.

  Other web communities: local associations, networking groups, industry directories or any site where you have an account, can log in and post content.

TIP!

The effectiveness of recommendations within this section depends on how well you've built your personal networks within the social networks. If you have no presence on Twitter, Facebook, Google+ or LinkedIn, social promotion won't work. Build up an engaged, relevant audience with consistent, positive interaction. Talk to people. Help people. Promote their content, then let them help you promote yours.

CAUTION!

Blog posts without pictures will not be as prominent or pretty when posted in Facebook, Google+ and LinkedIn. Make sure that each post has at least one image.

When posting to a network, you are basically adding a link and a teaser. The teaser is a headline and a short excerpt from the full post. There is no risk of a duplicate content penalty in Google, but you still don't want to put the entire post in the teaser. If the teaser is too long, the reader may glean all the meaning and value without clicking and becoming a visitor.

You'll also have an opportunity to mention others when posting in Facebook, Google+ and Twitter. Take this opportunity to share the post with one or two fans or friends who are likely to read, enjoy and comment on the post.

FORMATTING	SHORTCUT
bolding	Add an asterix (*) to both sides of the text Example: This text is *bold* This text is **bold**
italics	Add an underscore (_) to both sides of the text Example: This text is _italicized_ This text is *italicized*
strikethrough	Add a hyphen to both sides of the text Example: This text is -struck through- This text is ~~struck through~~
bullets	Alt + 8 adds a bullet point. Example: • point one • point two

Google+ allows you to add formatting to your headline and teaser: Bolding, italics and bullets. Take advantage of this formatting to draw attention to your teaser by bolding the headline and using bullets to summarize the main points.

If you are active within Facebook groups, LinkedIn groups or any other forums, you have another opportunity to promote your content. As long as the content is relevant to the topics within that group, feel free to share it there. If the post sparks comments or conversation, be prepared to respond. It's not polite to join a group and post content without engaging with people.

If you have both a personal following and a business with its own following, consider first posting the content on the business page, then sharing from your personal account (example: post on Orbit's Facebook page, then share the post from Andy's account). This will leverage your personal connections while guiding others toward the brand.

Once the post is live on Twitter and Google+, take a moment to search those networks for people who are likely to be interested in the topic of your post. If you wrote about technology solutions for executives, search for "CTO." If your article is about a new farmers market in Atlanta, search for gardeners in the area. Follow these people or add them to a circle; they may notice you, see the post, follow you back and possibly share it.

TIP!

After you post a nice piece of high-value original content, the timing is right to take deliberate steps to grow your social following. Just as the content on a web page determines the visitors' likelihood to convert, your most recent post on Twitter or Google+ will appear at the top of your stream and will determine the likelihood of a new potential fan to follow you or add you to a circle. They may be less likely to follow or circle you if your top post is irrelevant to their interests or about cats.

Tweet!

The next step is send out a series of Tweets. One Tweet isn't likely to be effective, so we recommend a series of Tweets spread out over time. Depending on your level of activity on Twitter, it may be appropriate to Tweet an article 4-6 times over two weeks or ten times over a month.

These Tweets should include various ways of summarizing the article. They should not all be the same. Although one of them may simply be the article headline and the link, others should include variations of the headline and/or other elements:

- **Mentions** of people at the end of the Tweet (see targeted sharing below) ⟶

Andy Crestodina @crestodina   1m
Nice Blogs Finish Last convinceandconvert.com/blogging-and-c...
cc: @manamica

- **Hashtags** of keyphrases or topics (but no need to overdo it) ⟶

Andy Crestodina @crestodina   1m
Nice Blogs Finish Last convinceandconvert.com/blogging-and-c...
#blogging

- **Quotes** from the article ⟶

Andy Crestodina @crestodina   1m
Nice Blogs Finish Last convinceandconvert.com/blogging-and-c...
"Only 34% of businesses align content with the buying stages"

CAUTION!

Your Twitter stream should not be dominated by Tweets promoting your content. No more than 20% of your Tweets should include links to your content. The remaining 80% should be conversations with your followers, promoting others' content, witty observations, inspirational quotes, thank you messages, etc.

Although a Tweet can include up to 140 characters (which should be plenty of room for your Tweets) try to keep the length down to 120 characters to make Retweeting easier and more likely. Why? When people Retweet something, they may want to add a little something to it. If you leave them some room, they are more likely to mention you.

It's not necessary (or possible) to summarize the entire article within these Tweets. The Tweet is simply intended to be a hook to entice the reader to click. For example, when Tweeting an article on five ways businesses can use Pinterest, consider sending a short Tweet that indicates the meaning of the article without giving too much away, such as "This is why I love Pinterest." This leaves a little mystery. It pulls the reader in. Although I may not be in the mood to read a top 5 list about Pinterest, I might want to find out what you love about it.

> *"Twitter is the greatest content distribution network out there for people who create content. Everyone gets that. Twitter didn't start out with that idea, but that's what it became because they kind of stepped back and let us use it the way we want to. What choice really, do they have?"*
>
> *- Brian Clark, Copyblogger*
> *(Internet Marketing for Smart People)*

TIP!

For a great overview on the mechanics of Twitter, see Jessica Hische's beautiful explanation, *Mom This is How Twitter Works*.

Although URL shorteners condense the link and allow for tracking, they also hide the domain name, and thus, remove information from the Tweet. Now that URLs in Tweets sent from Twitter.com are shortened automatically, you may find that URL shorteners are unnecessary or even less effective.

Example: Which of the following links is more compelling to the dentist that reads it?   bit.ly/38Ud8s   dentistrytips.com/blog...

Consider promoting your content through social channels one day before promoting it through email marketing. Readers from social sources are more likely to comment, and a post with a few comments will look better when the surge of email visitors arrive. If you moderate your comments before making them live, be prepared to approve comments quickly. If these comments include feedback for ways to make the content stronger, don't hesitate to do some quick editing before sending the mass email.

ADVANCED TIP!

If you track the clickthrough rates from Tweets using a URL shortener, you can see which Tweets generate the most clicks to an individual article, then use that Tweet as a subject line in your email marketing. Using Twitter to A/B test email subject lines is a fun but imperfect science, and only possible for companies with large followings.

Targeted Sharing

If you take a few minutes to find the people who are likely to be interested in your content, you'll get better results when you share. Part of the beauty of Twitter is that you can find almost anyone imaginable. So it's not difficult to find someone who's likely to care about your content.

Twitter itself has a notoriously bad search tool, but there are many other tools that make up for this. Here's an example of how I used one of those tools to find people and promote a blog post.

The post in this case is called "Web Marketing Poetry: SEO Advice in Rhyming Quatrains." It's a poem that compares the constraints of writing for search marketing to the constraints of rhyming in poetry. People interested in both SEO and poetry would love this one, right?

So I headed over to to one of the many Twitter search tools to look. In this case, I used FilterTweeps.com. In the Keywords in Bio search box, I entered "SEO poet" and clicked search.

Search Fields (advanced syntax)

All fields:

Name:

Keywords in Bio:

SEO Poet

Keywords in Location:

Order by: Followers ⬍ Desc ⬍

search

It turned out that, of the 140,000,000,000 people on Twitter, there are 31 who have "SEO" and "poet" in their bios. FilterTweeps listed them in order of largest following. Scrolling through and reading the bios, I saw that they were indeed people who are both poets and search optimizers, the perfect audience for my post.

Next I wrote a simple Tweet and mentioned a few of these people at the end.

Andy Crestodina @crestodina   13h
It's a poem about writing for SEO.
stumbleupon.com/su/1B9pMi/www.... cc: @SukhSandhu @egabbert
@steveakinsseo.

In less than an hour, Sukh Sandhu, the first person mentioned in the Tweet, visited the post and left a comment.

He also Retweeted it to his 27,000 followers and

SukhSandhu 5 pts
Its beautiful, It was fun reading this. Thanks for sharing :)
12 HOURS AGO   Like   Reply

then Tweeted that he had commented.

Sukh Sandhu @SukhSandhu retweeted to 27,238 followers:

crestodina Andy Crestodina
It's a poem about writing for SEO. stumbleupon.com/su/1B9pMi/www.... cc:
@SukhSandhu @egabbert @steveakinsseo.
Mar 31, 10:33 PM via web

Andy Crestodina @crestodina   13h
It's a poem about writing for SEO.
stumbleupon.com/su/1B9pMi/www.... cc: @SukhSandhu @egabbert
@steveakinsseo.
↳ Retweeted by Sukh Sandhu

Sukh Sandhu @SukhSandhu   12h
I just left a comment in "Web Marketing Poetry" fyre.it/SPh

 NOTE!

I would typically link directly to the article, but in this case, I hoped this article got traction within another network, StumbleUpon. So I used the link to the article within that network. This gave people the opportunity to "like" it on StumbleUpon, possibly leading to more traffic down the road.

There is absolutely nothing spammy about sharing your content with people whom you feel would enjoy it. In this case, I was confident that they would like the post and I simply invited them to read it, knowing we have similar interests (poetry and search marketing). In this case, Sukh literally thanked me for sharing it in his comment. Naturally, I thanked him for back for the comment and for sharing it on Twitter.

I have very low expectations when I do this targeted sharing, but it always seems to work. Usually, if I mention two or three people, one of them responds. And the entire exercise takes less than five minutes.

It's not surprising that targeted sharing is effective, because it is so precise. If you're a Star Trek fan who helps nonprofits with fundraising and one day you see a Tweet that days "Dr. Spock's Guide to Silent Auctions," wouldn't you click on it? You'd be thrilled to read it! And grateful to whomever shared with you.

Some commenting tools make this kind of sharing more likely. LiveFyre and Disqus are WordPress commenting systems that make the comments section more of a conversation. They let commenters login using Twitter or Facebook, which is both easier and pulls in their profile pictures. The tools also make it very simple for commenters to announce on Twitter or Facebook that they left a comment.

Email: Manual, Old School, Social Sharing

It's not fancy, but it's effective. Email your content directly to specific contacts. They don't need to be subscribed to your email list. You're just sharing something relevant along with a personal note with a high-value contact, who could be a prospect, a journalist, a job candidate or an industry thought-leader.

This is especially important for businesses where the value of a transaction is very high. If you sell helicopters or provide wealth management services, and you've created a relevant, informative article about the latest in in-flight controls or tax law changes, send the article to recent prospects individually via email. They are already in your funnel. Arguably, there are no readers more important than these.

If the potential reader is extremely valuable, you can use a URL shortener when creating the link for the email. If you use this shortened link no where else, you'll be able to see if the recipient clicked the link.

Example: If I wanted Seth Godin to review this book and I send him a link to a downloadable file, I might shorten the link through bit.ly before sending it to Mr. Godin. Since I would have used this link only in this way, I can check back on bit.ly to see the traffic. One click means Seth downloaded the book. Zero clicks means he didn't.

ECHO...Echo...echo

If you've done a good job promoting the content through social channels, it has likely been shared in the networks and Retweeted within Twitter. Now you have an opportunity to increase the visibility by creating a mini-echo chamber of conversation. Here's how:

- If the content was shared by others on Facebook and Google+, comment on the new shares with a thank you. If there's a conversation happening within the comments, jump in.

- If the content was Retweeted, thank the person who shared it. The thank yous and responses can easily triple the number of Tweets related to a piece of content.

- If the article generated comments, respond to them. Then find the commenters on the social networks and let them know you've responded.

- If the article generated lots of traffic, shares, comments, etc., Tweet about the popularity of the article: "Wow! Everyone seems to like this post..."

The idea is to create a small feedback loop and take advantage of any activity by responding. This can extend what is often a very short life of content within social networks. It increases the chance of content being noticed and becoming more viral.

Timing is important since within Facebook and Google+, posts that have lots of activity (likes, +1s and clicks) stay at the top of people's streams for longer. Be ready to have conversations, say thank you and respond to comments when social promotion begins.

Consider Tweeting links to articles published months or even years ago. These "from the archive" or "encore" Tweets can revive posts buried deep within your blog. If your audience has grown since they were first posted, it's likely that many of your followers haven't seen these yet. As long as the article doesn't contain out-of-date information, it may still be relevant and useful.

Guest Blogging

I consider guest blogging to be a content promotion tactic because it leverages the audience and influence of others to improve the visibility of content and companies.

There are two sides to guest blogging: publishing your content on other sites (being a guest blogger), and seeking content from others for your site (blogger relations and guest blogger outreach). They are both powerful content marketing tactics with search marketing and social media benefits.

To understand the benefits of guest blogging, especially when combined, let's imagine the processes and outcomes of two bloggers: one blogger who posts only on his own site, and another who embraces both approaches to guest blogging.

Round One: Both Bloggers Create Two Posts

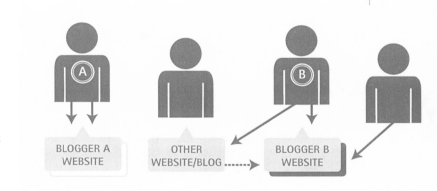

Blogger A has written two posts and publishes both on his blog.

Blogger B has also written two posts, but rather than post them both on her blog, she connects with another website owner or content manager who agrees to publish one of her posts. She asks only for a link back to her site in exchange. This link is indicated by the dotted line in the diagram above.

SCOREBOARD	POSTS	LINKS	SOCIAL CONNECTIONS
Blogger A	2	0	0
Blogger B	2	1	2

Also, she reaches out to another writer in her field. This writer submits a new, original post and Blogger B publishes it on her site. This guest post is indicated by the red box above.

Let's see how they're doing:

Although Blogger B only wrote two of the posts, she now has three posts associated with her brand. She also has a link and a few new friends.

Round Two: Both Bloggers Have Published Four Posts

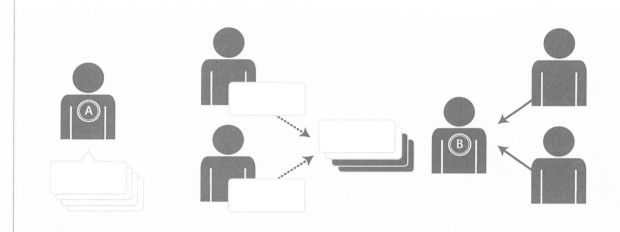

SCOREBOARD	POSTS	LINKS	SOCIAL CONNECTIONS
Blogger A	4	0	0
Blogger B	6	2	4

Blogger A has now written and published four posts, all on his own blog.

Blogger B has published two posts on external websites, both of which now have links back to her site. She's also connected with expert writers who have contributed two relevant posts that are now on her blog. And she's built connections with the people behind other websites relevant to her business.

Round Four: Both Bloggers Have Created Eight Posts

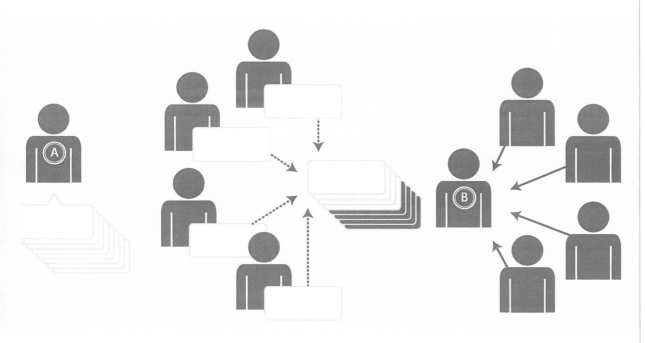

Blogger A has consistently produced and published content, but...

Blogger B has created a network of content, both on her site and linked to her brand. This has increased exposure to her content. She's also growing a network of connections with experts, which has increased her influence in her field. This is what great web marketing looks like.

Remember, search engine optimization is about great content and great links. Social media is about real connections with real people. Guest blogging provides both.

Target Host Blogs

Different blogs will have different benefits to your content marketing so it's important to understand the options and outcomes. There are generally two types of guest blogging opportunities: local social blogs or national topical blogs.

SCOREBOARD	POSTS	LINKS	SOCIAL CONNECTIONS
Blogger A	8	0	0
Blogger B	12	4	8

	LOCAL	NATIONAL
Primary benefit	social media	search engine optimization
Criteria	large social following and readership	authoritative domain, linking opportunity

Local and Social Blogs - Good for branding and networking (social media).

These could be high traffic, local sites such as local media sites. They may cover a broad range of topics but they are generally focused on your region. The ideal local blogs are those with large social media followings and lots of comments on previous blog posts. The readers of these blogs may be relevant people in your area that you'd like to meet in person someday.

TIP!

When possible, it's good to guest blog more than once on sites like these, so the readers see you repeatedly and become more likely to remember you.

National and Topical Blogs - Good for link building (SEO).

Although any guest blogging opportunity has some social benefit, sometimes guest blogging is more focused on the benefit of the possible link back to your site. For this reason, the size of the blog's readership or social following are less important and the authority of the domain is more important (more on measuring domain authority soon).

These sites may be tightly focused on your industry, such as trade publications or association websites. These may be websites of businesses like yours in other parts of the country. Regardless, the topics of the posts on these blogs are related to the topics that are important to your audience. The fact that these sites are topically related to your product or service means they offer a stronger SEO benefit. A link from a site that is relevant to your business is better than a link from a random or irrelevant site.

Example: If your business repairs HVAC systems for hospitals, look for links from mechanical contractor associations, repair safety sites or even healthcare blogs.

If you're able to find a site that meets both criteria, social and search, patiently cultivate a close relationship and seek to position yourself as a regular contributor or columnist.

TIP!

It's less important to blog repeatedly on these websites, since the value of the subsequent links is not likely to be as strong as a new link from a second, separate host blog. When your focus is SEO, one of your main goals is to increase the total number of websites that link to you. So you'd rather have two links from two different sites than two links from the same site.

How to Measure the Value of a Guest Blogging Opportunity...and a Link

In Chapter 1 we explored the research on why websites rank in search engines and we learned the importance of incoming links. We know that the quality of these links, not just the number of them, plays a huge part in search rankings. Not all links are created equal. If we're going to be effective in our efforts to improve our "link profile," we must learn to estimate the value of a possible link.

Here is an oversimplification that will help explain this concept: In the eyes of Google, the Internet is a network of authority and trust. Some sites are more trustworthy than others, largely because other trustworthy sites link to them. Sites that have few or no incoming links are not as trusted, because other sites have not passed along their trust through links.

> Links are votes of trust. All things being equal (of course, they never are), a site with more higher quality links will outrank a site with fewer, lower quality links.

Search engine optimizers call this trust "link juice." Some sites have a lot and others have very little. Ideally, trusted websites link to you and that juice flows through your site via internal links. A link from a trusted site may pass 1,000 times more trust than an unknown, untrusted site.

Link Metrics and Analysis

Open Site Explorer was created by SEOmoz and is an invaluable industry-standard tool for measuring link popularity and authority. In addition to showing the approximate raw number of incoming links, it shows several other metrics including domain authority, page authority, MozRank and MozTrust. The original metric for measuring trust and authority is Google's own PageRank (named after Google founder Larry Page), which is a simpler one-to-ten estimate of link popularity.

Unless you are a full-time search optimizer or really obsessed with link building, I encourage you to focus on Domain Authority when estimating a general value of a link or guest blogging opportunity. You certainly could consider other metrics when evaluating a possible website for guest blogging (some people pay attention only to PageRank or Alexa Traffic Rank), but for most web marketers, Domain Authority is sufficient. It's a good, general rating of the trustworthiness of a website.

How to Use Open Site Explorer

This tool is as easy to use as Google itself. Just visit the site and enter the address of the possible host blog. It will show you the number of incoming links, the number of domains with incoming links, the page authority and the domain authority. The higher the better.

If the domain authority is below 40, a link to your site from this site would have low value, unless the domain authority of your site is even lower. If it's in the 40-70 range, it's worth pursuing. If it's in the 70's or 80's, it's worth pursuing patiently and persistently. Links from sites in the 90-100 range are generally unattainable through guest blogging, but may be possible though "newsjacking" or other clever, well-timed PR techniques.

If you are not a paid subscriber to SEOmoz PRO, you will be able to use this tool only a few times each day from any given computer. I consider SEOmoz to be an indispensible tool for content marketing and recommend spending the $100 per month for the PRO subscription. It includes many useful tools. One tool tracks search rankings over time. Another tool makes prioritized recommendations for keyphrase usage on specific pages.

CAUTION!

Some blogs may add a tiny piece of code to their links that drastically reduce (if not completely eliminate) the value of a link. The code is robots="nofollow" and they add it to keep the value of their links to themselves and also to be less attractive to link spammers.

Although you may still want to guest blog for the social and branding benefits on sites that use this code, keep in mind that guest posts here will have little or no SEO benefit. Look at the HTML of other posts and examine the links to see if this code is there.

Therefore, the ideal link to your site and the ideal sites to target for guest blogging are:

- Sites that have high domain authority.
- Sites that allow you to use target keyphrases in the link to your site (remember the importance of keyphrases in anchor text from Chapter 2).
- Site that don't use the robots="nofollow" code within your link.

How to Submit Your Content

Once you've got a few host blogs in your sights, it's time to reach out and see if they are interested in your content. Keep in mind that the owners of popular sites with powerful domains are contacted regularly by eager content marketers. You need to be thoughtful and considerate when making contact with them, just as PR professionals are thoughtful and considerate when contacting journalists.

They might have a "guest blog for us" page with a contact form. If there are guest blogging guidelines posted, read them carefully. In other cases, you submit your request through a general contact form or to a general email address on a contact page. I've even seen hopeful guest bloggers approach website owners openly within comments on Google+ and on Twitter. It's a bold approach, but it's not usually effective.

Here are some DOs and DON'Ts to follow when submitting a possible guest post:

- **Don't waste their time**
  A little research and consideration go a long way. Make sure that you're submitting content that would make sense on the site and be interesting to its readers. I once absent-mindedly submitted a gritty Bruce Willis-themed web marketing article to a very pink, feminine web design blog. That didn't go well.

- **Do convey the value of the content**
  Take a moment to explain how the content fits within their blog and would be useful to their audience. You had better sincerely believe in the value of the content! Be confident but brief. A few sentences will do.

  If you optimized the content by aligning it with a keyphrase, mention that here. You can even mention the popularity of the phrase.

- **Don't be pushy**
  Remember they are the host and you are the aspiring guest. You're inviting yourself over to their home (or at least homepage). You should be very polite. Offer to let them make any edits, change the headline or images, even remove any links if they feel they are inappropriate. Be friendly.

- **Do offer to help promote it**
  If you have a significant social following, let them know you'll be promoting the article through your social networks. Of course you would do this anyway, but drawing attention to your ability to drive traffic will make your content more attractive.

If the post is likely to get comments, offer to be available once it goes live to add responses and answer questions within the comments.

- **Do follow up**
  Thank the host blog with an email. If the article ranks, let them know and they'll appreciate it. If you feel the post was successful, consider offering to write another. Now is the best time to grow the relationship with your new friends and collaborators.

If possible, submit the final, edited version of the content to the host blog in HTML format. It may take a bit of skill (or HTML authoring software like Dreamweaver), but it will make it easier for them to post and help assure that the links, formatting and images are kept in place. At the very least, submit the author box information as HTML, since it includes the all-important link to your site and the links to your social media profiles.

Don't be discouraged if you have trouble placing a post. You may submit an article to five or more blogs before it gets accepted. If you have trouble getting something published, consider these options:

- Write posts that are specifically tailored for the target blog. First research which headlines and posts are the most successful on their site (i.e., which ones get lots of comments).

- Submit ideas for posts to target blogs that relate to something they just posted within the last day. If they like the idea, you have a toe in the door.

- Network on social media with the editors before submitting.

- Submit posts to many potential blogs at once. Let each know that it's original content but you're submitting it to several other sites. First come first served!

- Submit posts to lower value sites.

- Rewrite the headline of the post or scrap it completely.

Carry a printed writing sample of one of your best articles with you. If you meet another blogger, a journalist or the manager of a website you'd like to submit to, hand them the sample and offer to follow up. These connections often happen at events, either randomly or through traditional stalking methods.

Be My Guest: Finding Great Guest Bloggers

When outside experts write for your blog, you add a new voice to your site, you add credibility, you leverage their social networks and *you get an article without spending the time and effort to write it yourself*. But you'll get few or none of these results unless you select your guest bloggers carefully.

The first two criteria should be obvious. You want great writers. They know their subject matter and they write posts with substance. They're skilled in crafting compelling content and they write posts with style. Read what they submit as if you were a visitor.

Ask yourself: Does the headline get your attention? Does the article hold it? Did you learn something from it? Would you be likely to comment or share it?

Social following, the third criteria for guest bloggers, is optional but highly desired: Do they have a large social following and are they willing to use it to drive some traffic your way? Look them up on Twitter, Facebook or Google+. Some social media professionals use Klout, the somewhat controversial social media metric, to estimate online influence.

Ask yourself: Do they have an audience? Are they engaged within social channels?

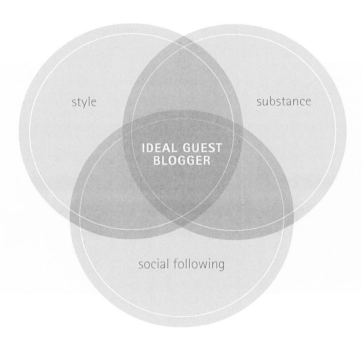

Two out of three may be ok.

If they don't meet these criteria, you'll need to politely decline ("Sorry, but this post isn't right for our audience right now.") or give them an opportunity to improve it ("This is a little light / isn't quite strong enough. Would you like to add more specifics / edit it down / add more examples / submit something else?").

Guest Blogging Guidelines

If you are serious about guest blogger outreach, you'll save time setting expectations by providing guest blogger guidelines, either as a file you can share or a web page on your site. Guidelines are becoming common on popular blogs. In many cases these sites are adding contact forms on "Write for Us" pages so that visitors can convert into qualified potential guest bloggers.

The guidelines below are basically a shorter version of the Article Checklist in Chapter 4. Feel free to use this worksheet or your own guidelines based on your standards for content aspects and quality.

- **Types of Posts** - Ask for submissions that appeal to your audience and align with other content on your site. Posts should fit nicely within your blog categories.

- **Tone and Style** - Conversational, approachable, helpful, useful, interesting.

- **Length** - 500 words.

- **Formatting** - Encourage the use of headers, subheaders and bullet lists.

- **Images** - Suggest (or require) that they submit an image with copyrights and sized to the appropriate width for your site.

- **Search Friendliness** - Suggest that they optimize the article for a relevant keyphrase. Provide guidelines for writing search friendly content if available.

- **Author Box Info** - Ask for two to three sentences about the author along with links to websites and any relevant social media accounts (Twitter, Google+, LinkedIn).

- **How to Submit** - Require interested bloggers to provide their content to you in a format that makes it easy to review and post. This may be through a web form, in a Word doc, HTML, a shared Google Doc, etc.

- **Originality and Reuse** - Require that the content provided by guest bloggers is unique and has not and will not be used elsewhere. You want to have exclusive use of the article.

Your guidelines may also highlight the benefits of being a guest blogger on your site. Assure the possible writer of acknowledgement, a great link and new audience. Remember, these guidelines are intended to make communication more efficient and lay the groundwork for collaboration.

Guest Blogging = Modern Day PR

The outcomes of guest blogging are virtually indistinguishable from the outcomes of PR. Technically it is just one PR tactic, but as the news media revenue model continues to evolve, crowdsourcing of content becomes more prevalent, and publishing content becomes easier for blogs and brands, guest blogging will be ever more important for PR professionals.

Currently, guest blogging as a tactic falls into a gap between the skill sets of SEO and PR practitioners. Although SEO pros know the value of links, they don't have access to the powerful host blogs since search engine optimizers don't typically create content. PR pros can create compelling content, but they don't typically understand the tactics and benefits of link popularity. Social media pros may be the first to bridge this gap.

Try it. You'll find that the principles of guest blogging align closely with the philosophy of content marketing in general: create, connect, collaborate and help others. It's fun.

You should reserve the right to edit guest posts. If you do make changes, the guest blogger shouldn't mind. In my experience, it's very common for host blogs to make significant changes to my submissions, such as changing the headline. Do I mind? Not at all. Except when they add a lot of bad stock photos. :)

5 Inspiration: Content Genesis

Science is work, often requiring long hours of effort with uncertain outcomes. But it's also punctuated by eureka moments. As a content marketer, you'll have many of both.

> *Writing is a means of getting things done or promoting ideas. Actual scientists spend lots of time writing grants to get research funding. They're promoting their ideas through writing, just like any content marketer.*

The inspiration for new content is part of the joy of content chemistry. Seeing a piece of content planned, created, promoted and measured is always satisfying, but for me nothing beats the big bang of a new idea.

Ideas for content can come from any direction. The more you write, the more open you'll become to new concepts. Also, the more you write, the more opportunities you'll have to repurpose content, as described in the Periodic Table of Content.

But if brilliance isn't forthcoming, there are many resources to trigger your imagination. In fact, there are so many "101 Ideas for Writing" articles, you could begin by writing a "Top 10 List of 101 Ideas for Writing" article.

Idea Templates and Headline Hacks

There are a few simple arrangements of words that are so successful as headlines that they are virtual templates for ideas. Here they are:

> **[number] of [blank] about [blank]**
> **What [blank] can teach you about [blank]**

Source: Danny Iny (Copyblogger)

Just because these are formulas doesn't mean the content will be low quality. We've all read, enjoyed, learned from and maybe been convinced by articles in this format. They are extremely versatile and can produce targeted, easy-to-consume content.

Jon Morrow wrote a whitepaper called *52 Headline Hacks: A "Cheat Sheet" for Writing Blog Posts that Go Viral*. It's possibly the best collection of headline ideas available. It separates these template headlines into six categories:

- **Thread Headlines** -
  What Keeps Your Readers Up At Night
  Example: 27 Complaints about Web Design Companies

- **Zen Headlines** -
  Promising Your Readers a Simpler Life
  Example: Perfect Profile Pictures: 9 Tips

- **Piggyback Headlines** -
  Riding on the Back of a Famous Brand
  Example: What Lady Gaga Can Teach Marketers

- **Mistake Headlines** -
  Irresistible Teasers from the Masters
  Example: 15 Grammatical Errors that Make You Look Silly

- **How-to Headlines** -
  The Oldie but Goodie That Never Fails
  Example: How to Write When You Have No Ideas And No Time

- **List Headlines** -
  Bite Sized Content That Readers Adore
  Example: 52 Types of Blog Posts that Are Proven to Work

Here are some additional ideas for content that are specifically designed to take advantage of the chemistry between social media and search engine optimization.

Interviews

Interviews with experts add credibility to any website. Text-based interviews can be an efficient way to produce excellent articles. If you interview people who are influential, they may help promote your content through their social networks.

- Email an expert five questions.

- Email five experts one question.

- Invite fans and followers to ask questions on Facebook and Twitter. Have experts within your business write answers or answer questions on video.

TIP!

Lee Odden recommends asking interview questions that include target keyphrases. If the reply includes the keyphrase, you may end up with compelling, natural language content that is also search friendly.

Video interviews are more difficult to produce, but often very engaging. Just think of the size of the viewership for content producers like Jay Leno.

Write for Each Stage in the Conversion Funnel

Every buyer of every product and every service goes through a series of steps: *awareness, interest, consideration and then the action of actual transaction.* From the impulse purchase of a Tootsie-pop in the checkout aisle to the government purchase of radar installations, every purchase goes through this funnel.

For most buying decisions, the interests, questions and concerns of potential buyers are consistent, making it possible to define the funnel and *then create content that aligns with prospects' interests and concerns.*

Audience seeks general information about the industry or the category of products or service.

Visitor has questions (or concerns) about the industry. Seeks general info about the company.

Visitor has specific questions (or concerns) about the actual product or service.

Visitor is confident enough to take action and make contact/purchase.

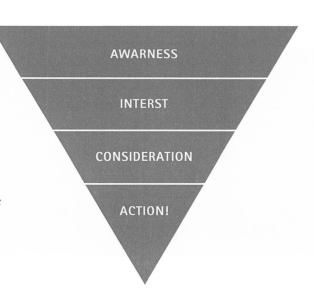

if you have more than one target audience or type of conversion, you may need to create more than one funnel. Each type of visitor has a separate set of interests and concerns that should be addressed with separate content. For example, one funnel may be for lead generation while a second funnel may be for newsletter subscribers.

Every great website first gives visitors the information they're looking for and then gently guides them toward the information it wants them to read. Ultimately, it leads visitors to the contact page and subsequent thank you page. Content needs to support this process at every step.

Once you've sketched out the conversion funnel and listed your audience's top interests and concerns, look at the content you've made available. Now ask yourself: Have you addressed all the stages in the funnel with content? If not, you know what to write next. Fill in the gaps.

For larger organizations, this works best when the marketing team is listening to the sales team. Once the marketing team finds out what questions are being asked during the process and what concerns prospects have, new content can then be created to fill gaps in the funnel.

Once the content is created, it goes into the blog where it can educate visitors and create more qualified leads. If it's really important, move it out of the blog and into the product or service pages. Better yet, the sales team can share it with prospects who are already in the pipeline.

Follow the Leader

A little research can lead to a lot of ideas. It's useful to look carefully at what is already working, whether it's on your site or possible host sites when you're guest blogging. Once you've done the research, you can choose a topic and a format similar to the posts and articles that have already been successful.

- Look at your own Analytics to see the top posts and pages on your site. Which pages are most frequently visited? Where are visitors spending the most time?
- When guest blogging on other sites, look through the older posts on the blog. Which articles have the most comments, shares, likes and +1s?

Make a list of the most popular or successful posts, then start breaking them down. Do they have similar headlines? Topics? Tone? Now you can start to see what interests the site's readers.

Reverse engineer this high-performing content and you'll find patterns that new ideas can fit into. This will help you find that great idea by narrowing your options and considering the context. You'll also have a structure that makes writing much faster and easier.

Just pick a popular blog and find a post that has been successful based on the number of comments and shares. Break down the length of the post, the length of the paragraphs and the sentences. Listen to the tone of the writing. Look at the supporting elements: examples, statistics, images, quotes, links, mentions and calls to action. Deconstruct the formatting: headers, subheads, bullets and bolding. If you found the post by searching for a keyphrase, examine the keyword usage.

Now consider making your next article conform to these attributes. It's likely that in doing so, you'll be adapting your own piece, making it more concise, more conversational, more scannable, more shareable and more effective.

Attend Events

Every event that you attend is an opportunity to create content. Mentioning speakers or other attendees you meet will give you reasons to share the post with others. They'll be likely to share it with their networks. If event summaries aren't relevant to your audience, consider making this a guest post on another local blog or industry blog. If there's a website for the event, they may also be interested in posting it.

Look in Your Outbox

Here's a well known blogger trick for getting new ideas: reading old emails. Scan through the last few hundred emails you've sent. Are there any topics that come up consistently? These are good candidates for web content.

While you're digging through these emails, notice the tone of what you've written. It's probably informal and concise. This is likely the same tone that your website visitors would appreciate.

You may have great communication skills and email etiquette, so don't set that aside when you write an article. Keep using that simple language and a friendly voice. Don't suddenly start writing like a PhD candidate just because it's an article. Be yourself. Write like you're sending an email.

Email is also a constructive way to overcome your own objections to content marketing. If while reading this book, you've said to yourself, "I don't have time to write" or "I don't know how to write," just look at all those messages in your outbox. You're already a writer! You may already be producing 1,000 words every day on the same topics and in the same tone that you should use as a content marketer.

To keep the tone of your writing conversational, read your articles out loud to a friend when you're done. The jargon and formality might jump out at you right away. Or have an editor from outside your industry review the article. Another tip: Each time you sit down to write, put this at the top of the page: "Dear Mom..."

So there you have it. You should now have a good understanding of how websites succeed through traffic and conversions. You should also know how content helps achieve these goals.

Ideally, at this point, you're excited to start mixing things up in the lab. You're ready to experiment with keyphrases, discover new connections and concoct a big batch of relevant articles.

Persist

Yes, it's going to be work. There is no secret formula. Content marketing isn't about just one thing. It's about 100 little things. And it's about doing these things well and doing them consistently. It may take time to find the style that works for you and gets a reaction from your audience. You'll need to keep at it if you're expecting big results. Persistence is the biggest factor in success, not just in web marketing but in every field.

> *"Marketing is a habit, not an event." -John Jantsch, Duct Tape Marketing*

You'll see small results right away - a few shares, more clicks, some new people accepting your invitation to be added to your list - but it will take time before you become an expert.

Some of the greatest content chemists of our time put in tremendous effort to get where they are. It took Chris Brogan 8 years to get his first 100 subscribers. Today he has hundreds of thousands of readers each month. Lee Odden of TopRank Online Marketing has written more than a million words during his career. Today he's one of the most sought after web strategists in the country.

You don't need to work for 8 years to get 100 subscribers or write a million words to get results. Thankfully, there are plenty of small incremental results to measure along the way. But it will take patience and effort. Keep going; you'll get there.

Fear Not

Almost nothing is as high-stakes as it seems. Yes, there are examples of spectacular failures in social media. There are nightmare stories of collapsing search engine rankings. But these stories are rare relative to the millions of businesses doing content marketing.

> *"Fortes fortuna adiuvat." Fortune favors the bold.*

Don't be afraid to try something new. Don't be afraid to write something provocative. If an article rubs a few people the wrong way, there are probably hundreds of other people who appreciate the candor. If you feel strongly about something, let it show through your words.

Have fun!

To me, web marketing is a game. I play it like a sport and Analytics is my scoreboard. I've chosen certain metrics that I like best and I try to make them move. It's actually easy to gamify your marketing because there are so many beautiful charts to look at! Thinking of it as a game, and making those charts and numbers move helps keep me motivated.

Everything you're about to do is measurable, and the results of your efforts make lovely charts. So pick out a few statistics and watch a few of the charts. Choose the ones that have an impact on your goals and start obsessing over them a little bit. Call it a "key performance indicator" if you want. Personally, aside from leads, some of my favorite stats are: newsletter subscribers, newsletter click-to-open rates, Google +1s and total visitors. If these numbers are growing, results will come. I'm always trying to break my high score.

So I watch the charts. I measure. I wonder. I tweak. I try something new and I measure again. And somewhere along the way, I forget that I'm working. I'm having fun.

If you're not having fun, you're doing it wrong.

Resources

A lot of things in this book are likely to change over the next few years. There are new social media tools, new ranking factors in search engine algorithms and new trends in what visitors expect from websites. Keep learning.

More Advice: The Orbit blog has posts on many topics that weren't covered here. We invite you to drop by to read our latest content marketing advice. You can also stay connected through our newsletter and social media:

http://www.orbitmedia.com/blog/

http://twitter.com/orbiteers

https://plus.google.com/116758072288598121083/posts

https://www.facebook.com/orbitmediastudios

Here is a list of some of the resources that I've used over the years to learn many of the things in this book. Many of these I still use every day. One of the wonderful things about content marketing is that the experts are all happy to teach what they know. They do it every day on their websites, in their videos, in their newsletters and at conferences.

I'd like to both thank and recommend the following websites and thought leaders. Believe it or not, I've never met any of them. But they've each had a profound effect on me. I'm grateful and, by way of thanks, I encourage everyone to read, watch, follow and subscribe to these wonderful resources, as I have.

- SEOmoz/Inbound.org and Rand Fishkin

- Copyblogger and Brian Clark

- HubSpot and Dan Zarella

- TopRank and Lee Odden, author of "Optimize" (highly recommended)

- Marketing Profs and Ann Handley, co-author of "Content Rules" (another book I am constantly recommending)

Here are some other superstar websites and experts I recommend taking a close look at, in no particular order:

Liz Strauss, Joe Peluzzi, Nick Kellet, John Morrow, Danny Iny, John Jantsch, Ross Hudgens, Ian Lurie, Danny Sullivan, A.J. Kohn, Jay Baer, David Meerman Scott, Chad Pollitt, and John Carlton.

Also a huge thanks to my partners and fellow content marketers here in Chicago, from whom I've learned so much, including Mana Ionescu of Lightspan Digital, George Zlatin and Taylor Cimala of Digital Third Coast, Brad Farris of EnMast, Gini Dietrich of Spin Sucks, and my partners in ContentJam, our content marketing event. This includes Tim Frick of Mightybytes, Jill Pollack of Story Studio and Hilary Marsh. Thanks to my designer, Bridget Gannon, who made this book look beautiful. And to my editor, Kim Bookless, who showed such persistence and clarity, making this book so much better and keeping me on track.

Lastly, thanks to my business partner, Barrett Lombardo, as well as Todd Gettelfinger and the rest of the Orbiteers. The work you do every day for our beloved clients is an inspiration to me.

Notes